Compliance in Today's Global Supply Chain

Compliance in Today's Global Supply Chain

Thomas A. Cook

CRC Press
Taylor & Francis Group
Boca Raton   London   New York

CRC Press is an imprint of the
Taylor & Francis Group, an **Informa** business

CRC Press
Taylor & Francis Group
6000 Broken Sound Parkway NW, Suite 300
Boca Raton, FL 33487-2742

© 2011 by Taylor and Francis Group, LLC
CRC Press is an imprint of Taylor & Francis Group, an Informa business

No claim to original U.S. Government works

Printed in the United States of America on acid-free paper
10 9 8 7 6 5 4 3 2 1

International Standard Book Number: 978-1-4200-8621-8 (Hardback)

Library of Congress Cataloging-in-Publication Data

Cook, Thomas A., 1953-
  Compliance in today's global supply chain / Thomas A. Cook.
     p. cm.
  Includes bibliographical references and index.
  ISBN 978-1-4200-8621-8 (hbk. : alk. paper)
  1. Business logistics. 2. Trade regulation. 3. Commercial policy. 4.
Exports--Management. 5. Imports--Management. I. Title.

HD38.5.C656 2010
658.7--dc22   2009042413

Visit the Taylor & Francis Web site at
http://www.taylorandfrancis.com

and the CRC Press Web site at
http://www.crcpress.com

To Kelly, who challenges, inspires, and motivates me to climb higher, do better, and shows the love and devotion we all need to emulate.

Contents

Foreword xiii

Overview xv

**1   The Importance of Trade Compliance Programs in Global Supply
        Chains** 1
    The Global Supply Chain 1
    The Basics Steps of Structuring and Implementing 2
        Awareness 2
        Senior Management 3
        Analysis and Review 3
        Person(s) Responsible—Team Initiative 4
        Resource Development 5
        Action Plan 5
        Standard Operating Procedures (SOPs) 6
        Training and Education 7
        Self-Audit 8
    Global Contract Management 8
        INCO 9
    Terms of Sale/INCO Terms 9
        Payment 11
        Freight 12
        Title 12
        Revenue Recognition (Exports Only) 12
        Compliance 13
        Insurance: Loss and Damage 13
    Resources Outline 13
        Magazines 14
        Associations 14
        E-Mail Newsletters 15

2   Export Logistics and Compliance Management 17
Export Logistics, Freight Forwarding, and Shipping.................................17
Export Freight Forwarding and Supply Chain Management 18
Shipping Costs..19
Shipping Cost Breakdown 21
Value-Added Services..23
Power of Attorney 24
INCO Terms in Logistics 26
Terms of Payment 27
Export Packing 28
Management Policy 29
Set Packing Guidelines 29
Packaging Resources 30
Managing Compliance and Documentation......................................30
Export Compliance...31
Census 31
Valuation 33
Harmonized Tariff Schedule/Schedule B Number 34
Bureau of Industry and Security (BIS)...35
Export Control Classification Number (ECCN) 35
Denied Party Screening 35
Office of Foreign Asset Controls 36
Export Documentation...37
FCPA Awareness and Adherence...38
Documentation and Letters of Credit 41

3   Import Management and Inbound Logistics 43
The Bureau of Customs and Border Protection (CBP) 43
Profile 43
The Department of Homeland Security (DHS) 44
Organizational Structure 44
Import Regulatory Issues...46
Import Management: Importer of Record vs. Ultimate Consignee 46
Reasonable Care 51
Meeting Reasonable Care Standards...51
Importer 51
Broker...52
Best Practices: Ten Steps to Achieve Import Compliance............................52
References..53
C-TPAT: Customs–Trade Partnership against Terrorism 54
Importer Self-Assessment (ISA) Program...54
Quick Response Audits...54
Global Security Awareness...55

Container Security Initiative..56
Advanced Manifest Notification Programs....................................57
Wheels Up or Four-Hour Advanced Notification............................57
Two-Hour Advanced Notification for Ground and Rail Shipments..58
Flexibility of Filing...64
Postloading Filing Privileges...64
Foreign Cargo Remaining On Board...65
Implementation Process of Final Rule..65
Methods of Filing ISF Data...66
Valuation Verification..66
Methods of Valuation...67
Assists..67
Royalties...67
Commissions...67
Customs Powers of Attorney..68
Revocation..69
Validating the Power of Attorney..72
Certificate of Registration..73
Foreign Shipper's Repair/Manufacturer's Affidavit............................74
Importation and Customs Clearance Process.....................................74
Record Keeping..78
Recommendations of Compliance...79
Importers...79
Customs Brokers..80
Methods of Storage of Records..80
Customs Bonds..82
Parties to a Bond..82
Types of Bonds..83
Amounts of Bonds..83
Invoices..83
Invoice Requirements...83
Duty Drawback..84
Harmonized Tariff System...85
Format..85
General Notes..85
Chapter Notes...86
Alphabetical Index...86
Techniques of Classification...86
GRI Consideration..86
Alphabetical Index...86
Chapter Notes...86
HTSUS Number Structure...86

4 Government Agencies Controlling Supply Chain Issues......................87
Government Agencies Involved in Exporting...87
    Department of Commerce: Bureau of Industry and Security...........87
    Department of Commerce: Office of Antiboycott Compliance 88
    Department of State: Directorate of Defense Trade Controls...........88
    Department of Commerce: Bureau of Census,
    Foreign Trade Division 88
    Department of Justice: Drug Enforcement
    Administration, Office of Diversion Control (Chemicals
    and Controlled Substances) 89
    Department of Health and Human Services: Food and Drug
    Administration (Drugs and Biologics, Investigational Drugs
    Permitted, Medical Devices)...89
    Department of Energy: Natural Gas and Electric Power 89
    Department of Energy: Nuclear Regulatory Commission: Office
    of International Programs (Nuclear Materials and Equipment,
    Technical Data for Nuclear Weapons) 90
    Department of Homeland Security: Customs and Border
    Protection (CBP) 90
    Federal Maritime Commission: Ocean Freight Forwarders 90
    Department of Commerce: Patent and Trademark Office 90
    Department of Homeland Security: Transportation
    Security Administration 91
    Department of the Treasury: Office of Foreign Asset Controls.........92
    Department of Interior: Fish and Wildlife Services 92
Government Agencies Involved in Importing 93
    U.S. Customs and Border Protection 93
    Food and Drug Administration 93
    Department of Agriculture, Animal Plant Health
    Inspection Service...94
    Consumer Products Safety Commission..94
    U.S. Fish and Wildlife Service..94
    Federal Communications Commission..95

5 Utilization of Technology Options...97
Technology Advantages 97
Service Providers and Technology...99
RFID: Trade Compliance and Import–Export Management....................99

6 Personnel Deployment, Training, and Best Practices 105
Where Should Trade Compliance Be Managed?.....................................105
Training and Education..106
    PACMAN Benefits...107

U.S. Export Compliance.com: A Solution for U.S. Trade
Compliance Education and Training..107
Benchmarking and Best Practices 109
Benchmarking 109
Best Practices in Trade Compliance... 110
What Are SOPs? 112
Why Create Trade Compliance SOPs? 113
What Needs to Be Included in My Trade Compliance SOPs? 113
Organized and Formal Education and Training 114
Putting Best Practices for Trade Compliance into an Action Plan 115
Concluding Remarks 116

Glossary... **119**

Key Acronyms **127**

Key International Web Sites... **131**

Appendix A: All About AES: The Automated Export System......................139

Appendix B: Supply Chain Security Best Practices Catalog.......................171

Appendix C: Foreign Corrupt Practices Act Antibribery Provisions 221

Appendix D: INCO Terms 2000 231

**Appendix E: Sample Documentation for an Export
and Import Shipment** 233

Index 255

About the Author 269

Foreword

I have read many of Tom Cook's books. I have seen him lecture and run seminars and business meetings. There is no one more fully informed with practical advice and counsel on how best to manage a global supply chain successfully.

Since the unfortunate events of 9/11, the global community, both in the United States and abroad, has realized the importance and relevance of introducing compliance and security in their global operations. Tom has taken a leadership position on this subject and has gained invaluable insight into corporations and just what it takes to raise the bar of compliance and security in their global operations.

This book addresses these issues in a comprehensive, no-nonsense approach that keeps the reader interested and fully engaged. It is detailed, articulate, and full of contemporary as well as timeless recommendations to help supply chain executives manage their global responsibilities.

As with all Tom's books and the work he does, I am a supporter and can earnestly recommend this book as an important tool in combating the effects of terrorism in managing your global supply chain.

Spencer Ross
President, World Trade Institute
Former Chairman, NY District Export Council

Overview

One of the newest and fastest growing corporate positions is that of *global trade compliance manager*. This position was once an insignificant factor in most corporations, but the events surrounding 9/11 changed that forever. *Compliance* became a household word in businesses involved in importing and exporting. As we approach 2010, this is still a work in progress.

While there are many resources for the compliance manager, this book will be the compilation and "go to" one-step resource for the executive engaged in global supply chains who wants to be compliant with government regulations. In addition, this book will provide a step-by-step blueprint for developing a compliance program and making it work cost-effectively within a corporation's supply chain operation. This book will become the "resident bible" for current and future managers of global supply chains.

When corporations begin setting up initiatives to become compliant, they often have to seek the support of outside counsel, consultants, and specialists, because there is no single resource to go to—to get the necessary answers to accomplish this work independently.

This book will provide the company and the manager responsible for supply chain compliance with the necessary tools to initiate all the steps to secure a corporate compliance program in their global supply chain.

Chapter 1

The Importance of Trade Compliance Programs in Global Supply Chains

Trade compliance has always been a relatively small part of any company's supply chain. The events of September 11, 2001, raised the bar of trade compliance forever. Those companies who do not elevate their participation in trade compliance will find in a very short time that it will be next to impossible to be engaged in global trade.

The Global Supply Chain

Supply chain executives have always had three primary responsibilities in managing their logistics program. The basis of the three primary responsibilities is first to understand that the basis of supply chain is to eventually move goods from A to B.

In moving goods from A to B, whether importing, exporting, warehousing, processing, etc., the intent of management is to do that in a manner that is:

- Timely
- Safe
- Cost-effective

Now it is time to not only accomplish these three elements, but also to include the additional elements of compliance and security.

This makes the *primary goal* of the trade compliance officer to ensure that the company's supply chain is secure and compliant, while at the same time ensuring that the three deliverables of timely, safe, and cost-effective logistics.

This is where the real challenge occurs. It is not easy to focus on two areas of responsibility: compliance and logistics. Often there can be a conflict between strict regulatory adherence and the free ability to move freight. In both areas, certain compromises need to be made to accomplish a balanced global supply chain that runs successfully and meets regulation responsibly.

The Basics Steps of Structuring and Implementing

The author outlines a ten-step strategy to structure and implement a trade compliance program. This can be accomplished as either a brand new initiative or an enhancement to a preexisting program. The ten steps, which are further outlined in greater detail throughout this book, can be summarized as follows:

1. Awareness
2. Senior management
3. Analysis and review
4. Person(s) responsible—team initiative
5. Resource development
6. Action plan
7. Standard operating procedures
8. Training and education
9. Self-audit
10. Stewardship reports

Awareness

Trade compliance begins with corporate supply chain personnel becoming aware of all the issues in compliance and security and understanding just where their company stands in the mix. This is being proactive.

Being reactive, after the fact, will cause delays, fines and penalties, and extra costs that are typically not anticipated and therefore not budgeted. There is certainly personal exposure as well: the boss isn't going to be happy, so getting the resume together may be the plan B. However, we also face personal risks where fines, penalties, and even prosecution may extend to individuals in tandem with the corporation for violation of federal regulations.

Awareness means having a consistent inbound flow of information and developing resources, so we know what the issues are, the most recent modifications, and ultimately, the options we have in mitigating these matters in our supply chains.

It is critical that the supply chain executive manage his or her responsibilities. This includes allocating as much as 10% of his or her time reading trade publications (such as *Managing Imports and Exports* (The World Academy), *American Shipper, Journal of Commerce*, and *Cargo Business News and World Trade*), reviewing Web sites, and attending trade compliance symposiums, training sessions, and conferences.

Information inflow is as important a skill set as knowing how to get goods cleared by Customs in China or dealing with the Food and Drug Administration (FDA) in the United States if we bring in food, pharmaceutical, or related merchandise. That information inflow will eventually cause the trade compliance manager to need to change some of the aspects of his supply chain. Such changes require the support of senior management.

Senior Management

All corporations have profit and cost centers managed by individuals with personalities, egos, and their own interpretations and ideas on how various responsibilities should be managed.

Compliance, security, and terrorism issues cross all boundaries within a corporation. Finance, legal, customer service, operations, logistics, traffic management, inventory, purchasing, manufacturing, and even the customers and suppliers are a few of these centers within typical corporations. In our practice, we have found that at all times the nature of people in corporations is to resist change.

When you discuss issues regarding terrorism, compliance, and security with a lot of uninformed executives, there will be a natural resistance to any infrastructure change recommendations put forth by compliance and security personnel. This is where the support of senior management is vital. Their support and avocation of compliance and security initiatives will break down the resistance and allow for constructive review and implementation.

As a matter of import and export regulation, it is clearly required that senior management be aware of the importance of regulatory compliance and institute internal controls to follow the same. Simply stated, those supply chain initiatives that carry senior management support will have a much more likely opportunity for successful implementation than those that do not. Having said that, one is more likely to obtain senior management support when senior management is made aware of the specific consequences of operating a nonsecure and noncompliant supply chain. *To move in that direction, a company must assess where it is. It needs to benchmark.*

Analysis and Review

In order to determine where they are, a company should conduct a process called a facilities review. This is a detailed analysis and mock audit of the supply chain and operations. This is typically best accomplished by engaging an independent consultant. This will afford a third-party analysis where "others" do it outside the corporation. They have no specific agendas that conflict with personnel or career matters and will have external reference points to utilize as benchmarks for where a company is. This necessary review will then provide the blueprint for actions to be taken later that will make the company's supply lines more able to manage the affects of terrorism, compliance, and security issues.

The review and scrutiny also responds to the various government agencies' doctrines of exercising due diligence, reasonable care, and supervision and control. A facilities review can also assess the relationships to vendors, providers, carriers, forwarders, and brokers—to ensure the strength of those links in the supply chain and add compliance and security to the business profile in lieu of weak links.

Accountable, responsible, and qualified personnel in the necessary trade compliance skill sets should handle the control and management of the reviews and benchmarking. Their experience and qualifications will ensure a successful trade compliance initiative.

Person(s) Responsible—Team Initiative

Irrespective of the size of the corporation or the supply chain, one person should be responsible for managing the risks of terrorism, compliance, and security. This person can be part of any profit or cost center—logistics, manufacturing, purchasing, legal/regulatory—it does not really matter, as long as he or she has the skill sets and capabilities necessary to manage the job. We do recommend, though, that this person work within a team approach. Individuals from all profit and cost centers, all divisions and disciplines, are involved.

Gaining cooperation will be more easily achieved when all interests—manufacturing, purchasing, customer service, legal, finance, logistics, etc.—feel that they will have influence, their ideas will be heard, and they can constructively provide input.

We are observing more companies creating positions in supply chain or import/export trade compliance and security at a faster rate today than at any other previous time in contemporary global trade history.

There is an organization—Professional Association of Import and Export Compliance Managers (PACMAN), based in New York City, with representation throughout the United States—that actually has a seminar structure, testing, and certification of supply chain managers (www.compliancemaven.com). This association teaches the skill sets for personnel who have these compliance and security responsibilities and offers instruction that helps a company meet the standards of exercising due diligence, reasonable care, and internal training and education.

These responsible personnel, who may have these responsibilities added to their job description, will eventually have to implement and affect corporate change. This will best be accomplished by creating a *plan of action*. The plan of action needs to state goals, objectives, the process of obtaining, time frames, and who has ownership of all the activity.

Resource Development

It is imperative that supply chain management develop resources to gain information. Quality information is the foundation for being informed. Being informed allows for good decision making. Good decision making allows supply chain managers the best opportunity to achieve successful and profitable global supply chains.

In every office I enter, where a first-class supply chain manager resides, you will see copies of many periodicals, such as *The Journal of Commerce, Managing Imports & Exports, and American Shipper.* These periodicals are read and distributed to all concerned fellow staff. Besides having good periodicals, working the Internet and going to key Web sites and being listed on certain mailings and e-mail blasts is very worthwhile.

In our studies, we identify that supply chain personnel should allocate at least 10% of their time reading and surfing resource material. The best supply chain managers are well read and informed. They recognize the value this brings into the negotiation process and have the ability to utilize that information inflow to the corporation's best advantage. Recommended key Web sites are provided at the end of the book in Appendix A, and recommended periodicals and e-mails are given at the end of this chapter.

As part of resource development, it is also important to actively participate in various organizations that interface with global supply chain issues. Below are some, to name a few:

National Association of Customhouse Brokers and Freight Forwarders (NCBFAA)
Council of Logistics Managers (CLM)
Professional Association of Import and Export Compliance Managers (PACMAN)
National District Export Councils (NYDEC)
Long Island Import/Export Association (LIEXA)
Air Forwarders Association (AFA)

In addition, there are literally hundreds of books that focus on various aspects of supply chain management that would work in the building of a library of core information. Three books that we would recommend are:

Mastering Import and Export Management (Cook, AMACOM Books)
Export/Import Procedures and Documentation (Johnson, AMACOM Books)
Extending the Supply Chain (Boyer, AMACOM Books)

Action Plan

Once the analysis is completed and the compliance person chosen, a plan will have to be developed utilizing an Excel spreadsheet.

Action	By When	By Who	Status
Create record keeping system	December 15, 2012	Lindsay	Draft done by December 2
Meet with Panalpina to review B/L info	December 10, 2012	Zack	Appointment set by Sam for December 2
Internal C-TPAT review committee meeting	November 25, 2012	Travis	Set for November 10
Meet with engineers to review ECCN classifications	December 20, 2012	Hunter	Sam to schedule

This example sets the stage for a system of responsibility and accountability and keeps everyone on the same page. It will allow the company to set an agenda of all that needs to be done, who will execute, by what specific timetable, and a status so all can see where they are. It should be updated on a weekly or an agreed periodic basis. Maintaining an "everyone on the same page" system will help ensure success.

The action plan will eventually lead the company and the individuals in charge of compliance and security to create standard operating procedures (SOPs).

Standard Operating Procedures (SOPs)

SOPs are a necessary component of any supply chain and are a key tool to successfully implement consistent behavior of personnel and how they act in purchasing, sourcing, and logistics. Their importance can be outlined in four areas:

1. They provide the blueprint for all to follow and become the internal resource for all personnel to look to for guidance of how to operate within the company's global supply chain.
2. They commit all the processes to a written format, which clearly outlines how a company and its personnel will function in its supply chain.
3. The SOPs then become a benchmark to meet the government's requirements for exercising due diligence and reasonable care.
4. Should supply chain personnel move on, there is written guideline for new personnel to follow.

In addition, if we are a public company, we will need to be concerned with Sarbanes-Oxley (SOX) regulations and our fiduciary responsibilities to create financial and operating guidelines, controls, and information flows back to corporate management. This affords a synergy between compliance and security management SOPs and SOX SOPs.

On the various government Web sites established guidelines are put forward by various agencies as starting points and benchmarks for creating written guidelines within U.S. companies.

We strongly advocate SOPs that are:

■ Easy to comprehend
■ Comprehensive
■ All-encompassing
■ Functional

Keeping in mind that, at the end of the day, logistics still has to move the goods from point A to point B, the SOPs should not be so restrictive that they impede personnel's basic responsibilities in international transportation services that encompass the global arena. There needs to be a reasonable compromise between security and compliance—that meets the regulatory requirements but still allows the freight to move safely, in a timely manner, and cost-effectively. A key element of implementing the SOPs will be educating and training the staff.

Training and Education

A cornerstone of any compliance and security program is having all the supply chain personnel specially trained in the basics of compliance and security. These basics include:

■ Logistics outsourcing
■ Choosing freight forwarders, brokers, and vendors
■ Classification
■ Valuation
■ Record keeping
■ Red flag management
■ Documentation
■ SOP development
■ Denied party screening
■ Crisis and risk management

These are but a few of the areas where personnel from all areas of a supply chain must be better informed and trained in what they need to know and how they need to operate.

Education and training is another benchmark of the government for a corporation exercising due diligence and reasonable care. At the end of the rainbow in education and training is the ability for a corporation to eventually "stand on its own," There are two excellent resources for education and training:

World Academy: www.theworldacademy.com
American Management Association: www.ama.net.org

Personnel need to be trained and retrained every one to three years. The landscape of global business changes in nanoseconds. What one learns today is outmoded the next season. Refresher courses and continuing education are a cornerstone issue of any program and best practices initiatives.

Self-Audit

The ultimate goal of this whole process, outlined in the ten steps, is for a corporation to run its global supply chain compliantly and securely on an independent basis. This means that the company can self-audit its import and export operations and feel confident in its personnel and SOPs, and that operations will run in accordance with the new post-9/11 regulations—and be cost-effective in competing in the marketplace.

One of the many benefits of becoming a member of Customs-Trade Partnership Against Terrorism (C-TPAT) is what is referred to as the importer self-assessment (ISA) program. In this program, an importer must demonstrate the capability to self-audit, self-regulate, and basically meets the steps outlined by Customs and Border Protection under the guidelines of this program. Once granted ISA status, CBP will keep "out of their face" and allow the importer to monitor itself independently—free from Customs' day-to-day scrutiny, which faces the overwhelmingly majority of importers. What a nice position to be in—a company that is so well organized in its compliance program that Customs affords it the ability to manage its own trade compliance program.

Global Contract Management

Every time a company engages in a corporate contract, whether for an export sale or an import purchase, it must create a checklist of six issues that must be successfully dealt with in that agreement. While these issues are independent from one another, they do have dotted lines of connectivity:

- **INCO terms (international commercial terms of sale)**
- **Payment terms**
- **Freight**
- **Insurance**
- **Title**
- **Revenue recognition**

While these areas have certain aspects of connectivity and are related to one another in an export sale or import purchase, they are also distinct issues that need to be resolved and worked out on their own merit.

One must also keep in mind that there is the strict interpretation of rules and regulations, and there is also the functionality of dealing with these rules and regulations while continuing to operate our supply chains compliantly, securely, and cost-effectively.

In addition, one must also pay attention to other governance, such as but not limited to:

Securities and Exchange Commission (SEC)
Internal Revenue Service (IRS)
Sarbanes-Oxley (SOX)
Generally accepted accounting principles
Uniform Customs and Practices (UCP)

INCO

The INCO terms primarily address a point in time in which responsibilities and liabilities pass between an exporter and an importer located overseas. They do not specifically address freight, title, payment, and revenue recognition, though by default they may have some bearing.

The INCO term does concern itself with liability for loss and damage. However, depending upon how payment is made, which must be factored in, when we look at the INCO term, we have to also consider *functional* supply chain management issues. The best example of this is when responsibility and liability pass to an importer where credit terms have been extended, such as in a FOB/FCA port of export sale, and sixty-day open account terms are also provided.

What would happen if the shipment was lost or damaged? How would the exporter protect itself? There are many options to this question, but they would depend upon how the supply chain operates. But having said that, the point being made is the showing of a conflict between the term of sale and the term of payment, where a point in time has passed between seller and buyer but exposure still exists for the seller.

Terms of Sale/INCO Terms

INCO terms are the internationally accepted definitions for terms of sale legislated by the International Chamber of Commerce (ICC). It is vital that U.S. companies are familiar with these terms, as they identify the precise moment when ownership of goods passes from seller to buyer. INCO terms further assign each party its respective performance responsibilities, elements of cost, and associated risks. The inclusion of INCO terms in a sales agreement commits the buyer and seller to a strict interpretation of these standard definitions.

Note that the following terms must designate a place or port to be valid.

EXW—Ex works: The seller's only responsibility is to make the goods available at his or her premises in a condition prepared for export. The seller is not responsible for loading the goods in the vehicle provided by the buyer, unless otherwise agreed. The buyer bears the full cost and risk involved in bringing the goods from there to the desired destination.

FAS—Free alongside ship: The seller's obligations are fulfilled when the goods have been placed alongside the ship on the quay (wharf). The buyer bears all costs and risks of loss or damage to the goods from that moment. Unlike FOB, FAS requires the buyer to clear the goods for export.

FOB—Free on board vessel: The goods are placed on board a ship by the seller at a port of shipment named in the sales contract. The risk of loss or damage to the goods is transferred from the seller to the buyer when the goods pass the ship's rail during loading. This term only applies to transportation by sea or inland waterway.

CFR—Cost and freight: The seller must pay the cost of freight necessary to bring the goods to the named destination, but the risk of loss or damage, as well as any cost increases, is transferred from the seller to the buyer when the goods pass the ship's rail in the port of shipment. Applicable for sea or inland waterway transport only.

CIF—Cost, insurance, and freight: This term has the same meaning as CFR, but with the addition that the seller has to procure marine insurance against the risk of loss or damage to the goods during carriage. The seller pays the insurance premium.

DES—Delivered ex ship: The seller makes the goods available to the buyer on board the ship at the destination named in the sales contract. The seller bears the full cost and risk involved in bringing the goods there.

DEQ—Delivered ex quay (duty paid): This term means that the seller must deliver the goods to the buyer on the quay (wharf) at the named port of destination, cleared for importation. The seller has to bear all risks and costs, including duties, taxes, and other charges for delivering the goods. This term should not be used if the seller is unable to obtain the import license. If the buyer is the party who will clear the goods for importation and pay the duty, then the term is changed to "duty unpaid." This term applies to sea or inland waterway transport.

DDU—Delivered duty unpaid: DDU means that the seller makes the goods available to the buyer at the named place (e.g., door—Tokyo, Japan) in the country of importation. The seller has to pay the costs and bear the risks involved in bringing the goods to that point. The buyer pays the costs and risks of carrying out Customs formalities, obtaining the import license and duties, taxes, and official charges payable upon importation in his country. This term may be used irrespective of the mode of transport.

DDP—Delivered duty paid: While the term *ex works* signifies the seller's minimum obligation, DDP, when followed by the buyer's location in the destination country, denotes the seller's maximum obligation. The seller provides the import license and is responsible for delivery, import duties, taxes, and other import-related charges. This term may be used irrespective of the mode of transport.

FCA—Free carrier: This term has been designed to meet the requirements of modern transport, particularly such multimodal transport as container or "roll on/roll off" traffic by trailers and ferries, as well as carriage by air. FCA is based on the same principle as FOB, except that the seller fulfills his or her obligation when goods are delivered into the custody of the carrier at the named point. If no precise point can be mentioned at the time of the contract of sale, the parties should refer to the place or range where the carrier should take goods into his charge. The risk of the loss or damage to the goods is transferred from the seller to the buyer at that time and not at the ship's rail. *Carrier* means a person by whom or in whose name a contract of carriage by road, rail, air, sea, or a combination of modes has been made.

CPT—Carriage paid to: Like CFR, CPT means that the seller pays the freight for the carriage of the goods to the named destination. However, the risk of loss or damage to the goods, as well as any cost increases, is transferred from the seller to the buyer when the goods have been delivered into the custody of the first carrier and not at the ship's rail. It can be used for all modes of transportation.

CIP—Carriage and insurance paid to: This term is the same as "carriage paid to," but with the addition that the seller has to procure transport insurance against the risk of loss or damage to the goods during the carriage. The seller pays the insurance premium.

DAF—Delivered at frontier: DAF means that the seller's obligations are fulfilled when the goods have arrived at the frontier, but before the Customs border of the country named in the sales contract. The term may be used for any frontier, including that of the country of export. Therefore, it is important that the frontier be defined precisely by naming the point and place in the term. The term is primarily intended to be used when goods are to be carried by rail or over the road, but it may be used irrespective of the mode of transport.

Payment

Terms of payment will be based on whatever both parties agree to and negotiate. Keep in mind that a receivable exposure may exist and your company's interest should be protected. This is an area that can be insured. Options for terms of payment may include advance payments, open accounts, forfeit, drafts, letters of credit, or credit cards.

Freight

Once again, this is determined by whatever both parties agree to, but the intent of freight payment should coincide with the INCO term and be built into the cost of goods sold to your foreign customers if you are selling, and built into your landed cost if you are purchasing. Either way, these charges should be accounted for and line itemed in your commercial invoice. Freight also can be prepaid or collected. This will have a bearing on potential financial exposures.

Title

Title is not determined by the INCO term. It is determined by the sales contract, sales agreement, or what you have in the commercial invoice. It should only pass on an export, once the contract has been satisfied—meaning you have delivered and they have paid.

This is often a very misunderstood point in financial arenas. The INCO term specifically stays away from property right issues in its intent and application. Title needs to be expressly written into your contract of sale, purchase order, or on the commercial invoice.

Revenue Recognition (Exports Only)

This is a more complicated area for an export. It is primarily covered under generally accepted accounting principles (GAAPs). For revenue to be recognized, there must be four things in place:

1. An impending sale (usually provided by a purchase order in hand)
2. An ability to meet that sale in inventory, manufacturing capability, or third-party purchase
3. A reasonable expectation that you will get paid (not only by the customer, but by the country of destination being able to transfer funds into U.S. dollars)
4. Delivery has been accomplished

Delivery is not very well defined, but by court precedence and rulings, it has been defined at the time the freight is tendered to the first carrier whose intent is to bring it to a point where it will leave the country.

From prior rulings and established precedence, there is also an onus on the corporation to be consistent in its revenue recognition practice. This has a potential major impact on Sarbanes-Oxley (SOX) compliance matters.

The more difficult area of the component is delivery. In most situations this is highly interpretative and subjective. Having said that, most companies have successfully defined this as when the goods are either loaded on the international conveyance or handed over to the inland carrier for international transport, or when they have an international bill of lading in their possession. This is where there is a connection to the INCO term.

The importance of this choice is that it be consistent and that documentation exists that an export will happen. Tie in the other two factors—contract completion and payment—and a company can meet this standard.

As an example, many companies have gotten themselves into trouble with the IRS and the SEC where an export has occurred, but the nature of the sale is one of goods on consignment or ones that are placed strategically in an overseas warehouse, available for the importer to access. In reality, the sale is specifically not made until the goods are removed from local inventory. The INCO term of the sale was FOB port of export and delivery has occurred, but the nature of the deal changes how this sale is really being made. The company takes the sale when the goods are exported, but really should not have done that until the goods have been extracted from inventory. Many companies have had major issues over this type of export.

Compliance

Making choices to ensure compliance is critical. In exports, we have the U.S. principal party in interest (USPPI) concern. This entity is the company that receives the primary benefit in an export transaction and is responsible for export compliance, including the information passed on to the government, where the goods are shipped, to whom they are going to, and how they will be utilized.

The government does not care if the INCO term is ex works, FOB, or FCA; it will still hold the USPPI responsible. This begs the question why a company would allow a third party not under its control to handle the shipment, by default creating significant compliance exposures. This is one more factor that must be considered when deciding which INCO term to use.

Insurance: Loss and Damage

Most customers will hold the exporter responsible for loss and damage, irrespective of the INCO term. For this reason, exporters should make sure the shipment is insured properly and with a secure underwriting facility. Ocean shipments, in particular, provide an array of critical exposure to shippers.

Resources Outline

A critical element of being compliant and secure is to have a regular and consistent flow of information from an array of reputable, comprehensive, and reliable resources, as outlined below.

Magazines

Air Cargo World
American Shipper
Asia Monitor
Breakbulk Connection
Cargo Business News
Cargo Security International Magazine
China Business Review
Emergency Preparedness News
Export Practitioner
Government Security News (GSN)
Global Logistics and Supply Chain
Inbound Logistics
Journal of Commerce (JOC)
Logistics Management
Logistics and Supply Chain
Logistics Today
Managing Imports and Exports
Marine Digest/Cargo Intelligence
Maritime Reporter & Engineering News
Material Handling Management
Modern Materials Handling
Supply and Demand Chain Executive
Supply Chain Management Review
Traffic World
World Trade

Associations

Air Forwarders Association (AFA)
American Association of Exporters and Importers (AAEI)
Association for Operations Management (APICS)
Association for Services Management International
Council of Logistics Management (CLM)
Council of Supply Chain Management Professionals (CSCMP)
Institute for Supply Chain Management (ISM)
Long Island Forum for Technology (LIFT)
National Customers Brokers & Forwarders Association (NCBFAA)
New York District Export Council (NYDEC)
Overseas Security Advisory Council (OSAC)
Professional Association of Import/Export Compliance Managers (PACMAN)
Traffic Club of Newark

E-Mail Newsletters

AAEI
AfA AIRMAIL
Air Cargo This Week Online
American Shipper
Cargo Business Newswire
GSN: Government Security News
JOC ONLINE
Logistics Management Online
Material Handling Management Briefing
Supply Chain Brain
Supply Chain Daily
Traffic World Daily Briefing
Transport Topics
World Trade eNewsletter

Chapter 2

Export Logistics and Compliance Management

Exporting is big business for companies located in the United States. Exporting is one of the areas within the global supply chain under scrutiny from the U.S. government. This chapter gives an overview of all one needs to know about the substance of exporting.

Export Logistics, Freight Forwarding, and Shipping

Another integral option to gain competitive advantage is through comprehensive logistics management. More often than not, logistical issues can be a significant expense to the exporter's landed cost. A higher than estimated landed cost may dissuade your company from exporting. This issue makes the U.S. manufacturer noncompetitive and, in many instances, is the last consideration of the U.S. exporter. Comprehensive logistics management should be part of the original scrutiny in the overall sales process to any destination. Anything you can do to lower the logistics costs, and help your customer achieve a lower landed price, will have a significant favorable impact on sales into the region, acknowledging that a good logistics program can be the factor that completes the sale and makes the trade a done deal. We need to understand the supply chain process in order to affect quality, comprehensive, and competitively priced transportation.

Export Freight Forwarding and Supply Chain Management

The quality of your freight forwarders and the delivery of the international services they provide can make or break your export operation. While at times they may seem to be nothing but a necessary evil, forwarders can be your best ally in mitigating the hazards of world trade and ensuring successful and profitable international transactions.

Like other key vendors, freight forwarders need to be managed and treated as partners with mutual goals, common direction, and a full understanding of what each party brings to the relationship—and ultimately the benefit to each other through the association. One of the most important services a forwarder can provide is advice and counsel. Most shippers utilizing a good forwarder will say the most important factors in their choosing that forwarder were level of experience, resources, and general working knowledge of international trade. Forwarders are also a great resource for problems that may occur with shipments. For a company experiencing a frequency of damage claims via a particular mode of transport, the forwarder can guide the company to make changes in packaging that better protect the cargo, leading to less frequency of damage claims. Less frequency of damage claims results in the customer satisfaction level being raised, as they are receiving a complete and intact shipment. The five key points in choosing a forwarder are:

1. Selection
2. Logistics consulting
3. Pricing
4. Value-added service
5. Setting performance standards selection

In determining what forwarder to choose, you have several resources:

■ Go to other shippers for referrals
■ Ask carriers for recommendations
■ Use industry-specific export links
■ Go to the National Association of Customhouse Brokers and Forwarders
■ Check the Export Yellow Pages
■ Check the American Export Register

For a referral, contact the World Academy (www.theworldacademy.com).

Potentially, there are another dozen resources to turn to, such as another shipper who has had firsthand experience with a freight forwarder. To determine which freight forwarder is best suited to meet your needs, you must set up some selection criteria. For example, a large shipper may have a fully staffed traffic department and may be fully capable of executing documentation and negotiating freight rates.

In this case, a freight forwarder might be needed for a niche type of activity, special tasks, and overall logistics consulting.

On the other hand, a small shipper may require the freight forwarder to execute every document, including the export invoice, certificate of origin, bill of lading, and electronic export information (EEI) transmission.

It is essential to note that even very large shippers have decided to purchase all services of the freight forwarder in lieu of establishing a fully staffed traffic department. At the same time, some qualified small shippers prefer to do much of the work themselves. Your company must survey its own needs to determine the criteria for its forwarder selection process.

Freight forwarders vary greatly from one another in skills, capabilities, and delivery of services. Some forwarders are specialists on certain trade routes and specific commodities. Some shippers may choose to use two or more forwarders for different areas. Most forwarders offer a menu of value-added services, such as warehousing and packing.

In creating criteria that fit your company, you might list the following:

- Documentation
- Rates
- Carrier and port selection
- Packaging
- Insurance
- Warehousing
- Electronic documentation capabilities
- Logistics knowledge
- Depth of compliance and cargo security knowledge
- Customs clearance and foreign country outreach
- Hours of operation

This list should be given to the forwarders in order to obtain proposals. The proposals received from the forwarders will serve as a gauge for evaluation of their services in the areas your company has identified as most important to its export program.

Shipping Costs

Pricing may vary between different forwarders. Price quotations should be obtained from a forwarder prior to export. The request for quotation should be all-inclusive, with the charges broken down by description. A one-line (all-inclusive) price should not be accepted, as it leaves room for later add-ons, resulting in additional bills and unaccounted for charges.

Quotes should include transportation rates, frequency of transit, and transit time. If the product has special handling requirements, that information should be provided to the forwarder prior to the quotation so it can include any additional costs associated with that handling. The request for quote should also request documentary requirements and destination country requirements to ensure the best information is received.

Jane,

Please provide a quote for the following:

    Fleece dog sweaters

    Value: $5,000

    1 box 150 lb

    Insurance

    Dimensions: 25 × 32 × 36 inches

    Pickup from: Melville, New York

    Destination: Zurich Airport, Switzerland

Please advise if there are any special requirements at destination.

Thanks,

T. Zan

T.

Per your request, please find the all-inclusive charges to pick up:

    1 box 250 lb (dimensions: 25 × 32 × 36) from Melville, NY to Zurich

    Airport with insurance:

        Air freight: $3.25/kg (weekly consolidation)

        Air freight: $3.80/kg (daily flight)

        Security fee: $25.00

        Service fee: $35.00

        AES/EEI transmission: $25.00

        Pickup Melville/transfer to JFK: $40.00

    Insurance: $15.00

Destination Customs will require an invoice and certificate of origin.

Regards,

Jane

Shipping Cost Breakdown

Domestic invoice total
Additional domestic costs that may be part of the forwarder's fee:

>   Warehousing
>   Inland freight
>   Export packing
>   Loading charges

Shipping and documentation:

>   Consularization/notarization
>   AES/EEI transmission
>   Certificate of origin
>   Packing list
>   Bills of lading
>   SGS inspection
>   Insurance certificate
>   Health and sanitary certificates
>   Miscellaneous

Banking and finance:
  Letter of credit
  Sight draft

Freight forwarding fees:
  Insurance
  Freight
  Security or fuel surcharges

Foreign import costs:
  Customs clearance
  Local delivery (inland freight)
  Import license
  Product registrations
  Storage
  Handling
  Documentation charges

Miscellaneous

INTERNAL QUOTATION WORKSHEET FOR EXPORTS

Date: _____

Customer name: _____

Destination country: _____

INCO terms (named place): _____

Payment terms: _____

Method of shipping: _____

Product details: _____

_____

Dimensions/weight of final package: _____

Selling price of goods: _____

Export packing: _____

Inland freight: _____

Ocean freight/air freight:

    Bunker adjustment fee (ocean)

    Currency adjustment factor (ocean)

    Loading fee (ocean)

    Unloading (ocean)

    Security fee (ocean and air)

    Fuel surcharge (air)

    Total freight cost: _____

Insurance: _____

Forwarding fees:

    AES filing fee

    Messenger/courier fee

Handling

Additional

Legalization fees

Total forwarding fees: _____

Transit time/frequency: _____

Total quotation: _____

Value-Added Services

Forwarders rates may vary, but pricing should not be the only factor taken into consideration when choosing a forwarder. Most forwarders use the same air carriers and the same steamship lines. Where forwarders truly differentiate themselves is in the value-added services they offer.

A forwarder may provide an array of services that may be considered standard or value added. For example, you may be entering a new market in a different country. In your analysis, you will need to be supplied with a significant amount of data. Your forwarder may be in a position to review your needs and provide feedback in areas such as the following:

- Logistics options
- Documentation requirements
- Packaging considerations
- Warehousing capabilities
- Labeling requirements
- Distribution systems
- Foreign agency outreach

Another potential value-added service is providing electronic documentation capability. This entails the retrieval of manual shipping data in an automated format with production of documentation and tracking in an automated mode. The range of data, equipment availability, and report formatting may vary from forwarder to forwarder. The bottom line is that the electronic documentation capability reduces costs and improves tracking capabilities in managing the export process.

The freight forwarder relationship needs to be managed to ensure your forwarder keeps its commitments to quality service, on-time performance, and quoted costs.

In maintaining the forwarder's performance:

1. Get all commitments, quotes, and proposals in writing.
2. Allocate time frames to export transactions. Maintain a diary and follow-up schedule to determine responsiveness and accuracy.

3. Have all export shipments quoted. If there is no time to quote, then have pricing made available as soon as practical.
4. Have your forwarder submit annual stewardship reports.
5. Require regular meetings with your forwarder. Gain access to senior management. Meet with the staff handling your account and not just the salesperson. Make sure those individuals understand your company's needs.

The effectiveness of the forwarder will depend on the level of accountability to which your company holds him. The forwarder should be viewed as a valuable partner in your logistics team. When utilized effectively, he can maximize profit, mitigate risk, and spearhead you into successful exporting.

Power of Attorney

Freight forwarders provide statements and declaration to the U.S. government on behalf of the exporter. Freight forwarders will require a power of attorney as their authorization to make these statements. In lieu of a power of attorney, a written authorization may be provided to the forwarder.

E.I.N. # _____ **CUSTOMS POWER OF ATTORNEY**

Check appropriate box:
- Individual
- Partnership
- Corporation
- Sole Proprietorship

KNOW ALL MEN BY THESE PRESENTS: That _____

(Full Name of person, partnership, or corporation or sole proprietorship (Identify))

_____

a corporation doing business under the laws of the State of _____ or a _____

(indicate state in which you are incorporated) *(if not incorporated state Individual or Partnership)*

doing business as _____ residing at _____

(Enter the name of the partnership or fictitious business name) *(if an individual, fill in your home address.)*

having an office and place of business at _____

_____ , hereby constitutes and appoints : American River Brokerage Services Ltd.

as a true and lawful agent and attorney of the grantor named above for and in the name, place, and stead of said grantor from this date and in all Customs Districts, and in no other name, to make, endorse, sign, declare, or swear to any entry, withdrawal, declaration, certificate, bill of lading, carnet or other document required by law or regulation in connection with the importation, transportation, or exportation, of any merchandise shipped or consigned by or to said grantor; to perform any act or condition which may be required by law or regulation in connection with such merchandise; to receive any merchandise deliverable to said grantor;

To make endorsements on bills of lading conferring authority to transfer title, make entry or collect drawback, and to make, sign, declare, or swear to any statement, supplemental statement, schedule, supplemental schedule, certificate of delivery, certificate of manufacturer, certificate of manufacture and delivery, abstract of manufacturing records, declaration of proprietor on drawback entry, declaration of exporter on drawback entry, or any other affidavit or document which may be required by law or regulation for drawback purposes, regardless of whether such bill of lading, sworn statement, schedule, certificate, abstract, declaration, or other affidavit or document is intended for filing in any customs district;

To sign, seal, and deliver for and as the act of said grantor any bond required by law or regulation in connection with the entry or withdrawal of imported merchandise or merchandise exported with or without benefit of drawback, or in connection with the entry, clearance, lading, unlading or navigation of any vessel or other means of conveyance owned or operated by

said grantor, and any and all bonds which may be voluntarily given and accepted under applicable laws and regulations, consignee's and owner's declarations provided for in section 485, Tariff Act of 1930, as amended, or affidavits in connection with the entry of merchandise;

To sign and swear to any document and to perform any act that may be necessary or required by law or regulation in connection with the entering, clearing, lading, unlading, or operation of any vessel or other means of conveyance owned or operated by said grantor;

To authorize other Customs Brokers to act as grantor's agent; to receive, endorse and collect checks issued for Customs duty refunds in grantor's name drawn on the Treasurer of the United States; if the grantor is a nonresident of the United States, to accept service of process on behalf of the grantor;

And generally to transact at the customhouses in any district any and all customs business, including making, signing, and filing of protests under section 514 of the Tariff Act of 1930, in which said grantor is or may be concerned or interested and which may properly be transacted or performed by an agent and attorney, giving to said agent and attorney full power and authority to do anything whatever requisite and necessary to be done in the premises as fully as said grantor could do if present and acting, hereby ratifying and confirming all that the said agent and attorney shall lawfully do by virtue of these presents; the foregoing power of attorney to remain in full force and effect

until the _____ day of _____ , 20 _____

or until notice of revocation in writing is duly given to and received by a District Director of Customs. If the donor of this power of attorney is a partnership, the said power shall in no case have any force or effect after the expiration of 2 years from the date of its execution.

IN WITNESS WHEREOF, the said _____

has caused these presents to be sealed and signed: (Signature) _____

(Signature of an officer of the corporation or another employee specifically designated by the articles of incorporation or resolution of the board of directors to sign power of attorney for that corporation; if a partnership, a signature of a partner; if an individual, the signature of that individual.)

(Capacity) _____ (Date) _____

(Title of the person signing item 11.)

WITNESS: _____ _____

(Name of witness) *(Signature of witness.)*

(Corporate Seal)

U.S. Census Bureau

SAMPLE FORMAT: Power of Attorney

POWER OF ATTORNEY
EXPORTER (U.S. PRINCIPAL PARTY IN INTEREST)/FORWARDING AGENT

Know all men by these presents, That _____, the (USPPI)
(Name of U.S. Principal Party in Interest (USPPI))

organized and doing business under the laws of the State or Country of _____
and having an office and place of business at _____
(Address of USPPI)

hereby authorizes _____, the (Forwarding Agent)
(Forwarding Agent)

of _____
(Address of Forwarding Agent)

to act for and on its behalf as a true and lawful agent and attorney of the U.S. Principal Party in Interest
for and in the name, place and stead of the U.S. Principal Party in Interest, from this date, in the United
States either in writing, electronically, or by other authorized means to:

Act as Forwarding Agent for Export Control, Census Reporting and Customs purposes. Make,
endorse or sign any Shipper's Export Declaration or other documents or to perform any act which may
be required by law or regulation in connection with the exportation or transportation of any
merchandise shipped or consigned by or to the U.S. Principal Party in Interest and to receive or ship
any merchandise on behalf of the U.S. Principal Party in Interest.

The U.S. Principal Party in Interest hereby certifies that all statements and information contained in the
documentation provided to the Forwarding Agent relating to exportation are true and correct.
Furthermore, the U.S. Principal Party in Interest understands that civil and criminal penalties, may be
imposed for making false or fraudulent statements or for the violation of any United States laws or
regulations on exportation.

This power of attorney is to remain in full force and effect until revocation in writing is duly given by the
U.S. Principal Party in Interest and received by the Forwarding Agent.

IN WITNESS WHEREOF, _____ caused these
(Full Name of USPPI/USPPI Company)

presents to be sealed and signed:

Witness: _____   Signature: _____
                                      Capacity: _____
                                      Date: _____

Regulations, Outreach, & Eduation Branch, Foreign Trade Division: 301-457-2238

INCO Terms in Logistics

INCO terms are the foundation of global trade. INCO terms fundamentally tell the seller and the buyer what their responsibilities and liabilities are to the export transaction.

INCO terms are global and are managed by the International Chamber of Commerce, consisting of over 130 countries. They transpose language, cultural, and legal issues local to all countries and peoples. This does not mean that an exporter does not have to take into account local issues when completing the transaction. It does mean the exporter can feel comfortable that an INCO term in the United States will have the same meaning to his customer in South Africa, Brazil, or the Netherlands.

In most U.S. companies, a salesperson or sales division, agent, or distributor begins the sales process. This is also where the terms of sale are generally concluded and agreed upon. Therefore, it is imperative that international salespeople understand INCO terms, particularly as they relate to transportation costs, export clearance, execution of export documentation, and foreign Customs clearance. The consequences of not comprehending the INCO terms may lead to internal aggravation between operations, finance, and sales due to unaccounted for transportation expenses. For example, under ex works, the seller is only responsible to make the freight available at his dock for pickup. A Cincinnati industrial products company enters into a contract for $30,000 under EXW Cincinnati. However, the customer calls and asks to have the treats delivered to the Port of Baltimore, essentially changing the INCO term to FCA Port of Baltimore. If the additional inland freight is not accounted for and billed to the customer, the additional charge would have to be absorbed by the seller, cutting into profit. The inland freight move could be as high as $700.

INCO terms must include a place name. An exporter in Riverside, California, sells pet shelters FCA California. Without naming a specific port, such as San Francisco, San Diego, Los Angeles, or Oakland, the exporter will not be able to account for the correct amount of inland freight to get the goods to the port of export. While there are thirteen standard INCO terms, normal business practice will create variations of the standard INCO terms, leading to countless options.

INCO terms are terms of sale that run in conjunction with a related but completely different subject: the terms of payment. In the introduction to the INCO terms, it is clearly stated that there are a number of problems that may occur that are not dealt with at all under the INCO terms. This is another reason why it is so important to train all staff involved in exports to understand the limitations of the INCO terms.

A pet products exporter sells FOB Norfolk. This means the seller is responsible to get the shipment to the point at which the goods are loaded on board the vessel. Once the shipment has passed the rail of the vessel, the seller passes the responsibility and costing to the buyer. The vessel leaves Norfolk and is moving across the ocean to the destination port. The vessel hits a tidal wave and sinks. While the INCO term was FOB Norfolk, the term of payment was sight draft sixty days. According to the INCO term, the risk of the international leg was for the account of the buyer. The buyer is obligated to pay for the goods, but he will never receive the goods.

This realistic example points out the conflict that arises in export shipments. While the term of sale and term of payment were clearly stated, there was a lapse in protecting the interest of the seller in the event the goods did not make it to the buyer. This could have been rectified by the seller requesting a copy of the buyer's insurance for the shipment and, even more airtight, requesting the buyer list the seller on the policy as a named insured. This would allow the seller to ready the next export for the buyer while collecting from the buyer's insurance company the claim for the lost shipment.

Terms of Payment

The exporter should control the terms of the sale as well as the terms of payment. The following factors must be considered in determining the terms of payment.

- Price and payment terms
- Competitive pressures
- Forwarder and carrier options
- Opportunities for loss and damage
- Previous experience with buyer
- City and country of destination
- Current economic and political situation in buyer's country

An additional consideration in controlling the terms of sale offers you, the exporter, both short- and long-term options for maintaining competitiveness. If you choose to sell on terms where all the basic shipping, documentation, insurance, and freight choices are in your control, then you have the ability to affect the CIP costs. You are not forced to accept a particular insurance company whose marine rates may be higher than you can obtain in the open market. If you are free to choose steamship lines, you have the option to look at carriers that may offer lower shipping costs. Each variable must be evaluated. Controlling the option to evaluate will afford more competitive choices, which will work to your company's advantage.

Another important consideration in determining the terms of sale is to look at the pitfalls of attempting a door-to-door sale, if required to do so, particularly in certain countries where Customs law and practice work to the disadvantage of the exporter.

The key here is to reduce your company's risk. You will never eliminate the risks, but you can manage the risks involved. Your company will need to make arrangements, either through the freight forwarder or the carrier, not to release the freight until the payment is made to the local representation. Quality local representation, good communication, and tight monetary controls will be critical to successful execution of this option.

Equally important is attention to the minute transactional detail for the passage of title and payment terms. Though title may transfer, responsibility, particularly fiscal responsibility, may not end.

Quality marine insurance affords protection to the exporter in all situations. The marine insurance contract should have features that protect the exporter, regardless of who is responsible to insure and where the title passes. Unpaid vendor and contingency insurance is part of a successful export program when a company is not responsible to insure, but may still have an insurable exposure due to payment terms or other factors. It will afford the exporter full transportation insurance in cases where it is not responsible for insurance but may be exposed to payment or contract terms.

Export Packing

Seventy percent of cargo losses in global trade can be attributed to loss or damage from controllable sources. Water damage, improper labeling, and poor handling make up most of the cargo losses that would be considered controllable. Specific actions taken by the shipper or the forwarder, prior to the international journey, may have prevented these losses from occurring.

International freight is subject to a number of impediments:

■ Salt and fresh water hazards (including condensation, humidity)
■ Multiple handling, dropping, and racking
■ Conveyance stress (truck, rail, ocean, and air)
■ Shock and vibration
■ Cultural and language differences
■ Customs and shipping delays
■ Pilferage and theft deterioration
■ Contamination and inherent vice
■ Acts of God and *force majeure*

The prudent shipper will purchase marine cargo insurance policies to protect its interest in the cargo on an "all risk" warehouse-to-warehouse basis. However, cargo insurance underwriters warrant that the cargo must be properly packaged for the international transit. This means the packing the shipper utilizes must be able to deal with all the hazards and impediments listed above. If not, a company's ability to obtain favorable settlement on a cargo claim may be diminished.

There are numerous options available to exporters and shippers to manage the export packing process to maximize the opportunities to move freight in a timely and safe manner through international transit. This important step in your company's export program is often referred to as cargo loss control management. Your company must manage its cargo loss control to mitigate these exposures. This is best achieved through management policy, packing guidelines, instructions to carriers and forwarders, and developing resources.

Management Policy

Management must recognize the value of cargo loss control and set a policy for all of the operational staff to follow. Money spent up front in better packaging, labeling, and handling systems will have future benefits that outweigh the up-front expenditures. Money spent on using better packing materials, labeling, and handling systems is a known cost and can be budgeted. Future losses due to damaged cargo, lost freight, and customer dissatisfaction cannot be budgeted and remain an unknown risk. By managing cargo loss control, your company can build the known costs of proactive loss control into the sales pricing. Successful shipping to overseas consignees will justify the costing in long-term relationships. Management must then set policy guidelines to instill a sense that all must be done, within cost-effective reasonableness, to ensure quality in export sales.

Steps in cargo loss control may become more cost-effective options for shipping, which ultimately will reduce the overall expense of an international shipment. An example of this is with unitization or consolidation. Unitization is the tying together of a smaller number of units into one handling unit, such as putting twenty small cartons on one pallet. The pallet causes an additional weight expense but goes a long way in reducing the handling of the individual cartons. If the unit load is shrink-wrapped, this will provide protection from moisture, contaminants, and pilferage.

Another example is by utilizing master shipping cartons, which are standardized in the freight industry, such as with E, EH, or D containers. Smaller cartons or shipping units can be repacked or consolidated in these standard cartons, preventing multiple handling and pilferage. Carriers offer rate discounts for these shipping containers that offset the initial outlay.

Set Packing Guidelines

Management must coordinate packing with sales, marketing, engineering, legal, and in concert with logistics. Packing that has a sales orientation that meets domestic market requirements may not hold well in the export logistics process. Packing that is export ready but does not conform to the marking and labeling requirements in the country of destination may arrive at the destination, but will not make it out of local Customs. Each country has its own marking requirements. These marking requirements are guided by the type of commodity that is being shipped.

Once management has coordinated this effort, export managers will need to set packing guidelines and standards. These standards must be both practical and cost-effective. Lines of accountability between all the vested interests will need to be established to ensure consistent compliance. Any export packing guidelines will need to be flexible, with standards that change from mode to mode, country to country, commodity to commodity, and all the many variables that could affect product outturn.

Standards should be committed to writing. We recommend the packing be part of the quoting process and included on export *pro forma* orders. This makes for a better sale and more clearly advises the overseas prospect just what it is buying.

Packing needs to be thought out with respect to the mode of transport and the carrier. Issues that may affect the freight include the environment the freight will pass through, the number of times the shipment will be handled, exposures to theft and pilferage, protection from the elements, and special handling requirements.

Exporters tend to choose the mode by cost. Exporters need to work with their forwarders to see if the forwarder and carriers are using the most direct route, utilizing consolidation, and where and how many points of transfer are involved.

Packaging Resources

Marine insurance cargo policies and international bills of lading refer to adequate or proper export packing. However, there is no set of guidelines for adequate packing. There are numerous resources that can be utilized to assist exporters in developing proper export packaging guidelines. Ocean, truck, rail, and air carriers may provide certain assistance. Insurance companies, forwarders, surveying firms, and consultants are also great resources. The following resources are also useful:

> Thomas Stowage: *The Properties and Stowage of Cargoes*—www.mdnautical.com
> IATA: *Cargo Claims and Loss Prevention Handbook*—www.iata.org/ps/ publications/cargoclaims.htm
> Joseph Hanlon: *Handbook of Package Engineering*—www.amazon.com
> David House: *Cargo Work for Maritime Operations*—www.amazon.com
> TAPPI: *Fibre Box Handbook*—www.tappi.org
> AMACOM: *Mastering Import and Export Management*—www.amanet.org (select AMACOM books)

For most exporters, export packaging will never be an issue until there is a problem. Proactive planning and implementing packaging guidelines as part of the overall export program can avoid many problems.

Managing Compliance and Documentation

Compliance and documentation are an integral part of your company's export program. The United States has regulations that must be followed by an exporter to ensure the export transaction is being handled in a legal manner.

The events of 9/11 changed how the government deals with export compliance, and the whole subject became more complex and comprehensive. Documentation is the key to moving the shipment through U.S. borders, the destination country's Customs, and to the customer's door. Together these two elements can make or break your company's export program.

Export Compliance

The responsibility for export compliance falls upon the U.S. principal party in interest (USPPI). The USPPI is the party in the United States that derives the greatest benefit, financial or otherwise, from the export transaction. Most often the USPPI is the actual shipper or manufacturer of the product and is responsible for arranging the export transportation. While this may seem pretty straightforward, there could be some confusion about the responsibilities of the USPPI in an ex works transaction where the foreign customer is responsible for moving the shipment.

The Foreign Trade Regulations view this type of transaction as a routed export. In a routed export, the foreign customer is responsible for selecting the forwarder. However, the USPPI still has the responsibility to comply with export regulations. This responsibility may only be transferred to the foreign consignee (foreign principal party in interest (FPPI)) if the USPPI receives something in writing from the FPPI stating that it will assume responsibility for determining licensing authority and obtaining any licenses if required.

In a routed export, the USPPI must provide the FPPI's forwarder with the information necessary to properly complete and transmit the Automated Export System filing of the electronic export information, which will be discussed in the next section.

The USPPI is responsible for following the rules and regulations of the following:

Department of Commerce: Bureau of Census
Department of Commerce: Bureau of Industry and Security (BIS)
Department of Treasury: Office of Foreign Asset Controls

There are other government agencies that cooperate with the above to enforce the regulations. Customs and Border Protection (CBP) works directly with these agencies to ensure exporters are complying with the law. Depending on your company's product, you may also be required to follow the laws of additional government agencies, such as the Food and Drug Administration, Fish and Wildlife Services, etc.

Census

Census is responsible for maintaining trade statistics for the United States. The Foreign Trade Regulations provide the basis for U.S. companies to report their export trade activity to Census. This is done via the Automated Export System (AES) reporting of the electronic export information (EEI). This information is required to be reported to Census prior to the shipment being delivered to the carrier in accordance with the advanced manifest filing regulations.

The AES reporting may be transmitted by your company as the exporter, or you may choose to delegate this to your forwarder. Regardless of whether your company is filing or your forwarder is filing, your company is required to accurately report the following information to Census:

- USPPI employer identification number
- Name, address, and contact information of the USPPI
- Ultimate consignee
- U.S. state of origin
- Country of ultimate destination
- Method of transportation and carrier details
- Port of export
- Related parties
- Domestic or foreign origin of goods
- Description of goods, unit of measure, and quantity
- Shipping weight
- Value
- Shipment reference number
- Hazardous materials
- Name, address, and contact information for authorized agent
- Product ECCN classification
- Export information code
- Commodity classifications (HTSUS/Schedule B number)

The information is transmitted to Census electronically. Upon receipt of the information, Census will send a response message indicating it has received the information in the required format. The response message will include an internal transaction number (ITN), which must be indicated on the transportation bill of lading as proof of filing.

The Foreign Trade Regulations stipulate fines for late filings. These fines begin at $1,100 to $10,000 per violation. In addition, for knowingly failing to file or for filing false information, the civil penalty may be as high as $10,000 per violation, and criminal penalties may be as high as $50,000 per violation, or imprisonment of no more than five years, or both.

AESDirect Shipment Record: KR111808 Page 1 of 1

Shipment Information		USPPI	
Filer ID:	#11-12345678	**Name:**	Kelly's Kreatures
Shipment:	#KR111808	**ID Number:**	#11-12345678
ITN:	X20081118123456	**Contact:** Kelly Raia	
Current Date/Time:	Wed Nov 18 17:32:03 2008 EST	**Phone:**	6313966800

Cargo Origin: East Moriches, NY

Departure Date: 111908

Trans Ref.: #125 12345678

Origin State: NY

Country of Dest.: GB

Export Port: 4701 JFK

Mode of Transport: Air (40)

Carrier SCAC/IATA: British Airways

Routed Transaction: No

Related Companies: No

Hazardous: No

Ultimate Consignee

Name: Sam's Salamanders

Contact: Edward Cullen

Phone: 011 2345678899

Address: 525 Shoreham Village

Essex, London, UK 2BH 35Z

Freight Forwarder

Name: American River International

ID Number: 11-12349876

Contact: Rosanne Esposito

Phone: 631-396-6800

Address: 1229 Old Walt Whitman Road

Melville, New York 11747

Commodities

Item	EIC Schedule B/HTS	Qty.	Gross Wt.	Value	Origin	License	Vehicle
1	3923290000	10,000	45 kg	$2,500	D	C33	No
2	4602900000	900	91 kg	$2,800	D	C33	No

Valuation

For AES purposes, the value to be declared in the filing should be the value to move the goods to the port of export (FCA/FOB). Many times the value is declared only as the invoice value. If your company's invoice reflects a delivery to customer shipment, then the value declared should be the invoice less the freight charges, clearance charges, etc. If your company's transaction is not an item for sale, a value must still be declared on the AES. The value stated should be the market value for the product if it were sold.

Harmonized Tariff Schedule/Schedule B Number

When exporting overseas, it is necessary to describe the commodities being shipped as either a Harmonized Tariff Schedule (HTS) number or a Schedule B number. This is a ten-digit number that provides a numerical description that matches up with the written description maintained by Customs and Census.

The HTSUS is specific to the United States and contains ninety-nine chapters. Chapters 1 to 97 deal specifically with commodities, while Chapters 98 and 99 deal with circumstances of import. The Schedule B system is very similar to the HTSUS, but tends to have more generalized descriptions. Additionally for U.S. importers, Customs only recognizes the HTSUS for Customs clearance purposes.

For purposes of filing the electronic export information, the HTSUS or the Schedule B number may be used. To illustrate the difference between the two systems, the HTSUS breakdown for the classification of dog treats might read "chicken flavored treats, beef flavored treats, duck flavored treats." The Schedule B breakdown would simply state "flavored treats."

These numbers can be accessed online as follows:

Schedule B: www.census.gov/foreign-trade/schedules/b/index.html
HTSUS: http://www.usitc.gov/tata/hts/bychapter/index.htm

Classification is not an exact science and requires interpretation of the rules and guidelines as established in the Census and Customs regulations. All guidelines need to be clearly understood prior to the ultimate selection of the HTS/Schedule B number, as this could lead to inaccurate reporting if the incorrect number were chosen.

Export Documents

4201	Saddlery and harness for any animal (including traces, leads, knee pads, muzzles, saddle cloths, saddle bags, dog coats, and the like), of any material:
4201003000	Dog leashes, collars, muzzles, harnesses, and similar dog equipment X
4201006000	Other X
2308009900	Other . . . . kg
2309	Preparations of a kind used in animal feeding:
2309100000	Dog or cat food, put up for retail sale . . . kg
230990	Other: Mixed feeds or mixed feed ingredients:
2309901010	Pet food, put up for retail sale . . . . kg
2309901020	Poultry feeds, prepared . . . . t

2309901030	Dairy cattle feed, prepared . . . . . . t
2309901040	Other livestock feed, prepared . . . . . t
2309901050	Other . . . . t
	Other:
2309903010	Milk replacer . . . . kg
2309908500	Other . . . . kg

Bureau of Industry and Security (BIS)

The Bureau of Industry and Security is responsible for implementing and enforcing the Export Administration Regulations, which regulate the export and reexport of most commercial items. This includes dual-use items that have commercial and military or proliferation applications.

Export Control Classification Number (ECCN)

The Bureau of Industry and Security maintains a list of items that are controlled for export from the United States. The Commerce Control List contains items that the U.S. government considers controlled and may only be exported from the United States by obtaining an authorization prior to export. The authorization may be in the form of a license exception or an actual license issued by the Department of Commerce.

Most products are not controlled for export. However, U.S. companies are still required to go through the ECCN determination process. If they do not find that their product falls under a specific listing on the Commerce Control List, the product may be designated as EAR99. This indicates the product is not controlled based on a commodity control. An EAR99 designation does not mean your company is off the compliance hook. Your company will still be responsible to determine if the destination country for the product falls under any government sanctions and if the buyer of the product is a denied party. For example, a cat collar may not be shipped to Cuba without receiving authorization from the U.S. government allowing such an export.

Denied Party Screening

Another element of export compliance is Denied Party Screening. These lists are maintained by five government agencies and contain a listing of the names of companies and individuals to whom U.S. companies may not ship product without prior authorization from the government. U.S. companies are required to screen these lists prior to export. The lists are not maintained on a central government database and require your company to review each individual list. There are software solutions available to manage this process that may include documentation capabilities as well.

Department of Commerce:
Denied Persons List
Unverified List
Entities List

Department of Treasury Office of Foreign Asset Controls:
Specially Designated Nationals List

Department of State:
Debarred Nationals List

Name and Address	Effective Date	Expiration Date	Type of Denial
A. ROSENTHAL (PTY) LTD. P.O. BOX 44198, 65 7TH STREET, DENMYR BUILDING, LINDEN, ZA	08/08/1997	08/08/2017	Standard
Appropriate *Federal Register* Citations: 62 F.R. 43503 8/14/97			
A. ROSENTHAL (PTY) LTD. P.O. BOX 97 292 INDEPENDENCE AVENUE, WINDHOEK, NA	05/20/1997	05/29/2017	Standard

Last modified: October 28, 2009.

Office of Foreign Asset Controls

The Office of Foreign Asset Controls administers and enforces economic sanctions programs against countries and groups of individuals such as terrorists, drug traffickers, and money launderers. The sanctions may be comprehensive or selective using the blocking of assets and trade restrictions to accomplish foreign policy and national security goals.

The Specially Designated Nationals List mentioned previously contains the names of organizations and individuals with whom transactions are prohibited. There are specific country sanctions that must be reviewed if your company is considering sales to any of the following countries: Balkans, Burma, Ivory Coast, Democratic Republic of Congo, Iran, Iraq, North Korea, Cuba, Sudan, Syria, and Zimbabwe.

The Office of Foreign Asset Controls maintains a user-friendly Web site (www. treas.gov/ofac) containing frequently asked questions and breakdowns on how the sanctions may affect your company's business.

Export Documentation

One of the major pitfalls in an international sale is the quality of the documentation supporting the transaction. A mistake in spelling, execution, language, or number of copies may cause substantial delays in the foreign Customs clearance and may require additional expenditures to complete the process. With the right approach and support from several resources, the process can be simplified.

Export documents:
  Electronic export information
  Commercial invoice
  Packing list
  Bill of lading
  Insurance certificate

Foreign Customs clearance documents:
  Commercial invoice
  Packing list
  Health/sanitary certificates
  Certificate of origin
  Certificate of free sale
  Inspection certificates
  Carnet

Payment documents:
  Letter of credit
  Bank draft
  Commercial invoice
  Packing list
Certificate of origin

Documentation examples are given in the Appendix E, page 233.

In addition to knowing the required documents, your company will need to know language requirements, number of copies, required signatures, notarization, consularization, and shipping instructions.

The two best resources of information for documentary requirements are your customer and your forwarder. If they do not have the answers immediately at hand, they have the resources to get those answers.

Additional resources for documentation requirements include:

- Trade Information Center—Department of Commerce
- Export Yellow Pages
- Official Export Guide
- USDA Foreign Agricultural Service
- Food Export USA
- State Export Promotion Agency
- World Trade Centers and Clubs
- U.S. Chamber of Commerce
- U.S. Council for International Trade
- *The Shipping Digest*
- *Mastering Import and Export Management* (AMACOM Books, www.amanet. org)

The key to successful documentation is to check with several resources. This double-check will ensure compliance with local regulations. Your company should set up documentation files on a country basis. This will facilitate compliance on repeat and future sales to that country. Keep those files updated on a regular basis.

Another helpful step is to send documents ahead of the export itself. Have your customer review the documents with his or her agent to see if there are any changes to the documentation required. It is much easier to change a document when the shipment is still in the United States than to change the document as the shipment sits in a foreign Customs warehouse.

Finally, your company should always retain one complete and legible set of documents in the transaction file in the unlikely event the originals are lost.

FCPA Awareness and Adherence

With U.S. global supply chains presently expanding their reach to an unprecedented scope and range, adherence to the growing list of security and compliance initiatives stipulated by an ever-increasing number of government agencies has created the need to invest in self-policing. Two twenty-first-century hot button issues—terrorism and corporate accounting fraud—intersect their way into global supply chain issues. There are many parallels between these issues, the challenges they present, and the means to create a proactive check and balance system to protect the supply chain from internal and external forces. With all of these new challenges, however, one cannot forget to incorporate preexisting laws into a preventative twenty-first-century supply chain compliance action plan. One law that must make its way into the foreground of such a plan is the Foreign Corrupt Practice Act of 1977 (FCPA).

The original purpose of the FCPA was to assign monetary penalties to U.S. companies and individuals found guilty of bribery. This act specifically targets unlawful payments to foreign government officials, politicians, or political parties for the sole purpose of obtaining or maintaining business. The Department of Justice (DOJ) has been the agency responsible for the enforcement of the FCPA and, along with the Securities and Exchange Commission (SEC), has fined numerous corporations and individuals excessive monetary penalties for their infractions. With Sarbanes-Oxley regulations fully embedded into the fabric of the corporate American consciousness and Homeland Security mandates to safeguard U.S. interests against terrorism just on the horizon, FCPA regulations may be taking a backseat on a list of priorities for exporters. However, not taking the proper precautions to mitigate the potential risk of exposure to FCPA violations may cause considerable problems for U.S. companies as their growth in the overseas market continues.

Violating these laws often results in stiff fines along with possible prison time. Some corporations have found this out the hard way. In December 2004 and February 2005, GE InVision, a subsidiary of General Electric, settled its cases with the DOJ and SEC. The FCPA violations cost the company a combined total of just under $2 million. The Titan Corporation and Schering-Plough are two additional companies just recently found guilty and were fined after being investigated for violations.

A U.S. company conducting business in a foreign country must ensure that none of its employees, subsidiaries, agents, or hired contractors violate FCPA laws. Investing in setting up a monitoring system that performs thorough screenings of all entities conducting business on behalf of the U.S. company is highly recommended. The internal policing of this issue must begin with identifying problematic persons or entities wanting to represent the company in a foreign market. Refusal to submit written compliance to FCPA guidelines, failing to maintain sufficient books or records, requesting payments for an undisclosed third party, or having any relationship with a member of a political party should serve as a red flag to exporters.

Maintaining an "out of sight, out of mind" mentality or pleading ignorance to situations occurring beyond a self-perceived arm's length will not navigate one through the stormy seas of a FCPA investigation. The concepts of maintaining self-awareness and establishing internal controls repeat themselves over and over again throughout sections of the Sarbanes-Oxley law. Applying these principles to a standard operating procedure in order to prevent FCPA violations is a worthy exercise to undertake.

Establishing criteria for self-policing the supply chain in order to expose potential FCPA issues can start by requiring that all contracts include concise FCPA compliance language. Companies should insist that all payments be made via check or wire transfer while steering clear of any party insisting on using offshore accounts. Another safeguard that can be applied is to ensure that all applicants for foreign office positions undergo thorough background checks confirming they do not hold any public office and do not have close ties to a foreign government.

Awareness of corporate responsibilities has become paramount in today's post-9/11, Sarbanes-Oxley world. The government has stepped up its vigilance in protecting both the homeland and public confidence in the American business system. U.S. exporters must take the necessary precautions to guard their supply chains from activities that not only pose risks to the United States, but also jeopardize the sanctity of their companies. By taking a proactive and organized approach, a corporation can build a system of checks and balances to simultaneously mitigate risks in areas of security, compliance, and accounting. Maintaining high compliance and security standards within a global supply chain not only best prepares an organization to deal with new twenty-first-century government initiatives, but also safeguards it against FCPA infractions and other laws from yesteryear.

Globalization has expanded the number of executives and venues that companies are engaged in. Executives are traveling the world, making deals, and making commitments on behalf of their companies. They are involved in millions of dollars in negotiations and contracts. There are several steps companies can take to ensure they are conducting business within the FCPA guidelines.

1. Corporations initiate FCPA guidelines in their Sarbanes-Oxley or supply chain compliance guidelines.
2. Executives receive awareness training and develop SOPs for dealing with potential FCPA scenarios that they may become part of.
3. Develop very specific SOPs and incorporate them into all operating guidelines that ensure compliance.
4. Ensure internal communications from senior management with nontolerant and strict penalty guidelines.
5. Conduct annual audits utilizing outside consultants, law firms, and specialists to analyze potential FCPA violations.
6. Establish internal resources and "call centers" in the event an executive needs assistance in how to deal with a potential FCPA violation or potential problem situation, without the threat of backlash.
7. Identify high-risk situations, countries, customers, etc., that may be more vulnerable to a FCPA violation, and proactively mitigate these hot spots.
8. Work with internal risk management to determine insurance options and alternative loss control procedures.

Companies that are proactive in FCPA management will be the ones that avoid the pitfalls and enjoy more successful international trade, freer of government scrutiny and interference.

Documentation and Letters of Credit

An important function of export documentation is to ensure that collection proceeds according to the agreed terms of sale and that the exporter receives payment.

In a typical letter of credit transaction, the exporter anticipates receipt of funds once the goods are shipped. In practice, the exporter will only receive payment once the required documentation is received *and* approved by the bank.

If your company is using a letter of credit in order to get paid, the following steps should be followed to minimize problems:

- Ensure that the names and addresses of the beneficiary and applicant are correct.
- Make sure that the type of credit, terms, and conditions conform to the sales contract or purchase order.
- Be sure that all conditions are acceptable. Can your company prepare/obtain the necessary documents to comply with the requirements?
- Be sure that the description of merchandise and unit prices conforms with the sales contract.
- Check that the amount of credit is sufficient to cover all costs.
- Confirm that the shipping and expiration dates are acceptable.
- Confirm that the points of shipping and destination are as agreed.
- Confirm that the country in which the credit is payable is acceptable.

Chapter 3

Import Management and Inbound Logistics

For the last forty-five years imports have continued to be an integral part of the supply chain in the United States, and they are consistently growing at unprecedented rates. This is mostly due to offshore operations and foreign purchasing gains. The complexity in Customs and other government agencies has matured and integrated itself into the everyday fabric of the import supply chain.

The Bureau of Customs and Border Protection (CBP)

Profile

- Established in 1789 by the second act of the First Congress, and is older than the Treasury Department, of which it is a part
- Principle source of revenue for the United States during its first 125 years of existence—95 to 99% of total government revenue
- In 2010 provides the nation with the second source of revenue, and will facilitate an estimated $2 trillion in legitimate trade this year while enforcing the trade laws that protect the economy, health, and safety of the American people
- Administers the laws, executive orders, and presidential proclamations governing the importation of merchandise and baggage, collection of duties, and taxes thereon

1. The entry, clearance, and report of arrival and the unloading of vessels, vehicles, and aircraft
2. The prevention and detection of smuggling operations and seizure of merchandise, vehicles, and vessels involved
3. The exclusion of entry of prohibited articles
4. The control of imports subject to established quotas
5. The verification of import statistics for the Bureau of Census
6. The administrative imposition and collection of penalties for violations of laws, including the granting of administrative relief under certain conditions

The Department of Homeland Security (DHS)

The recently established Department of Homeland Security brought together twenty-two different government agencies under a sweeping reorganization. The U.S Customs Service has been incorporated into the DHS after 213 years of existence under the Department of the Treasury. While retaining oversight of commercial processing of merchandise into the commerce of the United States and the revenue collection tasks associated with the collection of duties and taxes, Customs has now become increasingly responsible for homeland security under the new name of the Bureau of Customs and Border Protection (www.cbp.gov).

Organizational Structure

The Customs territory of the United States consists of fifty states, the District of Columbia, and Puerto Rico. U.S. Customs is an agency under the Department of the Treasury, headquartered in Washington, D.C.

These four personnel areas of CBP Management are found in Customs' headquarters in Washington:

Commissioner of Customs
Deputy commissioner
Commissioners staff
Assistant commissioners
CBP key locations

In an effort to disseminate hands-on expertise throughout the United States, the Bureau of Customs and Border Protection (formerly U.S. Customs) created five strategic trade centers to handle major trade issues, including fraud, antidumping, protection of patents, trademarks, and copyrights:

- Chicago: Canada and NAFTA
- Dallas/Ft. Worth: Mexico and NAFTA
- Los Angeles: Autos and parts
- Miami: Production equipment and critical equipment
- New York: Textile and steel

Twenty management centers oversee the management functions for Customs for specific port office locations.

- Customs has increased its arm's length control and expertise throughout the United States.
- The restructuring took place as of Customs fiscal year 1996 to amend this two-hundred-year-old agency to look and operate like a modern private sector organization.
- This restructuring abolished the management functions of seven regional offices and forty-two district offices and divided those responsibilities among the five strategic trade centers and the twenty Customs management centers.

MANAGEMENT CENTERS

Mid America: CMC/Chicago
East Texas: CMC/Houston
West Texas: CMC/El Paso
Southern California: CMC/San Diego
Mid Pacific: CMC/San Francisco
North Pacific: CMC/Portland
South Pacific: CMC/Los Angeles
South Florida: CMC/Miami
West Great Lakes: CMC/Detroit
South Texas: CMC/Laredo
Arizona: CMC/Tucson
Northwest Great Plains: CMC/Seattle
New York: CMC/New York
Mid Atlantic: CMC/Baltimore
Puerto Rico/Virgin Islands: CMC/San Juan
North Florida: CMC/Tampa
North Atlantic: CMC/Boston
East Great Lakes: CMC/Buffalo
South Atlantic: CMC/Atlanta
Gulf: CMC/New Orleans

Import Regulatory Issues

- Duty rates decrease on an average every year, creating a downward trend in the collection of duties and taxes.
- Anticipated revenue collection from fines and penalties associated with Customs audits offsets this decrease in collection of duties and taxes.

The Customs Modernization Act of 1993 was a congressional act that outlined and redefined current regulations and introduced new legislation in reference to the importer's responsibilities. The Mod Act introduced a warning prior to audit enforcement of the future Customs aggression toward increased compliance levels.

Phase I — Informed compliance: Legal responsibility of importer to seek formal training on import rules and regulatory issues, which will allow the importer to elevate the level of education and knowledge necessary to demonstrate reasonable care over their import transactions.

Phase II — Enforced compliance: Legal responsibility of Customs to enforce the rules and regulations established in the Customs federal regulations and thereto defined in the Modernization Act of 1993.

Import Management: Importer of Record vs. Ultimate Consignee

Many companies in the United States that play a role in the import equation are confused about their specific responsibility:

- Am I the importer, ultimate consignee, both, or something else?
- Do I have any liability as just the ultimate consignee of an import shipment?

Determining who the "Ultimate Consignee" is in an import transaction is a very important concern of U.S. Customs (CBP). Customs will go to great lengths to assure that importers correctly document the importer of record and the ultimate consignee on information passed to them, as goods cross into the United States.

**U.S. Customs and Border
Protection Office of Strategic Trade
Regulatory Audit Division**

**Treatment of Ultimate Consignee
Transactions in a Focused Assessment**

Introduction

A Focused Assessment (FA) provides U.S. Customs and Border Protection (CBP) with the ability to review and verify information disclosed to CBP for accuracy and completeness. During an audit, the auditor may review records where the auditee is the Importer of Record (IOR) and/or the Ultimate Consignee (UC). Many issues can arise during an audit involving the auditee's responsibilities for reporting entry information to CBP and for record keeping. This document addresses IOR and UC responsibilities and audit procedures.

Background

The entry statute (19 U.S.C. 1484 (a)) establishes responsibilities of the IOR as follows:

(a) Requirement and time

    (1) Except as provided in sections 1490, 1498, 1552, and 1553 of this title, one of the parties qualifying as "importer of record" under paragraph (2) (B), either in person or by an agent authorized by the party in writing, shall, using reasonable care —

        (A) make entry therefore by filing with the Customs Service —

            (i) such documentation or, pursuant to an electronic data interchange system, such information as is necessary to enable the Customs Service to determine whether the merchandise may be released from customs custody, and

            (ii) notification whether an import activity summary statement will be filed; and

        (B) complete the entry by filing with the Customs Service the declared value, classification and rate of duty applicable to the merchandise, and such other documentation or, pursuant to an electronic data interchange system, such other information as is necessary to enable the Customs Service to —

            (i) properly assess duties on the merchandise,

            (ii) collect accurate statistics with respect to the merchandise, and

            (iii) determine whether any other applicable requirement of law (other than a requirement relating to release from customs custody) is met.

The statute (19 U.S.C. 1484(a)(2)(B)) defines the term "importer of record" as the owner or purchaser of the merchandise or a licensed customs broker appropriately designated by the owner, purchaser or consignee of the merchandise. Statutory obligations make the IOR "accountable" for the declarations made at entry. However, while the entry statute clearly identifies the "accountable "party, liability for penalties may attach to any culpable party under civil penalty statute, 19 U.S.C. 1592 (a).

In some instances, in order to meet the burden of using reasonable care when making declarations at entry, the IOR or his agent must necessarily seek information from another source. Sometimes that is the UC. For example, the IOR may not be the owner or purchaser of the merchandise, but rather, a customs broker retained by a UC. In such a case, it is unlikely that the IOR will have sufficient information to meet its reasonable care obligation without obtaining information about the transaction from another party. The IOR is always "accountable." If the UC provides the IOR with information that is material and false and that information is used to make entry, the UC may be culpable under 19 U.S.C. 1592.

In addition to responsibilities as IOR, auditees may be subject to recordkeeping requirements in 19 U.S.C. 1508, which state:

(a) Requirements

Any —

(1) owner, importer, consignee, importer of record, entry filer, or other party who —

(A) imports merchandise into the customs territory of the United States, files a drawback claim, or transports or stores merchandise carried or held under bond, or

(B) knowingly causes the importation or transportation or storage of merchandise carried or held under bond into or from the customs territory of the United States;

(2) agent of any party described in paragraph (1); or

(3) person whose activities require the filing of a declaration or entry, or both; shall make, keep, and render for examination and inspection records (which for purposes of this section include, but are not limited to, statements, declarations, documents and electronically generated or machine readable data) which —

(A) pertain to any such activity, or to the information contained in the records required by this chapter in connection with any such activity; and

(B) are normally kept in the ordinary course of business.

Procedures

During an audit, the FA team will primarily address issues related to responsibilities of the auditee as IOR. Issues related to auditee's responsibilities as the UC will be addressed as needed on a case-by-case basis. The IOR will be held "accountable" for the declarations made at entry. Both the IOR and UC will be held responsible for maintaining records required by 19 U.S.C. 1508. If the UC provides the IOR with information that is material and false, that information is used to make entry, and the resulting errors have significant impact, the auditors will refer the information to appropriate action officials for possible action under provisions of 19 U.S.C. 1592.

The following three scenarios provide guidance to the auditors when the auditee is the UC but NOT the IOR.

Consolidated Entries with Multiple Ultimate Consignees

In the past, shippers and importers used consolidated release and entry summary for shipments that had multiple UCs arriving at the border in a single conveyance. But CBP's automated system has limitations that allow for the submission of only a single UC. Because only one UC can be designated for the consolidated shipment, a company may be listed as the UC on the consolidated entry summary in CBP's automated system but may not be responsible for all portions of the consolidated entry summary.

An audit sample may include a consolidated entry that identifies the auditee as the UC when other UCs are responsible for part of the consolidated shipment. When this occurs and the auditee is not the IOR, the auditee must arrange with the entry filer to provide information to CBP to prove that the auditee is not the UC responsible for all portions of the consolidated entry. The auditee is only responsible for those portions of the consolidated entry for which he is the UC. Under provisions of 19 U.S.C. 1508, the auditee must maintain records related to those portions of the entry for which he was the UC.

Unsolicited Merchandise on Entries Listing a Company as UC

Sometimes companies are listed as the UC on an entry when the company does not initiate or have any information about the specific import transaction. For example, a related company may send unsolicited prototypes or samples. This may also occur if unrelated entities send unsolicited merchandise (such as returned merchandise) to a company listed as UC on the entry. During an audit, the sample may include unsolicited entries where the auditee is listed as the UC but is not the IOR. If the auditee did not initiate the import transaction, has no records related to the importation, and can adequately explain the circumstances and its lack of records to support this transaction, the auditee will not be held responsible for records required by 19 U.S.C. 1508 or for accuracy or completeness of entry information.

Entries Initiated by the UC but Another Entity is IOR

In some cases, a company initiates an import or is in some way responsible for information related to the import, is listed as UC, but is not the IOR. For example, this may occur when the overseas supplier (or other entity) is IOR and handles the details of the importation. If these entries are included in an audit sample, the UC is responsible for maintaining and making available records required by 19 U.S.C. 1508.

The IOR is always accountable for entry information. However, if the UC provides the IOR with information, which is material and false, and that information is used to make entry, the UC may be culpable under 19 U.S.C. 1592.

In addition to the record keeping obligations and the situation where the Ultimate Consignee may be liable under 19 U.S.C. 1592 for false statements or omissions, the party being audited will be responsible for entry information or internal control of entry information provided to CBP only when designated as the IOR.

FOCUSED ASSESSMENT (FA)

Customs has endorsed the focused assessment approach as a more effective means in the audit process, rather than a detailed sampling of over one hundred files per importer combined with a wide range of scrutiny contained in most compliance assessment audits.

Customs will focus on key areas of compliance.

The outcome of the FA will categorize the importer as either high risk or low risk.

- Valuation
- Classification
- Record keeping
- Internal controls and supervision

- GSP declarations
- American goods/repair and return declarations

Reasonable Care

Reasonable care is defined as the degree of care that a person of ordinary prudence would exercise in the same or similar circumstances.

- Legal responsibility of the importer and his or her agent (Customs broker) to use in entering merchandise. Customs responsibility is to fix the final classification and value.
- Mandated by the Customs Modernization Act and passed into law December 8, 1993.

Meeting Reasonable Care Standards

Importer

- Consult with qualified experts such as Customs brokers, consultants, and attorneys specializing in Customs law
- Should seek guidance from Customs through the formal binding ruling program
- If using a broker, must provide the broker with full and complete information sufficient enough for the broker to make proper entry (import declaration) or for the broker to provide advice as how to make entry
- Obtain analysis from accredited labs to determine the technical qualities of imported merchandise
- Use in-house employees who have experience and knowledge of Customs regulations and procedures
- Must follow any binding rulings received from Customs
- Ensure that products are legally marked with the country of origin to indicate to the ultimate purchaser the origin of imported products
- Cannot classify own identical merchandise or value own identical merchandise in different ways
- Notify Customs when receiving different treatment by Customs for the same goods on different entries or different ports
- Examine entries (Import Declaration CF 3461) prepared by the broker to determine the accuracy in classification and valuation.

Penalty for importer's failure to meet reasonable care standards: domestic value or twice the duty, whichever is less. If duty-free, the penalty is calculated at 20% of the value.

Broker

- Considered an expert and hence must give competent advice
- Must exercise due diligence to ascertain the correctness of information that he or she imparts to a client
- Shall not knowingly impart to client false information relative to any Customs business
- Shall not withhold information from a client who is entitled to that information
- Establish internal procedures to limit advice being given by qualified licensed individuals
- Obtain and receive directly from importer complete and accurate information sufficient to make entry or to provide proper advice

Penalty for broker not meeting reasonable care standards: $30,000 per violation as provided for in 19 USC 1641 (the section of the law governing Customs brokers).

Best Practices: Ten Steps to Achieve Import Compliance

1. **Internal supervision and control.** Importers of record are responsible for the development and maintenance of internal standard operating procedures, which directly relate to the Customs clearance declaration process—a standardized measure to control the correctness of information being tendered to the U.S. Customs Service and all other government agencies in relation to entering the commerce of the United States. These SOPs should monitor all communications made on behalf of the importer of record in reference to all clearances, by both the broker and the importer.
2. **Harmonized classification.** Importers are responsible to ensure that every harmonized number declared on the import declaration is accurate based on the guidelines established in the Harmonized Tariff Schedule of the United States. Importers are also responsible to know the principles of classification to monitor and control the advice tendered by third-party service providers, such as customhouse brokers.
3. **Global security management C-TPAT participation.** A nationwide invitation has been sent to the importing community for voluntary participation in the Customs-Trade Partnership Against Terrorism (C-TPAT). There are significant advantages to voluntary participation that will expedite the Customs clearance process. Management of your import supply chain security procedures is a crucial part of the participation process. Development and enhancement demonstrating control measures that effectively monitor the safeguarding of cargo entering the commerce of the United States is the goal.
4. **Commercial invoice requirements.** Commercial invoice requirements as established in the 19 CFR 141.86 are a very major concern for the U.S.

Customs Service. The invoice is the engine that drives the international shipment and clearance procedures. Misleading and misstatement of facts could circumvent the governing authorities from properly exercising control of our borders, and result in major devastation of domestic property and even lives. Correct import declaration reporting information is founded on the contents of the invoice. Every importer is bound by basic bond conditions under CFR 113.62 for providing a complete entry and entry declaration information.

5. **Duty payment management.** Every importer's first bond condition is to pay duties, fees, and taxes on a timely basis. It is the importer's responsibility to establish and verify that all duties, fees, and taxes are being submitted in accordance with CFR 19113.62(a).

6. **Informed compliance.** It is the responsibility of every importer, as established in the Customs Modernization Act of 1993, to meet and maintain "informed compliance" standards of increased and current education and training on industry-specific topics associated with the duties and responsibilities of importers of record.

7. **Record retention.** Importers of record are responsible for establishing a record retention system that maintains all records relative to an import transaction for five years from the date of entry of the merchandise into the commerce of the United States.

8. **Valuation.** Importers of record are responsible for ensuring that proper valuation principles are applied to each import transaction and subsequent declaration, as outlined in the CFR 152. Falsely declared values corrupt trade statistics and possibly defraud the government out of revenue. Valuation verifications and the knowledge of valuation principles are crucial to safeguarding your company from unforeseen Customs penalties for misstatement of valuation facts.

9. **Country of origin marking.** Importers are responsible for ensuring that all merchandise is properly marked upon entry into the United States, as referenced in the 19 CFR 134. Documentation must also indicate the proper country of origin on all shipments.

10. **Power of attorney management.** All importers should properly manage the number of Customs brokers that are conducting Customs business on their behalf. It is imperative that proper control be established and maintained to ensure that qualified persons are presenting all declarations.

References

Customs Web site: www.cbp.gov
Customs Federal Regulations (CFR) Title 19
Harmonize Tariff Schedule of the United States 2005

C-TPAT: Customs–Trade Partnership against Terrorism

C-TPAT is a joint effort by Customs and the trade community to raise the level of security associated with the import and export supply chain of merchandise to and from the United States. Every importer, exporter, manufacturer, Customs broker, nonvessel operating common carrier (NVOCC), and warehouse proprietor should join this partnership in a proactive effort to raise the bar on security standards in the United States.

Benefits include the following:

- Decrease in delays of imported cargo due to examinations
- No in-house Customs audits performed on C-TPAT members
- Automatic mitigation to Customs fines and penalties
- More efficient import supply chain process

Exercise care in the application process to ensure that complete statements of facts are included in the partnership questionnaire and application process.

Tier 1: Certification
Tier II: Validation
Tier III: Exceeding minimum security practices

More information may be obtained at www.cbp.gov and industrypartnership@ dhs.gov. There are a lot of details involved in managing CTPAT, which is found at the Web site. The reader should navigate the Web site.

Importer Self-Assessment (ISA) Program

The Importer Self-Assessment (ISA) Program is a privilege offered to C-TPAT members, which contains the opportunity for an importer to perform a self-analysis of their compliance standards and provide their findings to Customs for review. This process could minimize dramatically Customs in-house presence in their overall focused assessment process. Importers are encouraged to seek the professional assistance of qualified individuals to perform or aid in this self-assessment process.

An importer who has not demonstrated informed compliance practice may not be able to meet the requirements of the Importer Self-Assessment Program initially and may require a compliance preassessment and education and training to incorporate compliant practice into their daily management efforts.

Quick Response Audits

Quick response audits (QRAs) are single-issue audits with a narrow focus. These audits are designed to address a specific objective within a short period of time. QRA is a term used to cover a variety of audits that will have limited objectives as opposed to the complete evaluation of a company's Customs and Border Protection (CBP) activities in the focused assessment program.

Because audit objectives vary among QRAs, a universal audit program cannot be established and used for all QRAs. Examples of a QRA might be an audit of an importer's CBP operations to determine if there is a potential for unlawful trans-shipment, or an audit of the company's controls concerning intellectual property rights.

Generally, QRAs originate from referrals by other CBP and Homeland Security offices utilizing risk management principles to identify specific companies involved in certain types of transactions.

One of the major benefits of the ISA program is that the ISA member company is withdrawn from the focused assessment audit pool. This means that because of the company's demonstrated compliance level and willingness to partner with CBP, the company will not be considered a candidate for routine focused assessments.

CBP has always stipulated that ISA membership did not grant total immunity from any CBP single focus inquiry where the identification of a specific risk by CBP was sufficient to warrant a review of the transactions associated with the particular issue. In such instances, CBP and the importer will work together to determine a mutually acceptable course of action whenever possible. However, it is unlikely that an ISA-approved company, with established internal controls, would be the subject of a referral audit.

If a company that is applying for ISA or is contemplating applying for the program is notified that it has been selected for a QRA, some element of the importer's transactions has been identified as a potential risk. Consequently, CBP will have to resolve the risk issue, either through the scheduled QRA or through the ISA review process. Any potential high-risk issues must be resolved before a company can be approved for ISA.

In some cases with a specific identified risk, it would be more practical and efficient to have the audit team that is scheduling the QRA conduct the review and furnish its results to the ISA review team. In other cases, it may be possible for the ISA review team to complete the audit work if it is within the scope of the ISA review process. The timing and identity of the specific audit team conducting the work will be decided on a case-by-case basis, depending upon the audit team best suited to do the work. In most cases, it will be in the best interests of the company that is applying for ISA to resolve the immediate issue before the actual ISA review. A resolution of an outstanding issue will expedite the ultimate decision of CBP as to the company's eligibility for ISA.

Global Security Awareness

Due to the events of 9/11, the Bureau of Customs and Border Protection has implemented a steadfast effort toward the awareness of global security issues. The realization that information was being received after merchandise had already arrived in the United States prompted several new initiatives.

Since December 2002, Customs has established the requirement that carriers submit a cargo manifest to Customs twenty-four hours prior to the lading on the vessel. The enforcement rules of this policy are as follows:

Twenty-four-hour advanced manifest rule — ocean
Wheels up or four-hour advanced manifest rule — air shipments
Two-hour advanced manifest rule — ground transportation

Customs has posted U.S. Customs personnel at foreign ports to screen high-risk containers before they are shipped, as part of the Container Security Initiative (CSI). U.S. Customs has also invested significantly in new detection technology for increased cargo screening both abroad and in the United States.

Effective import compliance management includes the following:

■ Maintain the flow of goods into the United States
■ Create standard operating procedures that will reflect a focus on Customs compliance and security

Import process objectives include the following:

■ Strategically planned
■ Efficient
■ Compliant
■ Secure

Security background investigations and cargo security validations should be incorporated into the entire import supply chain process:

■ Vendors ®
■ Foreign transport agents ®
■ Carriers ®
■ Brokers ®
■ U.S. delivery

Container Security Initiative

The Container Security Initiative is a program to enhance significantly the security of the world's maritime trading system. By working together, we can jointly achieve far greater security for maritime shipping than by working independently.

Recognizing that trade is vital to the world economy, U.S. Customs has proposed a four-part program designed to achieve the objective of a more secure maritime trade environment while accommodating the need for efficiency in global commerce. A critical element in the success of this program will be the availability of advance information to perform sophisticated targeting using risk management principles. The four core elements of CSI are:

- Use automated information to identify and target high-risk containers.
- Prescreen those containers identified as high risk before they arrive at U.S. ports.
- Use detection technology to quickly prescreen high-risk containers.
- Use smarter, tamper-proof containers.

The CSI program is quickly being adopted by mega seaports in Asia, Europe, and elsewhere in the world. Currently, the world's top twenty seaports have joined U.S. Customs in CSI to protect global commerce from the terrorist threat.

- The volume of trade moving throughout the nation's 102 seaports has nearly doubled since 1995.
- In 2006, U.S. Customs processed more than 214,000 vessels and 5.7 million sea containers.
- Approximately 90% of the world's cargo moves by container.
- Globally, over 48 million full cargo containers move between major seaports each year.
- Each year, more than 16 million containers arrive in the United States by ship, truck, and rail.
- Customs processed 26 million entries in 2006.
- More than 1.2 trillion in imported goods passed through the nation's 301 ports of entry in 2007.
- Almost half of incoming U.S. trade (by value) arrives by ship.

Advanced Manifest Notification Programs

The twenty-four-hour advanced manifest rule provides the Bureau of Customs and Border Protection with a window of twenty-four hours prior to the loading of a foreign vessel to review automated manifest information to make prescreening determinations related to examination of the merchandise.

Wheels Up or Four-Hour Advanced Notification

The wheels up or four-hour advanced manifest rule requires that an air shipment's manifest be electronically reported to CBP at the time the flight is wheels up, or at least four hours prior to the arrival of the shipments landing into the first U.S. port of importation.

Two-Hour Advanced Notification for Ground and Rail Shipments

This prearrival notification of manifest must be transmitted to CBP at least two hours prior to the arrival of a ground transportation or rail shipment across a U.S. border.

The Bureau of Customs and Border Protection has pushed the borders back to afford a greater ability of assessment of terrorist risk. The bar has been raised in the area of global security. CBP has begun to collect additional trade detail and data before cargo is being shipped by ocean freight into the United States. The following outline provides detail of how CBP will manage this initiative.

CBP Proposal for Advance Trade Data Elements

I. Background

U.S. Customs and Border Protection operates at the nexus of national security and American economic security. Designing approaches to ensure that U.S. Customs and Border Protection contributes fully to these goals is critical to fulfilling the agency's mission to secure the nation's borders and to facilitate the free flow of international trade.

Finding the right equilibrium is a challenge that requires CBP to consistently monitor and evaluate the processes and systems the agency employs to screen and clear the millions of import ocean cargo containers and millions of entries that cross our ports of entry every year.

In this environment Congress recognized the need for more robust security targeting and recently passed the SAFE Port Act. The SAFE Port Act sets forth the following requirement to enhance the capability of CBP's Automated Targeting System:

"Section 203(b): Requirement. — The Secretary, acting through the Commissioner, *shall require* the electronic transmission to the Department of *additional data elements for improved high-risk targeting, including appropriate elements of entry data* ... to be provided as advanced information with respect to cargo destined for importation into the United States *prior to loading of such cargo on vessels at foreign ports.*"

Prior to enactment of the SAFE Port Act, CBP had already undertaken an internal review of its targeting and inspection processes in recognition that physically examining every cargo container entering the United States would impose an unacceptable cost on the American economy. Consequently, CBP had implemented a comprehensive strategy designed to enhance national security while protecting the economic vitality of the United States. The Container Security Initiative (CSI), the 24-Hour Rule, and the Customs-Trade Partnership Against Terrorism (C-TPAT) are cornerstone approaches implemented to further this goal. Additionally, CBP has developed cargo risk assessment capabilities in its Automated Targeting System (ATS) to screen all maritime containers before they are loaded aboard vessels in foreign ports. Each of the initiatives is dependent upon data supplied by trade entities, including carriers, non-vessel operating common carriers, brokers, importers, or their agents.

The information that CBP currently analyzes to generate its risk assessment prior to vessel loading contains the same data elements that were originally established by the 24-Hour Rule. For the most part, this is the ocean carrier's or non-vessel operator's cargo declaration. While this was a sound initial approach to take after the tragic events of September 11th, internal and external government reviews have concluded that more complete advance shipment data would produce more effective and more vigorous cargo risk assessments.

In late 2004, the Departmental Advisory Committee on Commercial Operations of Customs and Border Protection (COAC) forwarded to the Department of Homeland Security and CBP one of its subcommittees' recommendations, which provided that: "For ATS to provide enhanced security screening, the system should acquire additional shipment data to be used in the pre-vessel loading security screening process." COAC recommended that CBP undertake a thorough review of the data element recommendations with the Trade Support Network to determine what data elements the government required to improve the agency's risk assessment and targeting capabilities.

Accordingly, CBP undertook further internal review and analysis of its targeting and inspection processes and worked with the Trade Support Network on this issue. CBP convened a group of its senior level field targeting experts to review existing screening and examination procedures, and to evaluate the information requirements necessary to ensure the foundation of the agency's targeting efforts. The group met over several months to make recommendations on data elements required prior to vessel lading, the processes and procedures utilized to screen and examine cargo, and the infrastructure that supports the ATS. The task force reviewed thousands of data elements for potential value as targeting keys, evaluated current targeting approaches, and recommended areas for improvement.

Based upon its analysis, CBP offers for the trade's consideration the following draft proposal to be used as a strawman to facilitate the development of regulations, in consultation with the trade community as provided by the new statutory mandate under the SAFE Port Act. In keeping with the parameters of the Trade Act of 2002, the additional data elements requested under this proposal will be used for security and enhanced targeting and are not intended for commercial or trade enforcement purposes.

CBP will post this document to the Customs and Border Protection Web site and will provide guidance on how to direct your comments on the proposal to the agency as the process moves forward.

II. Security Filing: Proposed Data Requirements

A. In addition to the current data elements specified under the 24-Hour Rule (19 CFR 4.7(a)), CBP proposes to require an additional set of data elements 24 hours prior to vessel loading. These data elements will be linked, via the Automated Manifest System (AMS) or Automated Broker Interface (ABI) to the existing 24-Hour Rule data collected in the AMS. This new Security Filing (SF) is focused on those specific data elements that further identify the entities involved in the supply chain, the entities' locations, as well as a corroborating and potentially more precise description of the commodities being shipped to the United States. This data will significantly enhance the risk assessment process by enabling CBP to more efficiently separate higher-risk shipments from lower-risk shipments that should be afforded more rapid release decisions. In addition, these additional data elements will enable CBP to make critical decisions during and immediately after elevated alert levels when business resumption is essential to the well being and security of the U.S. economy.

For maritime cargo that is destined to remain in the U.S., the data elements listed below will be required to be transmitted 24 hours prior to loading the U.S. bound vessel. As further described in Section III, this portion of the Security Filing will be required to be transmitted by the importer or its designated agent.

The following ten (10) data elements were selected because of their probative value and because of their ready availability in current logistics processes. (See Annex A in the following section of this chapter for proposed definitions of the data elements.)

1. Manufacturer name and address
2. Seller name and address
3. Container stuffing location
4. Consolidator name and address
5. Buyer name and address

6. Ship to name and address
7. Importer of record number
8. Consignee number
9. Country of origin of the goods
10. Commodity Harmonized Tariff Schedule number (6 digit)

B. In addition to the data elements outlined above, CBP will require ocean carriers to provide two additional data sets to complete the security filing:

Vessel Stow Plan
Container Status Messages

The **vessel stow plan** is used to transmit information about containers loaded aboard a vessel. The CBP proposal will require the vessel stow plan no later than 48 hours after the departure from the last foreign port. For voyages less than 48 hours in duration, the vessel stow plan must be transmitted to CBP prior to arrival of the vessel at the first U.S. port.
Vessel Stow Plan information consists of:

- Vessel name (IMO number)
- Vessel operator
- Voyage number
- Container operator
- Equipment number
- Equipment size/type
- Stow position
- Hazmat-UN code
- Vessel location—load/discharge ports

Container status messages serve to facilitate the intermodal handling of containers by streamlining the information exchange between trading partners involved in administration, commerce, and transport of containerized shipments. The messages can also be used to report terminal container movements (e.g. loading and discharging the vessel) and to report the change in status of containers (e.g. empty or full).
The container status messages data elements will provide CBP with additional transparency into the custodial environment through which inter-modal containers are handled and transported before arrival and after unlading in the U.S.
This enhanced view (corroboration with other advanced data messages) into the international supply chain will contribute to the security of the U.S. and in the international supply chain through which containers and import cargos reach U.S. ports.

The CBP proposal, currently undergoing further review, is focused on the following data elements of the existing container status messaging set.

- Equipment number
- Event
- Event date and time
- Event location
- Vessel

III. Security Filing: Responsible Parties

In developing regulations pursuant to the SAFE Port Act, CBP is required to follow the parameters of the Trade Act of 2002. The Trade Act of 2002 states that "the requirement to provide particular information shall be imposed on the party most likely to have direct knowledge of that information." (19 U.S.C. 2071 Note (a)(3)(B)).

In order to receive the Security Filing data, CBP will utilize existing modules of the Automated Commercial System (ACS): the Automated Broker Interface (ABI), and the Automated Manifest System (AMS). CBP proposes that current authorized transmitting entities for these modules (i.e. ABI filers and AMS participants) may transmit the Security Filing data. CBP is committed to integrating this data submission process with the future ongoing developmental work and implementation of the ACE.

Because of the similarity of the ten data elements of the Security Filing and entry data, importers may be interested in fulfilling both Security Filing and entry obligations at the same time by filing 24 hours before vessel loading. CBP will consider any comments in this regard within the context of existing statutory schemes and technological capacity.

Annex A: Proposed Data Definitions

Manufacturer/Supplier Name/Manufacturer/Supplier Address: Manufacturer/Producer/Grower/: Name and Address

The name and address of the entity that last manufactures, produces, or grows the imported commodity. These entities produce or grow raw materials that are shipped to the United States or transform raw materials into a finished product or article that is shipped to the United States. The transformation of the raw material may involve processing into finished goods, or the production of goods to be further assembled to create a finished product, or the assembly of goods into a finished product.

Seller Name/Seller Address: The last named overseas (foreign) sellers/addresses on the transaction invoice/purchase order.

Buyer Name/Buyer Address: The last named buyer and address 24 hours prior to foreign lading.

Ship To Name and Address: The named party and the address on the transaction that will physically receive the merchandise, which may be different from the consignee (e.g. de-consolidator warehouse).

Container Stuffing Location: The physical foreign location street, city, country, where the goods were stuffed into the container prior to the closing of the container.

Consolidator Name and Address (if applicable): Foreign receiving party that physically stuffs the container prior to receipt by carrier for shipment to the U.S. The consolidator's address identifies the physical location of cargo, which may differ from the usual manufacturer or shipper premises. Typically, this is a fixed location.

Importer (of Record Number): The unique identifying number of the entity primarily responsible for the payment of any duties on the merchandise, or an authorized agent acting on his behalf. The importer may be any one of the parties noted below:

- The consignee
- The importer of record
- The actual owner of the merchandise
- The transferee of the merchandise

For any of the above named parties, the unique identifying number, which can be the IRS, EIN, SSN, or the CBP assigned number, is required on the Security Filing.

Consignee (Number): The unique identifying number of the entity to which the goods are to be consigned. Typically, the consignee is the "deliver to" party at the end of the supply chain who has a fiduciary interest in the cargo. This is normally the party defined at the house bill level.

For the above named party, the unique identifying number, which can be the IRS, EIN, SSN, or the CBP assigned number, is required on the Security Filing.

Country of Origin: The country of origin of a good is the country in which the good is wholly obtained or produced, as defined in CFR 19 102.11, Subpart B—Rules of Origin.

Commodity 6-Digit HTS: Indicates the initial classification required of a shipment prior to entry being filed. Provides specific HTS identification of the commodity being ordered from the purchase order.

Importer Security Filing, formerly known as the 10 + 2 Program, was announced on November 26 as a interim final rule to be effective January 26, 2009. Eight mandatory data elements to be filed twenty-four hours prior to loading are:

- Seller
- Buyer
- Importer of record number/foreign trade zone applicant identification number
- Consignee number(s)
- Manufacturer (or supplier)
- Ship to party
- Country of origin
- Commodity Harmonized Tariff Schedule of the United States (HTSUS) number

Flexibility of Filing

- The rule provides flexibility for importers with respect to the submission of four of these data elements.
- In lieu of a single specific response, importers may submit a range of responses for each of the following data elements:

1. Manufacturer (or supplier)
2. Ship to party
3. Country of origin
4. Commodity HTSUS number

- The ISF must be updated as soon as more accurate or precise data become available and no later than twenty-four hours prior to the ship's arrival at a U.S. port.

Postloading Filing Privileges

- The ISF will also need to include two data elements that must be submitted as early as possible, but no later than twenty-four hours prior to the ship's arrival at a U.S. port.
- The data elements that are allowed to be filed after loading but twenty-four hours prior to arrival are:

1. Container stuffing location
2. Consolidator

Foreign Cargo Remaining On Board

■ The interim final rule requires five data elements in the ISF for shipments consisting entirely of foreign cargo remaining on board (FROB), shipments consisting entirely of goods intended to be transported in bond as an immediate exportation (IE), or shipments for transportation and exportation (T&E).

■ Importer Security Filings for IE and T&E shipments must be submitted no later than twenty-four hours before the cargo is laden aboard a vessel destined for the United States, and any time prior to lading for FROB shipments. The following five data elements must be submitted for FROB, IE, and T&E shipments:

> Booking party
> Foreign port of unlading
> Place of delivery
> Ship to party
> Commodity HTSUS number

Implementation Process of Final Rule

■ The interim final rule includes a delayed compliance date of twelve months after the interim final rule took effect (January 2010).

■ During that 12-month period, CBP will show restraint in enforcing the rule. CBP will take into account difficulties that importers may face in complying with the rule as long as importers are making a good faith effort and satisfactory progress toward compliance.

■ It is important to note that CBP has made several significant changes from the original proposed rule based on industry trade feedback.

CBP will conduct a review to determine any specific compliance difficulties that importers and shippers may experience in submitting all ten data elements, twenty-four hours before lading.

■ The Importer Security Filing and additional carrier requirements interim final rule has been submitted to the Federal Register and will take effect sixty days after publication.

■ CBP invites written comment on the data elements for which some type of flexibility has been provided, and on the revised Regulatory Assessment and Final Regulatory Flexibility Analysis.

■ Based on the information obtained during the structured review and public comment periods, CBP will conduct an analysis of the elements subject to flexibility. The analysis will examine compliance costs for various industry segments, the impact of the flexibilities, the barriers to submitting the data twenty-four hours prior to lading, and the benefits of collecting the data.

■ Based upon the analysis, DHS will determine whether to eliminate, modify, or maintain these requirements.

Methods of Filing ISF Data

The importer is responsible for filing the advanced data; however, the importer can delegate any party to transmit data on its behalf. It can be the freight forwarder, Customs broker, or other third-party designee.

Filing options are as follows:

1. Stand-alone AMS filing
2. Stand-alone ABI filing
3. CF 3461 filing by the broker of record
4. CF 7501 filing by the broker of record

Valuation Verification

The objective for the importer performing the valuation verification on an entry-by-entry basis is to arrive at the FOB (FCA) value in all cases.

CIF (CIP) duty paid delivered = Cost of merchandise + Insurance + U.S. duty calculation + U.S. delivery charge

CIF (CIP) = Cost of merchandise + Insurance + Prepaid freight

CF = Cost of merchandise + Prepaid freight

FOB (FCA) = Cost of merchandise dutiable value (7501 column 33)

FAS = Free alongside carrier – Cost of merchandise alongside the export carrier

Ex works (ex factory) = Cost of merchandise at shipper warehouse

Prepaid freight and insurance are nondutiable charges (NDCs). All NDCs can be deducted from the CIP (CIF) and CF terms of sale to arrive at the correct FOB value.

FAS and *ex works* are below the FOB value amount. There may exist values that must be added to these amounts to bring them up to an acceptable level as a true FOB value, such as packing charges, foreign inland freight, or assist values.

Packing charges, if not already included in the invoice value, must be added to the value.

Foreign loading/handling charges, in the case of FAS terms of sale, must be added unless the shipment is being transported on a through bill of lading.

Foreign inland freight is dutiable except for ex works transactions and shipments being transported on a through bill of lading.

For additional information review, see CFR 152 in the Customs Regulations.

Methods of Valuation

Transaction value: The price actually paid or payable between a buyer and seller of imported merchandise.

Transaction value of identical or similar: The price paid or payable between another buyer and another seller on merchandise entered at or around the same time, from the same region of the world, used on a separate importation for valuation purposes only (fair market value concept).

Deductive value: The price after importation and U.S. resale minus all nondutiable charges calculated back toward an acceptable value for Customs purposes.

Computed value: The sum of the cost of the merchandise, including raw materials, labor, production, assembly, and general, added together as a computed valuation for Customs purposes.

Value if no other value can be determined: Customs will appraise a value based on general industry knowledge without the benefit of specifics. An educated guess of the value.

Assists

Any materials, dies, molds, tooling, design work, or engineering work provided from the buyer to the seller of imported merchandise at a reduced cost or free of charge, with the exception of design work undertaken in the United States, is a dutiable charge And must be included in the entry declaration and commercial invoice computation.

Royalties

Royalty payments as a condition of sale of merchandise to the United States will be considered dutiable and included in the transaction value declaration to Customs upon importation into the commerce of the United States.

Commissions

Selling commission: Any commission that is paid as a condition of the sale or from the sale. Dutiable commission.

Buying commission: Any commission that is paid not as a condition of sale. A true buying agent will receive payment regardless of the existence of the sale. Nondutiable commission.

CFR Title 19 Part 152.103

Additions to price actually paid or payable. (1) The transaction value of imported merchandise is the price actually paid or payable for the merchandise when sold for exportation to the United States, plus amounts equal to:

  (i) The packing costs incurred by the buyer with respect to the imported merchandise;

  (ii) Any selling commission incurred by the buyer with respect to the imported merchandise;

  (iii) The value, apportioned as appropriate, of any assist;

  (iv) Any royalty or license fee related to the imported merchandise that the buyer is required to pay, directly or indirectly, as a condition of the sale of the imported merchandise for exportation to the United States; and

  (v) The proceeds of any subsequent resale, disposal, or use of the imported merchandise that accrue, directly or indirectly, to the seller.

(2) The price actually paid or payable for imported merchandise will be increased by the amounts attributable to the items (and no others) described in paragraphs (b)(1) (i) through (v) of this section to the extent that each amount is not otherwise included within the price actually paid or payable, and is based on sufficient information. If sufficient information is not available, for any reason, with respect to any amount referred to in this section, the transaction value will be treated as one that cannot be determined.

(3) *Interpretative note.* A royalty is paid on the basis of the price in a sale in the United States of a gallon of a particular product imported by the pound and transformed into a solution after importation. If the royalty is based partially on the imported merchandise and partially on other factors which have nothing to do with the imported merchandise (such as if the imported merchandise is mixed with domestic ingredients and is no longer separately identifiable, or if the royalty cannot be distinguished from special financial arrangements between the buyer and the seller), it would be inappropriate to attempt to make an addition for the royalty. However, if the amount of this royalty is based only on the imported merchandise and can be readily quantified, an addition to the price actually paid or payable will be made.

Customs Powers of Attorney

1. **Importer of record:** A person or party who is responsible for duties, fees, taxes, and penalties as a result of imported goods entering the United States.
2. **Customs broker:** A person or party who is licensed by the Department of Treasury to conduct Customs business on behalf of an importer of record.

3. **Bureau of Customs and Border Protection:** The enforcement agency that administers the laws governing importation of merchandise, baggage, and collection of duties thereon.

The penalty for conducting Customs business on behalf of an importer without a valid power of attorney is and amount of up to the value of the merchandise for each transaction or loss of broker's license, or both.

A power of attorney gives a broker the authority to become an extension of the traffic department of the importer. Exercise caution when executing a power of attorney.

Revocation

1. **Expiration date:** All powers of attorney should have a date of expiration as a supervision and control issue.
2. **Letter of revocation:** A letter to the port director of Customs stating an importer's request to revoke a previously issued POA will be in effect on the date that Customs receives the request.

Sample

IRS #_____

CUSTOMS POWER OF ATTORNEY

Check appropriate box:

_____ Individual

_____ Partnership

_____ Corporation

_____ Sole proprietorship

KNOW ALL MEN BY THESE PRESENTS: That

_____ (full name of person,

partnership, corporation, or sole proprietorship (identify)),

a corporation doing business under the laws of the State of

_____or a _____doing

business

_____as_____

_____ residing at

_____

_____

_____, having an office and place of business

at _____,

_____hereby constitutes and appoints each of the

following persons _____

_____.

CUSTOMS BROKERAGE SERVICE PROVIDER

As a true and lawful agent and attorney of the grantor named above for and in the name, place, and stead of said grantor from this date and in all Customs Districts, and in no other name, to make, endorse, sign, declare, or swear to any entry, withdrawal, declaration, certificate, bill of lading, carnet, or other document required by law or regulation in connection with the importation, transportation, or exportation of any merchandise shipped or consigned by or to said grantor; to perform any act or condition that may be required by law or regulation in connection with such merchandise; to receive any merchandise deliverable to said grantor;

To make endorsements on bills of lading conferring authority to transfer title, make entry, or collect drawback, and to make, sign, declare, or swear to any statement, supplemental statement, schedule, supplemental schedule, certificate of delivery, certificate of manufacture, certificate of manufacture and delivery, abstract of manufacturing records, declaration of proprietor on drawback entry, declaration of exporter on drawback entry, or any other affidavit or document that may be required by law or regulation for drawback purposes, regardless of whether such bill of lading, sworn statement, schedule, certificate, abstract, declaration, or other affidavit or document is intended for filing in any Customs district;

To sign, seal, and deliver for and as the act of said grantor any bond required by law or regulation in connection with the entry or withdrawal of imported merchandise or merchandise exported with or without benefit of drawback, or in connection with the entry, clearance, lading, unlading, or navigation of any vessel or other means of conveyance owned or operated by said grantor, and any and all bonds that may be voluntarily given and accepted under applicable laws and regulations, consignee's and owner's declarations provided for in Section 485, Tariff Act of 1930, as amended, or affidavits in connection with the entry of merchandise;

To sign and swear to any document and to perform any act that may be necessary or required by law or regulation in connection with the entering, clearing, lading, unlading, or operation of any vessel or other means of conveyance owned or operated by said grantor;

To authorize other Customs Brokers to act as grantor's agent; to receive, endorse, and collect checks issued for Customs duty refunds in grantor's name drawn on the Treasurer of the United States; if the grantor is a nonresident of the United States, to accept service of process on behalf of the grantor;

And generally to transact at the customhouses in any district any and all Customs business, including making, signing, and filing of protests under Section 514 of the Tariff Act of 1930, in which said grantor is or may be concerned or interested and which may properly be transacted or performed by an agent and attorney, giving to said agent and attorney full power and authority to do anything whatever requisite and necessary to be done in the premises as fully as said grantor could do if present and acting, hereby ratifying and confirming all that the said agent and attorney shall lawfully do by virtue of these presents; the foregoing power of attorney to remain in full force and effect until the ____ day of _____, 20__, or until notice of revocation in writing is duly given to and received by a district director of Customs. If the donor of this power of attorney is a partnership, the said power shall in no case have any force or effect after the expiration of two years from the date of its execution.

IN WITNESS WHEREOF, the said _____

has caused these presents to be sealed and signed:

(Signature) _____

(Capacity) _____(Date)

_____

WITNESS: _____

_____

(Corporate seal)

Customs Power of Attorney Completion Instructions

IRS# _____ *Please input your company IRS# for the entity acting as importer of record.*

Know all men by these presents that _____

_____ *Please state the full name of the importer of record that is issuing the Customs power of attorney.*

A corporation doing business under the laws and the state of _____
Please input the state in which your corporation filed for its corporate status.

Doing business as _____ *Only to be completed if there is a DBA name under which the importer conducts import business.*

Residing at _____ *Only to be completed if the importer is doing business from his home address.*

Having an office and a place of business at _____

Please state the full business address for the importer of record.
Hereby constitutes and appoints the following persons _____.

Please input the name of the Customs broker that the importer of record is granting the Customs power of attorney to. If this field is completed, please verify that this company is the same company you intend to represent you in your Customs business affairs.

Has caused these presents to be sealed and signed _____
Must be signed by a corporate officer of the importer of record.
Capacity _____ *Title of the corporate officer who signed the POA.*

Date _____ *This is the date that you want the power of attorney to go into effect.*

Please sign and return the fax copy and note the original will be sent in the mail to your attention. Please also endorse it and return it to the Alston Group as soon as possible to keep within the regulations.

Validating the Power of Attorney

Because the power of attorney (POA) can authorize the movement of conveyances and merchandise into the United States, it is critical that it be examined carefully. By ensuring that each POA is valid, the broker joins U.S. Customs and Border Protection on the national security frontlines in verifying the data used to screen what enters this country.

In addition to security, the broker's own professional business interests and continuing obligation to demonstrate "reasonable care" require verification of the POA grantor's identity and legal authority (position in a company or partnership) to enter into a POA.

Here are some ways the broker can validate a power of attorney:

■ To the greatest extent possible, have POAs completed in person so the grantor's personal identification (driver's license, passport, etc.) can be reviewed.
■ Check applicable Web sites to verify the POA grantor's business and registration with state authorities.

- If the principal uses a trade or fictitious name in doing business, confirm that the name appears on the POA.
- Verify that the importer's name, importer number, and Employer Identification Number (also known as the Federal Tax Identification Number) on the POA match what is in ACS.

Check whether the POA grantor is named as a sanctioned or restricted person or entity by the U.S. government. (See the Bureau of Industry and Security, U.S. Department of Commerce, Lists to Check.)

§ 141.43 Delegation to subagents.

(a) *Resident principals.* Except as otherwise provided for in paragraph (c) of this section, the holder of a power of attorney for a resident principal cannot appoint a subagent except for the purpose of executing shippers' export declarations. A subagent so appointed cannot delegate his power.

(b) *Nonresident principals.* Except as otherwise provided for in paragraph (c) of this section, an agent who has power of attorney for a nonresident principal may execute a power of attorney delegating authority to a subagent only if the original power of attorney contains express authority from the principal for the appointment of a subagent or subagents. Any subagent so appointed must be a resident authorized to accept service of process in accordance with §141.36.

(c) *Customhouse brokers.* A power of attorney executed in favor of a licensed customhouse broker may specify that the power of attorney is granted to the broker to act through any of its licensed officers or authorized employees as provided in part 111 of this chapter.

Certificate of Registration

A certificate of registration is a documentary tool that allows merchandise to be exported from the United States and returned to the United States without the payment of duty, on the value previously exported. Certificates of registration are originally intended for foreign commodities, yet they may also prove valuable for American-made products returning to the United States without proof of U.S. manufacture status.

- Articles are subject to examination prior to exportation and reimportation.
- Any value added to merchandise while outside the United States is dutiable upon return to the United States.
- It is to the exporter's advantage to utilize the privilege of a certificate of registration if there is a 1% chance that the merchandise will return to the United States.

Certificate of registrations are completed on a CF 4455.

Foreign Shipper's Repair/Manufacturer's Affidavit

A foreign shipper's repair affidavit is a documentary tool used by importers to declare to the United States the actual repair, further manufacturing, and added value to an imported item previously exported and now being returned. This document is prepared on the foreign shipper's letterhead and contains the following:

- Name and address of the shipper or manufacturer
- Detailed description of the commodity
- Valuation itemized listing of added values added due to repair, alteration, or further processing
- Date received into the commerce of the shipper's or manufacturer's country
- Value declared upon receipt of merchandise prior to repair, alteration, or manufacturing
- Name of responsible person with knowledge of the pertinent facts of the shipment

This document may be used when an exporter has failed to register merchandise prior to export as an alternative privilege. Customs will accept this in lieu of the certificate of registration, though the first preference is a CF 4455 registration, with an opportunity to examine merchandise prior to export.

Importation and Customs Clearance Process

1. Profile privileges
   a. Air shipment—wheels up policy: The broker can present or transmit Customs entry import declaration to the U.S. Customs Service when the airline has certified that the cargo has physically left the ground in the country of export.
   b. Ocean shipment—five-day policy: The broker can present or transmit the Customs entry import declaration to the U.S. Customs Service five days prior to the arrival of the importing vessel or carrier.
   c. Documentary requirements: The broker can submit fax or photocopies of the original import documentation for most import shipments. Original

documents may be requested for certain special classes of merchandise (textiles, quota items, restricted merchandise requiring commodity specialist review, etc.).

2. The right to make entry
   a. Every importer has the right to make entry—the right to import the merchandise into the commerce of the United States for consumption for its own use or for sale. This is the most common type of importation into the commerce of the U.S.—the consumption entry.
      1. Section 1321 sample shipment exemption: Merchandise valued under $200, and meeting sample definitions, is exempt from entry requirements.
      2. Informal entries: Merchandise not exceeding $2,000 is eligible for informal entry procedures.
      3. Formal consumption entries: Merchandise valued over $2,000 must be entered under a formal consumption entry.

3. Privileged entries
   a. Temporary importation entry: Merchandise entered into the United States temporarily without the payment of duties for a period not to exceed one year.
   b. Bonded warehouse entries: Merchandise imported and stored in a Customs bonded warehouse for a period of five years from the date of importation without the payment of duties, fees, or taxes. Duties are paid when the goods are withdrawn from the warehouse for consumption.
   c. In bond entries: The transportation of merchandise not yet cleared through Customs authority from one bonded location to another Customs bonded location. There are three main types of in bond entries:

      IT—Immediate transportation entry
      TE—Transportation and exportation
      IE—Immediate exportation

Import declaration (entry) is a two-part process:

Part I: Release phase (Customs Form 3461): The filing of documentation or the electronic transmission of information to determine whether the merchandise may be released from Customs custody can be done by either:
   – Prior to arrival (prefile)
      1. Upon takeoff of aircraft (wheels up)
      2. Five days prior to the arrival of the ocean carrier

- After arrival of the importing conveyance
- Release status notification
  1. Paperless release: No entry documentation need be presented; examination of cargo not required.
  2. Entry documents required (EDR): Declaration (CF 3461), invoice, packing list, bond, etc., must be submitted to Customs office for further review.
  3. General exam/conditional release: After EDR no exam required; shipment can be released.
  4. Intensive examination: Customs examination required.
  5. Release authorized: After intensive exam, if applicable.

Part II
Duty payment:

1. By electronic transfer (automated clearing house) from brokers or importer's bank account
2. By check directly from importer to Customs or broker to Customs

Entry summary filing:
1. Time to file entry summary and pay duty must be performed by the tenth business day from the date of release under Part 1.

   Failure to do so:
   a. Liquidated damages (penalty) against the importer
   b. Amount of penalty:

      Unrestricted merchandise = two times the unpaid duties
      Restricted merchandise = three times the import value

Liquidation is the final computation or ascertainment by Customs of regular and special duties accruing on an entry.

Protest is a formal disagreement with a Customs decision, to be filed within ninety days of the date of liquidation:

Allowed: Reliquidation to follow.
Denied: Importer can file a summons (legal action) against Customs in the Court of International Trade within 180 days of the date of denial.

Supplemental information letter (SIL) is a formal disagreement communication with Customs for entry details that is brought to CBP's attention prior to liquidation. Information that CBP did not have at the time of entry that is needed to properly liquidate the entry.

Postsummary Adjustment
Correction to an Entry Summary PEA/SIL Only

That Is Processed for Liquidation

Filer ⬜   Date ⬜

Entry number ⬜   Port ⬜

Importer number ⬜

Importer name ⬜

Narrative description   Reason code ⬜

⬜

Corrected duty amount: Total ascertained amount shown on corrected 7501

Duty ⬜   ⬜ Payment

⬜

HMF   Refund

MPF ☐

☐ N-revenue value over $10,000 (PEA only)

☐

Tax

☐ Nonrevenue SILs

Add ☐

☐ Bill

CVD ☐

Total paid, refund, or bill amount

Total ☐

☐

Customs and Border Protection only

Interest ☐

Total liquidation amount ☐

Reason Codes

11—Valuation	15—CVD	19—Other
12—Classification	16—Special trade programs	
13—Quantity	17—Interest only	
14—Antidumping	18—Nonrevenue	

Amounts on the worksheet should be the corrected duty amount—not the difference.

Worksheet should have the same ascertained amounts as the corrected 7501.

Record Keeping

All records that pertain to the merchandise and are maintained in the normal course of business:

- Must be maintained in the United States
- Need to have correctness of information and financial data information contained in the entry import declaration substantiated
- Must be kept for five years from the date of entry

Drawback claims must be retained for five years from the date of entry and for three years from the date the claim is paid. All records, including but not limited to the purchase inquiry, purchase order, commercial invoice, letter of instructions, CF 3461, CF 7501, brokerage communications, Customs communications, notice of liquidation, and other documents as outlined in CFR 163 on a list known as the (a)1(a) listing.

CBP's penalties for failure to keep records are:

1. $100,000 or 75% of dutiable value for each release for willful failure
2. $10,000 or 40% of the dutiable value for each release for negligence

Recommendations of Compliance

All records should be kept in a *centralized location* within the importer's establishment or designated record-keeping service provider.

Importers

Copies of import transactional communications must include the following:

1. Purchase inquiry
2. Purchase verifications
3. Purchase negotiations between the buyer and seller of importer merchandise
4. Purchase order communications
5. Commercial invoice
6. Packing list information
7. Special Customs declarations/certifications
8. "Customs Import Declaration" (CF 3461)
9. "Customs Entry Summary" (CF 7501)
10. All communication records between the Customs broker and import compliance/traffic department in reference to each import transaction
11. Supervisory communication detailing supervision and control of import decisions between the importer and broker/freight forwarder/consultants/attorneys
12. All records of communication received from U.S. Customs Service
13. All records of communication relating to any statements/acts made to U.S. Customs
14. Notice of liquidations communication records

15. Communications records detailing receipt of merchandise into the importer's establishments or designated receiving stations
16. Communication records detailing the disposition of the merchandise after receipt or distribution
17. Records indicating actual proof of purchase of imported goods
18. Records indicating contract of carriage agreements, airway bills, and bills of ladings
19. Records indicating the exact amount of prepaid international freight or insurance contained in the import sales transaction

Importers cannot delegate record-keeping duties to the Customs broker in lieu of maintaining records for themselves.

Customs Brokers

Copies of import transactional communications must include the following:

1. CF 3461 original (as prepared and released)
2. CF 7501 original
3. Airway bill or bill of lading
4. Invoices (rated)
5. Packing lists
6. Special Customs invoices
7. Importer letter of instructions
8. Importer communications—Inquiries and replies
9. Customs communications—Inquiries and replies
10. Copies of all accounting transactions in which the broker is involved (monies received from the importer or laid out on behalf of the importer)
11. Delivery orders and disposition of merchandise
12. FDA and all other government agency declarations and dispositions

Methods of Storage of Records

Customs Regulations state that if a record has been created in hard copy format, those records must be maintained in hard copy format. Records that were never created in a hard copy format may be maintained in an alternate format as approved by Customs prior to the actual storage.

If the importer wishes to maintain records in an alternate method, it can obtain preapproval from:

Bureau of Customs and Border Protection
    Director of Regulatory Audit Division
    Charlotte, North Carolina

Alternative method of storage—(1) *General.* Any of the persons listed in §163.2 may maintain any records, other than records required to be maintained as original records under laws and regulations administered by other Federal government agencies, in an alternative format, provided that the person gives advance written notification of such alternative storage method to the

Regulatory Audit, U.S. Customs and Border Protection
2001 Cross Beam Dr.
Charlotte, North Carolina 28217

… and provided further that the Director of Regulatory Audit, Charlotte office, does not instruct the person in writing as provided herein that certain described records may not be maintained in an alternative format. The written notice to the Director of Regulatory Audit, Charlotte office, must be provided at least 30 calendar days before implementation of the alternative storage method, must identify the type of alternative storage method to be used, and must state that the alternative storage method complies with the standards set forth in paragraph (b)(2) of this section. If an alternative storage method covers records that pertain to goods under CBP seizure or detention or that relate to a matter that is currently the subject of an inquiry or investigation or administrative or court proceeding, the appropriate CBP office may instruct the person in writing that those records must be maintained as original records and therefore may not be converted to an alternative format until specific written authorization is received from that CBP office. A written instruction to a person under this paragraph may be issued during the 30-day advance notice period prescribed in this section or at any time thereafter, must describe the records in question with reasonable specificity but need not identify the underlying basis for the instruction, and shall not preclude application of the planned alternative storage method to other records not described therein.

(2) *Standards for alternative storage methods.* Methods commonly used in standard business practice for storage of records include, but are not limited to, machine readable data, CD ROM, and microfiche. Methods that are in compliance with generally accepted business standards will generally satisfy Customs requirements, provided that the method used allows for retrieval of records requested within a reasonable time after the request and provided that adequate provisions exist to prevent alteration, destruction, or deterioration of the records. The following standards must be applied by record keepers when using alternative storage methods:
  (i) Operational and written procedures are in place to ensure that the imaging and/or other media storage process preserves the integrity, readability, and security of the information contained in the original records. The

procedures must include a standardized retrieval process for such records. Vendor specifications/documentation and benchmark data must be available for Customs review;

(ii)   There is an effective labeling, naming, filing, and indexing system;

(iii)   Except in the case of packing lists (see §163.4(b)(2)), entry records must be maintained in their original formats for a period of 120 calendar days from the end of the release or conditional release period, whichever is later, or, if a demand for return to Customs custody has been issued, for a period of 120 calendar days either from the date the goods are redelivered or from the date specified in the demand as the latest redelivery date if redelivery has not taken place;

(iv)   An internal testing of the system must be performed on a yearly basis;

(v)   The record keeper must have the capability to make, and must bear the cost of, hard copy reproductions of alternatively stored records that are required by Customs for audit, inquiry, investigation, or inspection of such records; and

(vi)   The record keeper shall retain and keep available one working copy and one back-up copy of the records stored in a secure location for the required periods as provided in §163.4.

Customs Bonds

A Customs bond is a contract that obligates the importer to perform certain functions in the importing process. These, among others, include:

- The obligation to pay duties, taxes, and fees on a timely basis
- To pay as demanded by Customs any additional duties, taxes, and fees subsequently found due
- To file complete entries
- To produce documents where Customs releases the merchandise conditionally
- To hold the merchandise at the place of examination until the merchandise is properly released
- To, in a timely manner, redeliver merchandise to Customs custody, where, for example, the merchandise is admissible or, more commonly, where it does not comply with the country of origin's marking rules

Parties to a Bond

- Principle (importer)
- Surety (insurance company)
- Beneficiary (U.S. Customs Service)

Commercial bond paper is typically used.

Types of Bonds

- Single-transaction bond—Covers one particular entry at one port.
- Continuous bond—Covers all entries at all ports for one year.

Amounts of Bonds

Single transaction bond:
  Unrestricted merchandise = Value + duties, fees, and taxes
  Restricted merchandise = 3 × the value

Continuous bond: Ten percent of all duties, fees, and taxes paid in the preceding calendar year. If no duties, fees, and taxes were paid, then 10% of the estimated duties, fees, and taxes to be paid in the current calendar year.
Breach of bond: Penalties (liquidated damages) assessed in the following amounts:
  Unrestricted merchandise = Entered value plus all duties, taxes, and fees
Restricted merchandise: 3 × the value of the imported articles

Invoices

Invoices are the nucleus of the Customs entry declaration:

Commercial: A document prepared by the overseas shipper or seller that contains pertinent information related to the transaction of sale between the buyer and seller of imported merchandise.
Pro forma: A document prepared by the importer of record that contains pertinent information related to the transaction of sale between the buyer and seller of imported merchandise.

Invoice Requirements

- Invoice requirements, as set forth in the CFR Part 141.86, are a very crucial element of the Customs clearance process.
- Many penalty case situations develop and stem from incorrect invoices submitted on behalf of imported Merchandise.
- It is the importer's responsibility to present to the broker a proper invoice as established in the mentioned Customs Regulations.
- It is the broker's responsibility to ensure that a proper invoice is received from the importer for presentation purposes to CBP. If the invoice is incomplete or in violation of the rules and regulatory standards noted in Part 141.86 of the Customs Regulations, the broker is to request from the importer a corrected invoice.
- Failure to correct the importer is a lack of reasonable care on behalf of the broker. The broker would then face possible fines and penalties as liquidated damages in connection with the specific Customs clearance.

Specific invoice requirements include:

1. Port of entry to which the merchandise is destined
2. Name and address of the importer of record
3. Name and address of the ultimate consignee (if different from item 2)
4. Name and address of manufacturer/shipper
5. Detailed description of the merchandise, including the name by which each item is known in the country of sale
6. Unit price of the merchandise in the currency of sale
7. Total value of the merchandise, indicating the terms of sale associated with the actual purchase (CIP, CPT, ex works, etc.)
8. Country of origin of the merchandise
9. Statement of use in the United States, depending on the type of entry filed
10. Any rebates offered on imported merchandise between buyer and seller
11. Any discounts from price
12. Any values of assist, such as dies, molds, tools, or engineering work provided to the manufacturer to assist in the production of the imported merchandise
13. Packing list (itemizing each net packed item)
14. Must be in the English language
15. Must be endorsed by the person or party who prepared the invoice

Care must be exercised by foreign manufacturers and shippers in the preparation of invoices and other documents for entry of goods into the United States. Each invoice must contain information required by law and regulation outlined in CFR 141.86.

Every statement of fact contained in the invoice or document must be true and accurate. Any inaccurate or misleading statement of fact in an invoice or document presented to a Customs officer in connection with an entry, or the omission thereof, may result in delays in merchandise release, detention of the goods, or a penalty against the importer under provision USC 1592. The importer will be required to prove that it exercised reasonable care to avoid sanctions on future import transactions.

Duty Drawback

Drawback entries are a request for a 99% refund of duties paid on merchandise that is exported or destroyed under Customs supervision within three years from the date of importation.

Unused merchandise (same condition): Merchandise that is imported and exported in the same condition and unused within three years of the date of importation.

Rejected merchandise: Merchandise that is imported not conforming to the importer's standards of approval and then exported within three years of the date of importation.

Manufacturing drawback: Merchandise that is imported and used in the production or manufacture of a U.S. product and then exported from the United States within five years of the date of importation, and so used in manufacture within three years of the date received at the manufacturing site.

Drawback entries are filed on CF 7551, 7552, and 7553. They must be filed and approved prior to export unless a waiver of prior notice is approved allowing the goods to be exported without examination.

An exporter may qualify for a drawback refund even if it was not the original importer of record who paid the original duty.

Harmonized Tariff System

The HTSUS is a very detailed reference and guide to proper classification of merchandise upon entry into the United States. All articles subject to Customs clearance need to be properly classified for such clearance. Good references to HTSUS are:

1. Hard copy reference—Book format
2. Online reference—Customs Web site (www.cbp.gov)

Format

The General Rules of Interpretation (GRIs) is Customs formal guide of interpretation for classification purposes. Classification is not an exact science. A Customs classification agent is required to interpret in many cases the determining factors of what is being imported. There are differences in interpretations in most cases, so Customs regulatory procedures are to follow the guidelines of interpretation established in the HTSUS under the GRIs.

General Notes

General notes are located directly after the GRIs to provide ease in the usage of the reference itself. General notes provide explanations and definitions to special tariff treaty programs (i.e., GSP, NAFTA, CBERA, etc.). The general notes also contain clear definitions of symbols and abbreviations used throughout the reference material.

Chapter Notes

The HTSUS is formatted in numerical order by chapters. Each chapter deals with a specific class of merchandise. Each chapter is preceded by an instruction to the chapter entitled "Chapter Notes." These notes provide a very detailed level of understanding related to specific commodities. Definitions to terms and clarification principles are contained in this section.

Alphabetical Index

The alphabetical index is located at the rear of the HTSUS to provide a reference to respective headings (first four digits of the classification number).

Techniques of Classification

GRI Consideration

The most difficult task in classification principles is determining what it is that you are classifying. In that determination, one must consider the GRIs for interpretation.

Alphabetical Index

Once the interpretation is clear, one must reference the alphabetical index to determine the proper heading for the commodity classification.

Chapter Notes

Prior to selection of the HTSUS number, one must reference the chapter notes to ensure that there does not exist any interpretative notes that would prevent the usage of the intended classification number. The chapter notes will also provide a clear definition to terms mentioned in the chapter.

HTSUS Number Structure

Heading and subheading: First eight digits of the HTS number.
Statiscal suffix: The last two digits of the HTS number.
Article description: A detailed description of articles for classification purposes.
Rates of duty:
General: Normal trade relations countries.
Special: Special tariff treaty program designations.
Column 2: Rates of duties related to non-NTR countries.

Chapter 4

Government Agencies Controlling Supply Chain Issues

There are over one hundred government agencies that are involved in import and export supply chain management issues. This chapter reviews the key government agencies that supply chain executives should pay attention to and be aware of in their role in global operations and regulatory interface.

Government Agencies Involved in Exporting

Department of Commerce: Bureau of Industry and Security

The Bureau of Industry and Security (BIS) is responsible for implementing and enforcing the Export Administration Regulations (EAR), which regulate the export and reexport of most commercial items. Often these items are referred to as dual use, meaning items that have both commercial and military or proliferation applications, but purely commercial items without an obvious military use are also subject to the EAR. The EAR does not control all goods, services, and technology. Other U.S. government agencies regulate more specialized exports.

Dual-use items and strictly commercial items may be controlled for export. The BIS maintains the Commerce Control List, which specifically lists products controlled for specific destinations.

Department of Commerce: Office of Antiboycott Compliance

During the mid-1970s the United States adopted laws that seek to counteract the participation of U.S. citizens in other nation's economic boycotts and embargoes. The antiboycott laws were adopted to encourage and, in specified cases, require U.S. firms to refuse to participate in foreign boycotts that the United States does not sanction. These laws have the effect of preventing U.S. firms from being used to implement foreign policies of other nations that run counter to U.S. policy.

It is especially important that companies train all departments to ensure that the receipt of documents containing such boycott statements is recognized and, where necessary, reported to government authorities.

Department of State: Directorate of Defense Trade Controls

The U.S. government views the sale, export, and retransfers of defense articles and defense services as part of safeguarding U.S. national security and furthering U.S. foreign policy objectives. The Directorate of Defense Trade Controls (DDTC) is charged with controlling the export and temporary import of defense articles and defense services covered by the U.S. Munitions List (USML).

Companies that export items covered by the USML are required to register with the DDTC as well as apply for a license prior to export. Licenses may cover physical products as well as technical assistance agreements and manufacturing licensing agreements.

Department of Commerce: Bureau of Census, Foreign Trade Division

The Census Bureau is responsible for collecting, compiling, and publishing export trade statistics for the United States. The export trade data reported are referred to as electronic export information (EEI). The EEI is also used for export control purposes to detect and prevent the export of certain items by unauthorized parties or to unauthorized destinations or end users. The EEI is required to be filed through the AES. The AES is an electronic method for filing the EEI directly with the U.S. Customs and Border Protection (CBP) and the Census Bureau.

Electronic filing strengthens the U.S. government's ability to prevent the export of certain items by unauthorized parties to unauthorized destinations and end users, because the AES aids in targeting and identifying suspicious shipments prior to export and affords the government the ability to significantly improve the quality, timeliness, and coverage of export statistics. AES serves as an information gateway for the Census Bureau and CBP to improve the reporting of export trade information, customer service, compliance with and enforcement of export laws, and to provide paperless reports of export information.

Department of Justice: Drug Enforcement Administration, Office of Diversion Control (Chemicals and Controlled Substances)

The Drug Enforcement Administration's (DEA) Office of Diversion Control is responsible for two distinct issues: the diversion of controlled pharmaceuticals and the diversion of controlled chemicals.

Under federal law, all businesses that manufacture or distribute controlled drugs, all health professionals entitled to dispense, administer, or prescribe them, and all pharmacies entitled to fill prescriptions must register with the DEA. Registrants must comply with a series of regulatory requirements relating to drug security, records accountability, and adherence to standards.

The DEA is obligated under international treaties to monitor the movement of licit controlled substances across U.S. borders and for issuing import and export permits for that movement. The Drug Enforcement Administration requires an export permit for the export of controlled substances. Part of the permit application process requires certification by the authorized importer on how the goods will be applied exclusively to medical or scientific use within the country of destination, that they will not be reexported from such country, and that there is an actual need for the controlled substance for medical or scientific use.

Department of Health and Human Services: Food and Drug Administration (Drugs and Biologics, Investigational Drugs Permitted, Medical Devices)

Firms exporting products from the United States are often asked by foreign customers or foreign governments to supply a certificate for products regulated by the Food and Drug Administration (FDA). In many cases, foreign governments are seeking official assurance that products exported in their countries can be marketed in the United States or meet specific U.S. regulations, such as current good manufacturing practice (cGMP) regulations.

The FDA issues export certificates for food, dietary supplements, cosmetics, gelatin material, pharmaceutical products, human drugs and biologics, animal drugs, and products for research.

Department of Energy: Natural Gas and Electric Power

The Office of Natural Gas Regulatory Activities identifies developing export and international business opportunities for U.S. private industry and develops programs and implements policies that will enhance the U.S. energy industry's ability to compete in foreign markets. It promotes technologies and solutions that will improve the global environment and increase U.S. energy security.

Prospective importers and exporters of natural gas must obtain federal authorization for importing and exporting.

Department of Energy: Nuclear Regulatory Commission: Office of International Programs (Nuclear Materials and Equipment, Technical Data for Nuclear Weapons)

The U.S. Nuclear Regulatory Commission (NRC) was created to enable the nation to safely use radioactive materials for beneficial civilian purposes while ensuring that people and the environment are protected. The NRC regulates commercial nuclear power plants and other uses of nuclear materials, such as in nuclear medicine, through licensing, inspection, and enforcement of its requirements.

Commodities falling under NRC export licensing authority include nuclear reactors, uranium enrichment facilities, uranium and plutonium conversion plants, lithium isotope separation facilities, equipment, component parts and assemblies that are especially designed for exclusive use in any of these facilities, source material, and by-product material.

Department of Homeland Security: Customs and Border Protection (CBP)

Customs and Border Protection officers maintain a presence in every U.S. port of entry. With this amount of manpower, CBP acts as the enforcement arm for many government agencies. CBP officers are cross-trained in export regulations to enhance enforcement efforts and to act as the gatekeepers on behalf of other government agencies.

Federal Maritime Commission: Ocean Freight Forwarders

The Federal Maritime Commission (FMC) is an independent federal agency responsible for the regulation of ocean-borne transportation in the foreign commerce of the United States. The FMC regulates ocean freight forwarders and non-vessel operating common carriers (NVOCCs). These are considered to be ocean transportation intermediaries (OTIs). An OTI license is required of any individual or entity that is resident in or incorporated in the United States and performs OTI services in the foreign commerce of the United States. Ocean freight forwarders arrange space for shipments on behalf of shippers as well as prepare and process the documentation and perform related activities pertaining to those shipments. An NVOCC is a common carrier that does not operate the vessel and is a shipper in relation to the ocean common carrier.

Department of Commerce: Patent and Trademark Office

The U.S. Patent and Trademark Office (USPTO) is an agency of the U.S. Department of Commerce. The role of the USPTO is to grant patents for the protection of inventions and to register trademarks. It serves the interest of inventors and businesses with respect to their inventions, corporate products, and service identifications. It also advises and assists the president of the United States, the secretary of commerce, the bureaus and offices of the Department of Commerce, and other agencies of the government in matters involving all domestic and global aspects of intellectual property. Through the preservation, classification, and dissemination of patent information, the office promotes the industrial and technological progress of the nation and strengthens the economy.

In discharging its patent-related duties, the USPTO examines applications and grants patents on inventions when applicants are entitled to them; it publishes and disseminates patent information, records assignments of patents, maintains search files of U.S. and foreign patents, and maintains a search room for public use in examining issued patents and records. The office supplies copies of patents and official records to the public. It provides training to practitioners regarding requirements of the patent statutes and regulations, and it publishes the *Manual of Patent Examining Procedure* to elucidate these. Similar functions are performed relating to trademarks. By protecting intellectual endeavors and encouraging technological progress, the USPTO seeks to preserve the U.S. technological edge, which is key to our current and future competitiveness. The USPTO also disseminates patent and trademark information that promotes an understanding of intellectual property protection and facilitates the development and sharing of new technologies worldwide.

The right conferred by the patent grant is, in the language of the statute and of the grant itself, "the right to exclude others from making, using, offering for sale, or selling" the invention in the United States or "importing" the invention into the United States. What is granted is not the right to make, use, offer for sale, sell, or import, but the right to exclude others from making, using, offering for sale, selling, or importing the invention.

Department of Homeland Security: Transportation Security Administration

The Transportation Security Administration (TSA) is responsible for ensuring the security of all modes of transportation, including cargo placed aboard airplanes, and particularly focuses on passenger-carrying planes.

TSA worked closely with Congress for more than six months to significantly strengthen security in air cargo through the 9/11 Commission Bill, which was signed into law on August 3, 2007. TSA had to meet the mandates of the law and screen 50% of air cargo on passenger-carrying aircraft within eighteen months and 100% within three years.

TSA already has in place a multilayered, high-tech, industry-cooperative approach, utilizing surprise cargo security inspections called strikes, covert testing, security directives, and 100% screening at 250 smaller airports. In 2009 TSA also eliminated all exemptions to screening of air cargo for the first time and increased the amount of cargo that is subject to mandatory screening.

With TSA's new air cargo regulation, TSA will be doing a hundred thousand more background checks, specifically on cargo employees who screen cargo or have knowledge of how it is going to be transported or actually transport the cargo. The rule requires more robust checks and more visibility on the shipping companies and their employees. Additionally, we have extended security areas at the airport to include air cargo areas.

Department of the Treasury: Office of Foreign Asset Controls

The Office of Foreign Assets Control (OFAC) of the U.S. Department of the Treasury administers and enforces economic and trade sanctions based on U.S. foreign policy and national security goals against targeted foreign countries and regimes, terrorists, international narcotics traffickers, those engaged in activities related to the proliferation of weapons of mass destruction, and other threats to the national security, foreign policy, or economy of the United States. The sanctions can be either comprehensive or selective, using the blocking of assets and trade restrictions to accomplish foreign policy and national security goals.

Prohibited transactions are trade or financial transactions and other dealings in which U.S. persons may not engage unless authorized by OFAC or expressly exempted by statute. Because each program is based on different foreign policy and national security goals, prohibitions may vary between programs. OFAC regulations provide for general licenses authorizing the performance of certain categories of transactions. OFAC also issues specific licenses on a case-by-case basis under certain limited situations and conditions.

Department of Interior: Fish and Wildlife Services

The U.S. Fish and Wildlife Service issues permits under various wildlife laws and treaties. Permits enable the public to engage in legitimate wildlife-related activities that would otherwise be prohibited by law. Permits for import and export are issued by International Affairs. International Affairs is responsible for administering documents under the Convention on International Trade in Endangered Species of Wild Fauna and Flora (CITES) for the United States. These permits are issued to import and export species that are protected by CITES and other wildlife conservation laws.

A permit or license may be issued to qualified applicants for the following activities: to engage in business as a wildlife importer or exporter, import or export wildlife at other than a designated border or special port, and export and reexport certain CITES wildlife.

Government Agencies Involved in Importing

U.S. Customs and Border Protection

U.S. Customs and Border Protection (CBP), a division of the Department of Homeland Security, is responsible for protecting the borders of the United States against the instruments of terror and the illegal importations of persons and contraband while fostering positive economic revenue through the collection of duties and taxes. Global security initiatives have become the additional focus of CBP since the events of September 11, 2001.

In addition to the compliance affirmations of import declarations submitted by importers related to lawful importations into the commerce of the United States, CBP monitors the advanced manifest filing of import cargo manifests. CBP also serves as the enforcement agency for other government agencies that report to the Department of Homeland Security, such as the Department of Agriculture, Federal Communications Commission, and Fish and Wildlife Service. CBP is also responsible for the safe and secure management of one of the most successful partnerships between any government agency and the international trade community in the history of our nation, the Customs-Trade Partnership Against Terrorism (C-TPAT).

Customs and Border Protection is also very active in the compliance assessment process of importers, exporters, and Customs brokerage providers that conduct Customs business in the international supply chain process. Customs works diligently with importers on such efforts as selective focused assessment audits, the importer self-assessment program, and duty drawback recovery management programs.

Food and Drug Administration

The Food and Drug Administration (FDA), a division of the Department of Health and Human Services, is responsible for the affirmation of compliance of regulated articles described as food products, pharmaceuticals, medical devices, articles of human consumption, cosmetics, and beverages, among other articles. FDA entry declarations of compliance must be filed by the importer or broker prior to CBP entry release eligibility. FDA release may not be completed until after CBP release, and in many cases CBP requires that FDA declarations be submitted prior to any action taken by CBP.

The FDA also administers an import safety program under the title of the Twenty-Four-Hour Prior Notice Program, which requires food article imports to submit advance notification to the FDA to ensure that U.S. importers, foreign food manufacturers and U.S. food facilities are registered with the FDA for such imports. The FDA has made tremendous amendments to their supervision and compliance affirmations of food imports into the commerce of the United States in an effort to protect the U.S. food supply chain process relative to imported foodstuffs.

Department of Agriculture, Animal Plant Health Inspection Service

The Department of Agriculture, Animal Plant Health Inspection Service (APHIS), a division of the Department of Homeland Security, is responsible for monitoring the imports of agricultural, animal, and plant products that enter the commerce of the United States. Certain items require import permits due to the derivatives of their origin. The Department of Agriculture monitors the compliant importations of such products in an effort to protect the commerce of the United States from the importations of such products that may cause harm to the United States.

The Department of Agriculture is responsible for the management of the solid wood packing certification efforts, among others. The Department of Agriculture is also responsible for managing the newly implemented initiative of governance of the Lacey Act, which will require increased import reporting of species identification of many articles of plant derivatives, such as paper and paper products.

Consumer Products Safety Commission

The Consumer Products Safety Commission (CPSC) is responsible for the management of the Import Products Safety Program that was brought to world attention as a result of several incidents, such as high lead levels in paints used on imported toys for children. The CPSC will regulate and require that certain articles contain general conformity certificates with import documents to affirm that quality testing is performed on imported products. Products that are imported without this certification will be refused admission into the commerce of the United States and ordered for immediate export.

The CPSC will be supported by the compliance enforcement efforts of the U.S. Customs and Border Protection to ensure that compliance standards are met in this effort. The CPSC will continue to monitor its delegated list of products that require such certification to keep current and consistent a list of articles that need such governance.

U.S. Fish and Wildlife Service

The U.S. Fish and Wildlife Service (FWS) monitors the import and export of endangered fish and wildlife products into and out of the United States. Fish and Wildlife pays specific attention to species identified as endangered that require CITES certification to properly import such goods into the United States. The importation of articles under the jurisdiction of FWS without proper certification and approval will be subject to immediate seizure and confiscation by FWS in association with U.S. Customs and Border Protection.

Many imports that contain elements or parts of endangered specifies are seized annually due to lack of knowledge of importers as well as intentional fraudulent attempts. FWS is active in the affirmation of imported leather products, rugs, footwear, belts, and cultural articles that have traditionally been the focus of prior investigations and seizures.

Federal Communications Commission

The Federal Communications Commission (FCC) is an independent U.S. government agency. The FCC was established by the Communications Act of 1934 and is charged with regulating interstate and international communications by radio, television, wire, satellite, and cable. The FCC's jurisdiction covers the fifty states, the District of Columbia, and U.S. possessions.

The FCC is directed by five commissioners appointed by the president and confirmed by the Senate for five-year terms, except when filling an unexpired term. The president designates one of the commissioners to serve as chairperson. Only three commissioners may be members of the same political party. None of them can have a financial interest in any commission-related business.

As the chief executive officer of the commission, the chairman delegates management and administrative responsibility to the managing director. The commissioners supervise all FCC activities, delegating responsibilities to staff units and bureaus.

The FCC Consumer and Government Affairs Bureau (CGB) educates and informs consumers about telecommunications goods and services and engages their input to help guide the work of the commission. CGB coordinates telecommunications policy efforts with industry and other governmental agencies—federal, tribal, state, and local—in serving the public interest.

Chapter 5

Utilization of Technology Options

Global supply chain technology has advanced a hundred-fold since the events of 9/11. Those companies that have integrated software solutions into the import and export process are much more secure and advanced than those that run only on manual systems. This chapter reviews the options and offers some exciting technology options.

Technology Advantages

Technology provides the user with the following primary benefits:

- Savings
- Reduces risk

These benefits can be achieved through the following:

- Efficiencies in operation
- Reduction in human errors
- Closing of gaps in communication and information transfers
- Ease of supervisory controls
- Chain of custody management
- Ease of paying attention to government regulations in an automated format
- More timely updates and notifications for changes

- Access to management reports
- Supervision and control over third-party providers
- Access to due diligence and reasonable care standards

Trade compliance is best gained in corporate supply chains in two ways:

1. Purchased from independent software providers
2. Acquired through third-party providers that offer the software as part of their services

The primary benefit of option 1 is that these choices typically provide an array of options and comprehensive customization. The downside is cost. These systems can cost in the high six figures.

The primary benefit of option 2 is reduced cost. The disadvantage is a system that is designed for your specific needs and nuances in your global supply chain.

Some technology providers with recognized trade compliance programs include these representatives of hardware, software, and technology products used by supply chains.

Questaweb
Compliant One (American River International)
GT Nexus
GT Trade Services
eCustoms
Compliance 11
MK Denial
2020 Software
Export compliance
Documents for exports
Powerdms
Axiom
Haynesboone
Import-export software
PSI software
QAD
Tradepointe
JP Morgan Chase
ASCI of Miami
Nextlinx
FTZ software
Editrade
Aberdeen

Service Providers and Technology

Freight forwarders, customhouse brokers, and all other kinds of service providers have taken the lead in innovating and bringing technology solutions to principal import and export companies. The logistics industry (service providers) is enhancing its use of technology by:

- Creating more efficient freight handling and data transmissions
- Developing defined EDI or Internet interfaces with its customers' import-export order entry systems
- Providing linkage into warehousing, inventory management, and shipping functions
- Establishing systems for tracking freight and dealing with customer service issues
- Establishing and monitoring compliance controls
- Becoming an integral partner with its clients as an information resource
- Having programs that ease the knowledge of preparation and execution of international documentation
- Affording access to government reporting requirements and export licensing matters

RFID: Trade Compliance and Import–Export Management

Radio frequency identification (RFID) has taken hold in global supply chains in a number of areas that can benefit trade compliance and logistics capabilities. RFID, utilized by the government and commercial industries, should be investigated by all companies operating in the global arena as a way to enhance security and compliance management and, at the same time, gain certain efficiencies in their operations.

RFID is beginning to make its way into the mainstream consciousness with tangible purposes and real benefits. Walmart has led the charge on the commercial side. In 2005 Walmart advised its top one hundred vendors that they must use RFID tags as a prerequisite for doing business with the company. Other mainstream giants such as Best Buy and Target have followed suit. The two most prohibitive obstacles in the path of RFID—international standardized acceptance and cost per tag—are beginning to yield to the inroads created by the retail superpowers. These pressures from top-level commercial players have made the "pie in the sky" concept of integrating real benefits derived from RFID technology seem much more attainable. The military and several government agencies have been watching the progress from the sidelines.

They have identified RFID as a potential asset to assist in national security and provide a platform to enforce tighter compliance standards on importers and exporters. The government drawing a regulatory line in the sand with RFID as its mandatory centerpiece in the near future should not be considered that far away.

In April 2002, U.S. Customs and Border Protection introduced a government program called Customs-Trade Partnership Against Terrorism (C-TPAT). C-TPAT is a voluntary joint government-private sector program designed to create a standardized level of security in the international supply chains of U.S. companies. Supply chain service providers, including ocean carriers, airlines, freight forwarders, and Customs brokers, are also participants in this initiative. The C-TPAT program began with U.S. importers disclosing a working profile of their international supply chain. All supply chain components, including manufacturers, overseas agents, carriers, and the warehouses and U.S. corporate offices themselves, are required to submit a detailed self-assessment of standard operating procedures pertaining to supply chain compliance and security. The supply chain "links" use the C-TPAT security criteria, created by U.S. Customs and the trade community, as a guide. Once companies receive confirmation of membership to C-TPAT, they must commit to maintaining a minimum level of security and compliance in order to retain membership to the program.

In March 2005, Customs announced new minimum security requirements for applicants and members of the program. The new requirements came in the form of seven-point container inspections prior to loading at origin, as well as using PAS ISO 17712 security seals on ocean containers. Although the C-TPAT program has been considered very successful by amassing a pool of over nine thousand members within a four-year period, the General Accounting Office (GAO) issued a critical assessment of C-TPAT in 2005. The GAO stated that the scope and methodology that Customs uses to measure its validation processes of importers is inconsistent. This inconsistency comprises the validity of the data compiled from the importer's C-TPAT profiles, which are collectively used to analyze the importing community's level of security as a whole. Customs responded to the GAO by issuing "tiered benefits" and more stringent program requirements for participants.

This back and forth between government watchdogs and Customs represents a probable vicious cycle for years to come. Every time the program is critiqued, Customs will try to patch up the issue that caused the criticism. Customs will be open to this type of periphery subjective influence until it is able to (1) make the program universally mandatory instead of voluntary and (2) include the use of RFID technology (or an equivalent) as a basic required element importers must adopt for C-TPAT consideration. Until Customs does this, the program will always be chasing its own tail to substantiate its existence as a post-9/11 supply chain preventative measure. For this reason, U.S. Customs is keeping a close eye on the progress RFID is making in staking its claim in mainstream acceptance.

U.S. Customs Commissioner Robert C. Bonner announced during a 2005 Customs Trade Symposium in Washington that he was ready to take the C-TPAT program to the next level, which he called C-TPAT Plus. C-TPAT Plus entails no inspection upon arrival and immediate release for low-risk shippers that use RFID-like technology. The technology must include the ability to detect and record whether tampering has occurred with a container seal after being affixed at the point of origin. Importers that employ the RFID, or "Smart Box," technology in their supply chain security profiles are promoted to "green lane" clearance status by Customs.

In 2008, CBP secured new regulations that control the additional flow of information from overseas suppliers to U.S. Customs (CBP), known as 10 + 2, or now Importer Security Filing (ISF), which could very readily be assisted by RFID technology interface. These new regulations became effective in January 2009.

The years 2005 to 2009 saw U.S. government agencies in the infancy stages of realizing the potential of RFID technology.

In January 2008, the U.S. Department of Homeland Security began testing … RFID technology as part of its US-VISIT program to efficiently and correctly identify visitors at U.S. border crossing points. Each person crossing over the border is given an RFID tag that contains a unique serial ID number that links the visitor's photo, fingerprints, and basic personal information to the US-VISIT database. As part of the US-VISIT initiative, all non-U.S. visitors have digital fingerprints and photos taken prior to entrance into the country. The information gathered as part of US-VISIT in conjunction with RFID technology serves as a means to better enhance and strengthen national security efforts. In addition, foreign visitors who apply for U.S. visas are simultaneously enrolled in the US-VISIT program.

As a result of this program and with the aid of RFID, the additional information made available about foreign visitors uncovered suspicious details about certain people that was previously unattainable. In cases where the additional information raised red flags, seven thousand visa applications were denied and six hundred people were stopped from entering the country. There have been thirty-nine arrests that can be attributed to the additional information provided by utilizing this program and RFID technology.

In 2006–2007, the Department of Homeland Security (DHS) began testing another form of RFID technology by embedding RFID chips into immigration documents at five crossing points on the Mexican and Canadian borders. Customs and Border Protection Form I-94A is coated with the RFID chip and serves the purpose of improving the efficiency and timeliness in which foreign visitors can enter and exit the country. The ultimate goal of this program is to come as close as possible to automating the Customs border crossing process. With each DHS immigration program described above, personal information attained with RFID is kept to a minimum and the foreign visitor can only can tracked within the borders of the United States.

Recently, the GAO found that the U.S. Army is failing to maintain accurate inventory controls of items shipped to repair contractors. The GAO noted that this lack of supervision and control places these items at risk of loss or theft. In December 2005, the GAO issued a report stating: "Although the DOD (Department of Defense) policy requires the military services to confirm receipt of all assets shipped to contractors, the Army is not consistently recording shipment receipts in its inventory management system."

Basing their findings on the Army's 2004 shipment data as documented in DHS case studies, the agency found that the Army could not successfully reconcile shipment records with receipts for over 42% of unclassified secondary repair item shipments and 37% of the classified secondary repair items. The combined value of these items was just under $500 million. The GAO also notes that the Army lacks in documentation control and fails to follow up on confirmations of receipt.

Implementing basic RFID technology could assist the Army with this problem in two ways. Primarily, the Army's ability to mark inventory with RFID tags would enable tighter inventory and item reconciliation controls, as well as upgrade the security of these goods from theft or loss. Secondarily, converting to a RFID controlled system would transfer a manually heavy, time-consuming process out of human hands and into the arms of automated efficiency. For this reason, among others, the Department of Defense and the U.S. military are pilot testing several RFID programs with the intent of integrating the technology to improve their supply chain practices.

A.T. Kearny, a management consulting firm, recently conducted a thorough research initiative regarding RFID's potential benefits. Their extensive study found that logistics executives from some of the world's largest importers and exporters, (ranging from retail to high-tech industries) cited inventory management and container security as top flight issues regarding their international supply chain. The A.T. Kearny study also concluded that RFID technology provides more than tampering alerts. RFID was actually found to provide tangible monetary savings in the form of inventory reduction and out-of-stock reductions, as well as preventing the loss of containers and theft. Other recent studies, performed by Stanford University and the business systems integration consulting firm BearingPoint, pointed to similar findings. All three groups individually pointed to key benefits and savings per container to the importer when utilizing RFID technology, in the range of $400 to $1,800 per container shipment.

So what are the obstacles from launching this technology? The formidable issue delaying a massive RFID international explosion is a universal standard format that countries and corporations can agree upon and commit to. China's ultimate decision regarding its role in the RFID standardization will have both substantial commercial and political implications.

The RFID market in China has led to delegations involving its most revered business leaders and high-ranking government officials. With China as the centerpiece, representatives from the RFID industry organization EPC Global have been working toward finding a universally acceptable standard for RFID to further its acceptance as a vital fixture of the twenty-first-century supply chain model. EPC Global has been working very closely with the International Organization for Standardization (ISO) for approval of universally acceptable RFID standards.

The Chinese government has been very supportive of EPC Global's efforts, and ISO approval will even better its standing. China may also receive pressure for accepting a standardized RFID platform from the commercial side. Walmart is

China's number one exporter of goods. Taken alone, the company represents more export volume to China than the total dollar volume of exports from Germany or Britain. While the company is not specifically mandating that China itself become RFID compliant, the fact that a majority of its top suppliers are China based and have moved to satisfy their ever so important client proves that Walmart can single-handedly influence foreign economic policy in yet another arena, albeit indirectly. However, nationalism runs strong in China, and any move by Walmart will be met by a rapid-fire response. Controversial Chinese businessman Edward Zeng, the founder and CEO of Beijing-based Sparkice, has been pushing the government of his country to adopt a China RFID standard as opposed to the more conventional and accepted EPC Global American version. Zeng has been lobbying the Ministry of Information Industries (MII) to reject the American version in favor of the version developed by Sparkice. His rationale for this direction ranges from issues of national security to nationalism and, ultimately, to the fact that Zeng stands to gain substantially from China using Sparkice's proprietary IP, which would position him as the largest RFID market in the world. The standardization issue will have to wade through Beijing's ministries, committees, and commissions to see the light of day. For this reason alone, acceptance of a RFID standard in China is quite a ways off.

Integrating the RFID technology into the ocean container shipping industry will not be a tireless undertaking either. Currently, the security methods for ocean containers mainly consist of disposable plastic bands and metal bolts securing the doors. These bands and bolts also have unique identification serial information printed on them that represent the seal number. At the ports of entry or departure, the seal's serial number and container number are recorded manually and then inputted into the carrier's database. There are obvious limitations to this method of container seal security. For instance, the carrier cannot determine time, date, or location of a seal or door being compromised.

The inspection of the container at the pier is a manual, time-consuming endeavor. In addition, the seals do not meet U.S. Customs Service Container Security Initiative minimum requirements. RFID technology would enhance security, automated and instantaneous seal serial number data transfer to the carrier's database, and immediate recording of a breach with the seal or container door. As mentioned previously, another advantage of utilizing RFID is U.S. Custom's stamp of approval recognizing compliant supply chain practice.

The pharmaceutical industry is unique to all others in its interest in utilizing RFID technology. Its interest in this technology is how RFID protects the sanctity of its shipments as well as maintaining traceability of its products at a bottle, jar, or even blister package level. What the pharmaceutical manufacturers desire to have is a RFID environment that would provide an efficient, cost-effective product recall management system. The prospect of guaranteed integrity of the product through the supply chain to the end user is of great interest to the industry. In years past, when a manufacturer announced recall of a product, the response was for pharmacies and retailers to strip the product clean from the shelves and dispose of it immediately.

Although this was considered a mandatory action for the interest of public health and safety, these actions cost the industry millions of dollars. For example, a given manufacturer must issue a product recall because of an irregular production event affecting two hundred bottles. The manufacturer that has employed RFID technology at the bottle level can target specific units it feels are dangerous, as opposed to wiping out an entire lot when a small percentage of the bottles caused an issue. Even though this technology would safeguard the products tremendously, the issue of tagging individual units as opposed to individual pallets or boxes is daunting from an expense standpoint.

Supply chain executives must continue to give this issue the attention it deserves. Keeping tabs on how this technology progresses with mainstream accessibility and applicability is a necessity for corporate logistics decision makers. Staying current by building and maintaining a relevant supply chain infrastructure with current technology available is an intelligent, cost-effective strategy to adopt. Having this type of approach is far less expensive than being forced to take expensive reactive measures after neglectfully falling behind. It is better to be proactive now than reactive at a later time, when it might be too late or too costly. Eventually, RFID will be a function of competitive advantage.

Although the realization of full-scale international RFID acceptance is not right around the corner, it is far from miles away. The concept of widespread RFID integration will inherit substantial credibility when viable return on investment can be substantiated. As soon as corporate models illustrating how the efficiencies created by RFID translate into real monetary savings are published and accessible to the public, the technology will have guaranteed its own future.

Several government agencies and industries have taken note of the vast potential of this technology and how it can enhance national security, protect the international supply chain, and promote sizable efficiencies in inventory control and management. With support and encouragement from the diverse and influential elements of government and the private sector, acceptance of a basic RFID environment is something to expect in the years ahead.

Chapter 6

Personnel Deployment, Training, and Best Practices

Supply chain personnel strategically placed and operating in key venues will make a global operation run the most effectively. The author elaborates and places focus on personnel issues in operating global supply chains in this chapter.

Where Should Trade Compliance Be Managed?

Our experience has evidenced that trade compliance best operates as part of supply chain management and global logistics. Other options, such as finance, legal, and corporate compliance, lack direct responsibility for the movement of freight. The business processes of trade compliance influence freight movement significantly. This dictates that the personnel who move the freight also have responsibility for trade compliance.

While some may be concerned about potential conflicts of interest, our experience has shown that with trained quality personnel, this point becomes moot. When other disciplines manage trade compliance, they are typically too quick to use the literal definition of regulatory controls rather than functional working options that allow success in both areas simultaneously—moving the freight and being compliant and secure.

Placing trade compliance control in a supply chain area provides the following benefits:

1. Logistics expertise is a necessary element of managing trade compliance. You need to understand what a bill of lading is, what a delivery receipt does, and how the Automated Export System functions.
2. Logistics managers typically chose service providers. Service providers are a critical component of the supply chain and must be part of and included in any trade compliance program. They must be kept to certain standards, which are best controlled by those managing and directing their services.
3. Logistics managers utilize software to support their supply chain responsibilities. The technology can be adapted to include compliance software to deal with regulatory controls.
4. Most compliance initiatives from government agencies are directed to transportation companies, professionals, and the like.

Training and Education

The skill sets of global trade are diverse. They are also a moving target and must be kept abreast of on a consistent basis. The author recommends that all persons with trade compliance responsibilities become certified in import-export compliance management. One program that comes highly recommended is the Professional Association of Import and Export Compliance Managers (PACMAN). This organization offers two-day programs that are followed up with take-home exams. It exercises the very best option to demonstrate due diligence and reasonable care for supply chain personnel to evidence this ongoing education and training.

PACMAN offers professional certifications in international logistics compliance management that serve as an acknowledged representation of informed compliance by government agencies such as U.S. Customs and Border Protection and the Bureau of Industry and Security.

You can demonstrate your industry expertise with:

- Certification of compliance management in import-export C-TPAT compliance
- Three-year certifications of compliance management
- Master certifications—available for compliance management representatives who have exceeded the standardized level of compliance expertise
- Compliance resource and best practices—available to all certified members
- Customized training—available upon request

Specific professional compliance certification programs include:

- C-TPAT certified compliance certifications
- Import compliance certifications

- Export compliance management certifications
- Import-export compliance management certifications

Redeem your professional certification now as an immediate representation of your professional experience and industry awareness.

PACMAN Benefits

C-TPAT Certification, Validation, and Web Portal Management Guidance PACMAN is an educational venue that affords real-time access to industry shared best practices in the areas of C-TPAT management. Its programs are structured to include government presentations and industry expertise directly related to validation, certification, and Web portal management.

Industry's Best Practices Import and Export Compliance Forum PACMAN creates a user-friendly access forum for industry compliance managers to dialogue, strategize, and share best practice compliance solutions to its membership base. Your challenges, obstacles, and current issues may be mitigated and avoided based on your interaction with this hands-on environment.

Industry Expert Advisory Assistance on Global Supply Chain Issues PACMAN provides access to an industry expert advisory board that provides international supply chain expertise to association members through immediate access Web, e-mail, and phone communications.

PACMAN Acknowledged Professional Practitioner Certification Award is acknowledged throughout the international supply chain community as an affirmation of compliance expertise. The value of informed compliance on export and import reasonable care standards is magnified with your participation in the PACMAN association.

Online training is also available. Though not the best option, compared with face-to-face training, for those with restricted schedules, this does present a viable alternative.

U.S. Export Compliance.com: A Solution for U.S. Trade Compliance Education and Training

Every company's management wants to have complete confidence in its trade compliance effort with respect to the International Traffic in Arms Regulations (ITAR) and Export Administration Regulations (EAR). The question is: Is that an achievable goal? Do you have concerns about your staff not having the necessary skills and up-to-date knowledge needed to keep your company in compliance? Do two-day training seminars leave you feeling as though you need more. Maybe historically your company has performed compliance training in-house, but every time you turn around you realize that your training materials are two years out of date or missing vital updates. Perhaps you've come to realize that training course development and delivery is not your core competency; after all, you are a compliance expert, and developing and maintaining curriculum draws you away from important compliance license issues. There is a turnkey solution that over one thousand companies worldwide and all of the top fifty aerospace and defense companies routinely rely upon to bring much needed ITAR and EAR compliance best practices and respected world class training and education and industry certification inside their organizations.

What does ITAR compliant or ITAR certified mean? The International Import-Export Institute (IIEI), part of nationally accredited Dunlap-Stone University, is recognized the world over as the premier online provider of specialized education and training that addresses critical U.S. government regulations, from Export Administration Regulations (EAR) to the International Traffic in Arms Regulations (ITAR) to the Office of Foreign Asset Controls (OFAC) and other regulatory agencies, and more. Recognized by the U.S. government and governments around the world for its international trade certification programs, the IIEI's is the unquestioned industry standard in over ninety countries.

Whether you are part of a large, global multinational corporation with a thousand ITAR- or EAR-compliance-related employees or a small company with a part-time compliance person, the IIEI has education and training programs and college degree options to fit your exact needs. Whether you have one employee that needs to learn trade compliance basics or advanced professionals that need to validate their expertise of the complete ITAR or EAR, or perhaps a group of employees dispersed globally that to need to prepare for the Certified U.S. Export Compliance Officer' examination, the IIEI can help you.

The IIEI's ITAR and EAR trade compliance and curriculum experts are constantly updating and revising the courses they offer to reflect the latest knowledge as the regulations change. For example, from January 2004 to July 2008, the Understanding the ITAR course (IIEI-306) was updated thirty-two times and had two major revisions, resulting in the 6-week course being new and fresh every 4½ weeks over a 4-year span. No in-house training is typically able to do this. This same course is now using topical case studies to demonstrate concepts in real-world terms.

Whatever your needs, the IIEI can help—from export compliance, to import certifications, to specialized training for empowered officials, to knowledge about agreements under the ITAR and many other topics.

The IIEI offers its Managed Trade Compliance Training Program. Used by larger companies that have operations dispersed geographically but want to have an integrated tightly monitored program, it is an effective way to outsource the training and education and maintain control at the same time. The IIEI assists companies in designing their unique annual education and training program to meet each individual's specific needs and then manages its implementation. Your management receives regular updated reports on the status throughout the year. This frees up your compliance management to proactively focus on mission-critical export licensing issues and concerns.

IIEI helps bring critical ITAR and EAR compliance knowledge into your organization. With its advanced online classroom model, IIEI can cost-effectively educate your staff, large or small, without disrupting your business and help you validate that your employees possess the requisite knowledge your company needs to reduce your trade compliance risk and validate that your company is ITAR compliant.

Benchmarking and Best Practices

When systems, standard operating procedures (SOPs), and personnel are in place, the prudent company establishes internal controls and processes that measure the levels of success and steps necessary to raise the bar of excellence—all discussed in this chapter.

Benchmarking

Every trade compliance program requires management to make sure the structure and the deliverables of the initiative are contemporary and comprehensive—and that they are working successfully. For public companies, a standard in Sarbanes-Oxley compliance requires this audit process. For all other companies, it is a prudent business practice.

Trade compliance has been a work in progress for over twenty years, with a significant focus starting after 9/11. Customs, commerce, and state are creating the rules, the standards, and all the governance as we speak. That fact makes it imperative to take steps to ensure that your trade compliance program is relevant—today and for the future.

Options in benchmarking include:

- Use outside consultants
- Handle internally

The upside of outside consultants is:

- Immediate expertise
- Unlimited and qualified expertise
- View into other organizations
- Access to personnel with significant skill sets
- Access to technology options
- Nonagenda approach to analysis
- Turnkey capability in problem resolution

The only downside is cost.

Internal options exist only if you have personnel with the necessary skill sets, time, and inclination to handle benchmarking. Costs could be a potential benefit as well. But you will lose the benefit the expertise consultants can provide regarding insight into other corporate trade compliance programs.

Best Practices in Trade Compliance

It is very important for trade compliance managers to raise the bar of practices, procedures, and business processes in the global supply chains their company operates in. There is no better thought process to accomplish this than by creating a best practices culture throughout the organization. Here is an outline on just how to proceed in accomplishing that.

There are three key elements to managing a trade compliance program:

- Taking ownership
- Creating SOPs
- Education and training

Once a company decides to invest in a trade compliance program, senior management must delegate the day-to-day responsibilities to one individual. This individual will take ownership of the trade compliance responsibilities to make sure that procedures are internally developed and promoted throughout the organization.

But even before this designation has occurred, senior management must be committed to the trade compliance program. This factor is critical to a successful corporate program. Monies, time, and effort will have to be expended. Personnel will have to be educated. SOPs will have to be established and implemented. Internal systems of coordination and communication will have to be heightened. To accomplish these, senior management must first be committed. They will need to understand the consequences—fines, penalties, and potential loss of export-import privileges—on both a corporate and personal level of exposure.

Once the commitment is obtained, the organization of the compliance effort must be accomplished. Many corporations create committees made up of supply chain individuals from various concerns, such as but not limited to:

- Traffic and logistics management
- Legal/corporate counsel
- Customer service
- Finance/accounting
- Supply chain staff
- Manufacturing and inventory
- Marketing and sales management
- Import-export operations
- Corporate compliance

But at the end of the day, the final responsibilities must come down to one individual. Through the committee, many responsibilities may be delegated, but only one individual will have the overall responsibility, answering to senior management to ensure corporate export compliance. We refer to that individual as the *trade compliance officer*. This person can come from an array of disciplines, but experience shows that logistics expertise provides the best foundation. The key to trade compliance is understanding that you are responding to rules governing the sale, then movement of the goods. The key word being *movement* or, in corporate terms, *logistics*.

A background of logistics expertise in the compliance person's resume offers one an insight into the various service providers that are utilized and their compliance habits and freight capabilities.

Most corporations utilize the services of freight forwarders and Customs brokers. The interface with these entities becomes a critical factor in overall export compliance. They are advisors. They are document preparers and handlers. They execute logistics. They advise on product classifications. They are an integral link in the export supply chain, and therefore *de facto* become an integral part of export compliance. Having a logistics professional involved in the evaluation, choice, and selection of these service providers, and now in evaluating their contribution to compliance management, is a key factor.

The trade compliance officer must be organized with an ability to articulate detail. Export compliance requires paying attention to detail. It requires internal coordination on a number of levels. It requires quality, timely communication—in writing and in oral presentation. The trade compliance officer will have to address a subject to personnel of all levels—from senior management to warehouse and dockworkers and everybody in between. Clear, concise, no nonsense, and down to earth communication will determine the success of any trade compliance initiative.

Having ownership will prevent finger pointing and act as a centralized point within the company that all can turn to for compliance management. The SOPs and training will give this authority to the compliance officer for all to follow. The officer's basic knowledge of preparing SOPs and developing in-house education and training programs is a valuable asset.

Knowledge of the following areas will be very important:

- Schedule B, HTSUS classifications
- Commercial invoice valuations
- Transfer pricing
- Documentation requirements
- BIS, DOT, TSA, Treasury, and DOC rules and regulations
- ITAR, State Department
- Census Bureau
- Denied Parties List
- Utilization of technology in global trade

- Service provider selection
- U.S. Customs and Border Protection
- Foreign Trade Regulations
- Record keeping
- Communication skills
- Resource development

These are but a few of the necessary areas, skill sets, knowledge, and capabilities the compliance officer will have to master.

A key factor in developing an expertise in these skill sets will be in developing numerous resources and access to key consultants, government officers, and trade personnel. The best resources are quality consultants and forwarders/brokers that have internal expertise. Many of the large accounting firms have capabilities, and many law firms offer these services. Developing retainers with these type of companies and tying them into availability and an extension of the compliance officer are key to a successful compliance initiative.

Developing external resources to obtain compliance data is critical for every compliance officer. Every government agency has Web sites that have significant reams of compliance data and are all great resources. Two of the best are www.doc.bis.gov and www.cbp.gov.

Magazines and periodicals such as *American Shipper, Journal of Commerce, Cargo Shipping Worldwide*, and *TWA Managing Imports and Exports* must be subscribed to. Attend trade seminars and programs having compliance subject matter. The World Academy, American Management Association, and UNZ & Co. are a few options. Having trade compliance ownership is a huge responsibility. Developing the right partners, service providers, and the critical resources will make the job much easier.

Once the position is solidified, the next step is to create a set of standard operating procedures (SOPs).

What Are SOPs?

The SOPs become a written internal communication that outlines the operating guidelines that corporate personnel must follow in managing trade compliance responsibilities. They are created by operating staff, endorsed by the legal and accounting departments, and given full authorization when signed off by senior management (preferably the COO, president, or CEO). The SOPs work in conjunction with other corporate operating guidelines developed for supply chain management and can be ISO 9001 certified.

For public companies, the SOPs are a necessary element in the functionality of Sarbanes-Oxley (SOX) requirements. If a public company is truly to be SOX compliant, then the supply chain must be part of the business process, procedures, and controls adhered to by the balance of the corporation.

The SOPs reflect the specific products, services, culture, and operating profile of the corporation they represent and establish a framework that global logistics, purchasing, customer service, sales, finance, and manufacturing can operate within.

Why Create Trade Compliance SOPs?

There are numerous and varied reasons to create the SOPs:

- They ensure that an entire company and its personnel are on the same page when it comes to trade compliance management. If the SOPs are in written form, concise with clear definition, the opportunity for deviation, misinterpretation, and misuse is minimized.
- They provide a forum for consistent operating procedures between different divisions and profit centers, where the tendency might be to personalize or differentiate operational guidelines to suit one's needs.
- They provide a written explicit guideline that demonstrates due diligence, reasonable care, supervision, and control in how the supply chain operates.
- They serve as an internal resource for corporate personnel to have import-export regulation type questions answered, and for defined interpretations of any trade compliance issue.
- They establish a forum for continuity when personnel change positions, move on to other areas, or leave the company.
- They establish lines of responsibility and accountability internally and with all the transportation and logistics providers in the global supply chain.

SOPs for trade compliance are really the only way an exporter can exercise supervision and control over its personnel, operations, and providers/carriers.

What Needs to Be Included in My Trade Compliance SOPs?

Each company must determine what has to be included in its SOPs that is unique to its products, values, and global supply chains. Having said that, there are a number of areas that would be typically included:

- Personnel responsibilities—by name and title
- Emergency response numbers
- Basic guide to the Export Administration Regulations (EAR), CBP, and other government agencies involved in your supply chain
- Denied Parties List
- Schedule B classification
- Export Commodity Control Numbers (ECCNs)
- Shipper's export declarations (SEDs)

- Automated Export System (AES)
- Commercial invoice preparation
- Valuation issues
- Money transfer and financial considerations
- Third-party vendor, carrier, and service provider responsibilities

These are but a few of the more important topics that should be included in export compliance SOPs. Each company has to look at its own set of circumstances and create their SOPs accordingly.

An excellent resource for creating export compliance SOPs is *Mastering Import and Export Management* (AMACON Books, www.amacon.pub). The BIS Web site (www.bis.doc.BIS.gov) has an entire tutorial on developing export compliance SOPs.

Another good source for export compliance management is the Professional Association of Import and Export Compliance Managers (www.compliancemaven. com).

Developing resources is a vital element of managing any export compliance program.

Organized and Formal Education and Training

The trade compliance officer needs to obtain certification in compliance management. The organization PACMAN (www.compliancemaven.com) provides instruction, testing, and then a network of resources for the continual need for more information, updates, and timely news briefs.

The world of compliance and security is one that is a work in progress. Small changes occur daily, large ones weekly, and huge ones quarterly. This makes the trade compliance officer's job more difficult. The key to mitigating the difficulty is to establish both formal and informal training programs—both taken externally and arranged in-house.

The trade compliance officer is not the only one who needs compliance and security training. It extends to all personnel who interface and interact within and without the global supply chain, such as but not limited to:

- Senior management
- Divisional and business unit managers
- Traffic and logistics
- Supply chain
- Manufacturing and inventory
- Warehousing
- Customer service
- Finance

- Legal
- Corporate governance and compliance
- Purchasing
- R&D, engineers, technicians, and scientists

There is total connectivity between all these corporate entities. And like links in a chain, trade compliance is only as strong as its weakest link.

Internal seminars, briefings, and awareness training are all key ingredients to a successful best practices trade compliance program.

Putting Best Practices for Trade Compliance into an Action Plan

For import and export companies, the supply chains of the world changed forever on 9/11. Such companies are now faced with an entire new set of regulations in compliance and security, combined with increased government scrutiny (with what can be best described as a work in progress) with modifications, different interpretations, and new laws (obstacles and barriers) coming up every day. Supply chain managers need to now be regulatory and legal superstars in the maze of logistics, inventory, purchasing, and operational responsibilities.

Pre-9/11, the risks of global trade—political, economic, carriers, forwarders, agents and distributors, Customs or the BIS, weather, acts of God, cultural, language and legal differences, handling, storage, terrorism, war, SRCC, our own internal politics of silos and fiefdoms—faced import and export companies.

These risks have not changed. In fact, such companies now face an array of new challenges:

- Patriot Act
- Export Administration Act
- C-TPAT
- USPPI for SED filing
- USPPI for carriers
- Bioterrorism Act
- Reorganization of the government with DHS
- Deemed exports
- Enhanced plant and warehouse security measures
- Twenty-four-hour manifest rules
- CSI
- Focused assessments
- ISA
- Green lanes
- Personnel hiring screening

- Technology security: Firewalls and spam
- Enhanced Denied Parties Screening
- Foreign Corrupt Practices Act
- Sarbanes-Oxley issues
- Safe Port Act
- 10 + 2 (ISF)
- Post-9/11 Commission recommendations

The onus is on import and export companies to manage global supply chains in a safe, timely, and cost-effective manner, but still be compliant, secure, and eliminate the exposures faced through terrorism.

These companies will be managing their trade compliance initiative with an eight-step program to raise the bar of best practices in their company overall. But one must keep in mind that the key to get to such status is the ability to work through the trade compliance with all that has been outlined in the preceding chapters.

The timing of strategies and action steps is not necessarily one of immediate expediency, as one can outline an action plan that spans a year, nine months, eighteen months—whatever works in the specific nuances of your global supply chain.

Keep in mind that the government has the approach of "point of discovery," meaning that it is even more concerned with what you do as a supply chain executive and corporation—from the point in time you first become aware that you are nonsecure and noncompliant—and not as much with what has happened in the past. This does not eliminate the consequences of prior history, but it can significantly mitigate them.

Here is a final thought on this subject: we have choices, both as an individual and as a corporation that is engaged in supply chain activities. If you are reactive to the regulatory climate that now prevails, you will be a slave to the process—with unknown consequences and uncontrollable costs. But if you are proactive, you will better control the destinies of your imports and exports and seriously reduce the costs, exposures, fines and penalties, and ultimate loss of the supply chain—becoming disabled. Therefore, be proactive, it is a better option. Then the question of the day becomes: Run your company by "good luck" or run it by better management?

Concluding Remarks

Trade compliance today and beyond will be a critical component in the management of global supply chains. This book is the very best foundation for a company to institute a trade compliance program and for the new trade compliance offer—as a recipe book for the structure and implementation of every concept and regulation that needs to be integrated into the supply chain, they have the responsibility to make compliant and secure. Due diligence, reasonable care, supervision, and control are no better outlined anywhere than in the preceding chapters of this book.

While there are no guaranteed formulas for success in anything, this book truly provides the reader and the serious company/individual with material, information, content, and actions to follow that will come very close to a 100% guarantee of success. Read it and read it again. Copy it and use it as a training manual. Be successful with it!

TAC

Glossary

Abandonment: Refusing delivery of a shipment that is so badly damaged in transit it has little or no value.

Acceptance: An international banking instrument known as a time draft or bill of exchange that the drawee has accepted and is unconditionally obligated to pay at maturity.

***Ad valorem*:** A tariff that is calculated based on a percentage of the value of the product.

Advising bank: A bank operating in the exporter's country that handles letters of credit for a foreign bank by notifying the exporter that the credit has been opened in its favor.

Agency for International Development (AID) shipments: The Agency for International Development is a U.S. government agency created to provide relief to developing countries who must purchase products and services through U.S. companies. Specialized export documentation is necessary to complete the transactions.

All-inclusive: Term of sale used to notate "all charges are included."

Allowance: Typically afforded a consignee as a "credit" or "deduction" on a specific export transaction.

All-risk cargo insurance: A clause included in marine insurance policies to cover loss and damage from external causes during the course of transit within all the terms and conditions agreed to by the underwriters.

Arbitration: Wording included in export contracts introducing an independent third-party negotiator into the dispute resolution in lieu of litigation.

Arrival notice: Advice to a consignee on inbound freight. Sometimes referred to as a pre-alert. Contains details of the shipment's arrival schedule and bill of lading data.

"As is": An international term denoting that the buyer accepts the goods as is. It is a connotation there may be something wrong with the merchandise, and the seller limits its future potential liability.

Automated Broker Interface (ABI): The electronic transmission and exchange of data between a customhouse broker and CBP.

Automated Export System (AES): The electronic transmission of the shipper's export declaration to Census, BIS, and CBP.

Automated Manifest System (AMS): The electronic transmission of a carrier/vessel's manifest between the carrier/steamship line and CBP.

Balance of trade: The difference between a country's total imports and exports. If exports exceed imports, a favorable balance of trade, or trade surplus, exists; if not, a trade deficit exists.

Barter: The direct exchange of goods or services without the use of money as a medium of exchange and without third-party involvement.

Bill of lading: A document that establishes the terms of a contract between a shipper and a transportation company under which freight is to be moved between specified points for a specified charge. Usually prepared by the shipper on forms issued by the carrier, it serves as a document of title, a contract of carriage, and a receipt of goods.

Bond: A form of insurance between two parties obligating a surety to pay against a performance or obligation.

Bonded warehouse: A warehouse authorized by Customs authorities for storage of goods on which payment of duties is deferred until the goods are cleared and removed.

Break bulk cargo: Loose cargo that is loaded directly into a conveyance's hold.

Bretton Woods Conference: A meeting under the auspices of the United Nations at Bretton Woods, New Hampshire, in 1944, that was held to develop some degree of cooperation in matters of international trade and payments and to devise a satisfactory international monetary system to be in operation after World War II. The particular objectives intended were stable exchange rates and convertibility of currencies for the development of multilateral trade. The Bretton Woods Conference established the International Monetary Fund and the World Bank.

Bunker Adjustment Fee (BAF): Fuel surcharge issued by a steamship line.

Bureau of Industry and Security (BIS): Department of Commerce agency responsible for Export Administration Regulations, formerly known as Bureau of Industry and Security.

Carnet: A Customs document permitting the holder to carry or send merchandise temporarily into certain foreign countries without paying duties or posting bonds.

Certificate of origin: Document used to certify the country of origin for a product.

Clingage: When shipping bulk liquids, the residue remaining inside the conveyance after discharge.

Combi: An aircraft with pallet or container capacity on its main deck and belly holds.

Commission agent: An individual, company, or government agent that serves as the buyer of overseas goods on behalf of another buyer.

Commodity specialist: An official authorized by the U.S. Treasury to determine proper tariff and value of imported goods.

Consignment: Delivery of merchandise from an exporter (the consignor) to an agent (the consignee) under the agreement that the agent sells the merchandise for the account of the exporter. The consignor retains the title to the goods until the consignee has sold them. The consignee sells the goods for commission and remits the net proceeds to the consignor.

Consolidator: An agent who brings together a number of shipments for one destination to qualify for preferential rates.

Cost, insurance, freight (CIF): A system of valuing imports that includes all costs, insurance, and freight involved in shipping the goods from the port of embarkation to the destination.

Countertrade: The sale of goods or services that are paid for in whole or part by the transfer of goods or services from a foreign country.

Credit risk insurance: Insurance designed to cover risks of nonpayment for delivered goods.

Currency: National form for payment medium: dollars, pesos, rubles, naira, pounds, etc.

Destination control statement: Specific wording included on a commercial invoice and bill of lading advising goods are subject to export control laws and diversion contrary to U.S. law is prohibited.

Distributor: A foreign agent who sells for a supplier directly and maintains an inventory of the supplier's products.

Dock receipt: Documented receipt the shipment has been received by the steamship line.

Domestic international sales corporation (DISC): Established in 1971 by U.S. legislation, DISCs were designed to help exporters by offering income tax deferrals on export earnings. DISCs were phased out in 1984.

Draft: Negotiable instrument presented to the buyer's bank for payment.

Drawback: Duties to be refunded by government when previously imported goods are exported or used in the manufacture of exported products.

Dumping: Exporting or importing merchandise into a country below the costs incurred in production and shipment.

Duty: A tax imposed on imports by the Customs authority of a country. Duties are generally based on the value of the goods (*ad valorem* duties), some other factor such as weight or quantity (specified duties), or a combination of value and other factors (compounded duties).

Embargo: A prohibition on imports or exports as a result of a political eventuality.

European Community (EC): The twelve nations of Europe that have combined to form the world's largest single market of more than 320 million consumers. The EC includes Belgium, Denmark, France, Greece, Ireland, Italy, Luxembourg, the Netherlands, Portugal, Spain, the United Kingdom, and West Germany.

Export: To send or transport goods out of a country for sale in another country. In international sales, the exporter is usually the seller or the seller's agent.

Export-Import Bank of the United States (Ex-Im Bank): Ex-Im Bank facilitates and aids the financing of exports of U.S. goods and services through a variety of programs created to meet the needs of the U.S. exporting community. Programs, which are tailored to the size of a transaction, can take the form of direct lending or loan guarantees.

Export management company: A private company that serves as the export department for several manufacturers, soliciting and transacting export business on behalf of its clients in return for a commission, salary, or retainer plus commission.

Export trading company: An organization designed to facilitate the export of goods and services. It can be a trade intermediary that provides export-related services to producers or can be established by the producers themselves, though typically export trading companies do not take title to goods.

Ex works (EXW) from factory: The buyer accepts goods at the point of origin and assumes all responsibility for transportation of the goods sold. Also: ex warehouse, ex mine, and ex factory as defined in INCO terms.

Fair trade: A concept of international trade in which some barriers are tolerable as long as they are equitable. When barriers are eliminated, there should be reciprocal action by all parties.

Federal Maritime Commission (FMC): Agency issuing rules and regulations for ocean transportation.

Force majeure: Expressed as "acts of God." Conditions found in some marine contracts exempting certain parties from liability for occurrences out of their control, such as earthquakes and floods.

Foreign Commercial Service: Department of Commerce agency assisting in promoting exports of U.S. products.

Foreign Corrupt Practices Act of 1977: U.S. legislation with stringent antibribery provisions and guidelines for record keeping and internal accounting control requirements for all publicly held corporations. The act makes it illegal to offer, pay, or agree to pay money or any item of value to a foreign official for the purpose of getting or retaining business.

Foreign Credit Insurance Association (FCIA): An insurance program, previously government managed and underwritten, now privately held, that insures commercial and political risks for U.S. exporters.

Foreign sales agent: An individual or company that serves as the foreign representative of a domestic supplier and seeks sales abroad for the supplier.

Forfaiting: The selling, at a discount, of a longer-term receivable or promissory note of a buyer.

Franchising: A form of licensing by the service sector for companies that want to export their trademark, methods, or personal services.

Free alongside (FAS): A system of valuing imports that includes inland transportation costs involved in delivery of goods to a port in the exporting country, but excludes the cost of ocean shipping, insurance, and loading the merchandise on the vessel.

Free domicile: Terminology used for door-to-door deliveries.

Free on board (FOB): A system of valuing imports that includes inland transportation costs involved in delivery of goods to a port in the exporting country and the cost of loading the merchandise on the vessel, but excludes the cost of ocean shipping and insurance.

Free port: An area such as a port city into which merchandise may legally be moved without payment of duties.

Free trade: A theoretical concept to describe international trade unhampered by governmental barriers such as tariffs or nontariff measures. Free trade typically favors the reduction or elimination of all tariff and nontariff barriers to trade.

Free trade zone (FTZ): A port designated by the government of a country for duty-free entry of any nonprohibited goods. Merchandise may be stored, displayed, or used for manufacturing within the zone, and reexported without the payment of duties.

Freight all kinds (FAK): A mix of cargoes traveling as one.

General Agreement on Tariffs and Trade (GATT): A multilateral treaty to which eighty-five nations (or more than 80% of world trade) subscribe; it is designed to reduce trade barriers and promote trade through tariff concessions, thereby contributing to global economic growth and development.

Generalized System of Preferences (GSP): Notes duty-free/reduced tariffs on imports from the countries listed on the GSP list.

Harmonized Tariff System of the United States (HTSUS): System of classifying products imported into the United States by number.

Harter Act: Legislation protecting a ship owner from certain types of claims that are due to actions of the crew.

Hazmat: Hazardous materials regulated by various government agencies, DOT/CFR Title 49, IATA, IMCO, Coast Guard, etc. Personnel who interface with hazmat cargoes need to be certified to do so.

Hedging: A mechanism that allows an exporter to take a position in a foreign currency to protect against losses due to wide fluctuations in currency exchange rates.

Hold: The space below deck inside an oceangoing vessel.

Igloo: Container used in air freight.

Import license: Government license issued for particular products and required by the importer prior to importation.

In bond: Transportation of merchandise under custody of a bonded carrier.

INCO terms: Terms of sale issued by the International Chamber of Commerce.

Inherent vice: Capability of a product to produce damage to itself. Example: Metal will rust and fruit will spoil.

Integrated carrier: Carrier acting as the pickup agent, air freight carrier, Customs clearance agent, and delivery agent. Examples: UPS, Federal Express.

Intermodal: Covering more than one mode of transportation.

Irrevocable letter of credit: A letter of credit in which the specified payment is guaranteed by the bank if all terms and conditions are met by the drawee (buyer). *See also* revocable letter of credit.

ISO 9000: Issued in 1987 by the International Organization for Standardization, ISO 9000 is a series of five international standards that establish requirements for the quality control systems of companies selling goods in the European Community. It now includes many additional countries and companies throughout the world.

Joint venture: A business undertaking in which more than one company shares ownership and control.

Known shipper: FAA ruling requiring forwarders and carriers to know the shipper of a product before accepting goods for shipment.

Letter of credit: A document is issued by a bank per instructions from a buyer of goods that authorizes the seller to draw a specified sum of money under specified terms, usually the receipt by the bank of certain documents within a given period of time.

Licensing: A business arrangement in which the manufacturer of a product (or a company with proprietary rights over certain technology, trademarks, etc.) grants permission to some other group or individual to manufacture that product (or make use of that proprietary material) in return for specified royalties or other payment.

Limits of liability: When goods are insured, they are subject to the limits of liability set forth within the policy or contract.

Logistics: The science of transportation covering the planning and implementation of specific strategies to move materials at a desired cost.

***Mala fide*:** Misrepresentation or in bad faith.

***Maquiladora*:** A tax-free program allowing the import of materials into Mexico for manufacturing of goods for export back to the United States. Now declining in importance as a result of NAFTA.

Marine insurance: Insurance covering loss or damage of goods during transit. It covers all modes of transport.

Market research: Specific intelligence about the market in which a seller proposes to sell goods or services. This information is gathered through interviews, commissioned surveys, and direct contact with potential customers or their representatives.

Marks and numbers: The references made in writing to identify a shipment on the exterior packing, typically referenced in the documentation.

No license required (NLR): Designation of a product not found on the Commerce Control List or a product that does not require a license authorization prior to export.

Nonvessel operating common carrier (NVOCC): Ocean freight consolidator.

North American Free Trade Agreement (NAFTA): An agreement that creates a single unified market of the United States, Canada, and Mexico.

Office of Foreign Asset Controls (OFAC): Department of Treasury office issuing regulations on transfers/funding of money.

Open account: A trade arrangement in which goods are shipped to a foreign buyer without guarantee of payment. The obvious risk this method poses to the supplier makes it essential that the buyer's integrity be unquestionable.

Order bill of lading: Negotiable bill of lading made out to the order of the shipper.

Overseas Private Investment Corporation (OPIC): A government-sponsored organization that promotes investment in plans and equipment in less developed countries by offering guarantees comparable to those of the Ex-Im Bank.

Paperless release: Electronic release of a shipment by CBP prior to hard copies being presented.

Phytosanitary: Type of certificate issued for particular commodities.

Political risk: In exporting, the risk of loss due to such causes as currency inconvertibility, government action preventing entry of goods, expropriation, confiscation, or war.

Power of attorney: A document that authorizes a Customs broker or freight forwarder to act on the exporter's or importer's behalf on issues relative to Customs clearance, transportation, documentation, etc.

Premium: Insurance dollars paid to an underwriter to accept a transfer of risk.

***Prima facie*:** At face value.

Product registration: Requirement to register a product with a particular government agency prior to import.

***Pro forma* invoice:** (1) Invoice prepared by the supplier to the buyer, usually as a means to secure financing. (2) Invoice prepared by an importer when the supplier's invoice does not meet the invoice requirements set forth by CBP.

Protectionism: The setting of trade barriers high enough to discourage foreign imports or to raise the prices sufficiently to enable relatively inefficient domestic producers to compete successfully with foreign producers.

Purchasing agent: An individual or company that purchases goods in its own country on behalf of foreign importers, such as government agencies or large private concerns.

Remarketers: Export agents, merchants, or foreign trading companies that purchase products from an exporter to resell them under their own name.

Revocable letter of credit: A letter of credit that can be canceled or altered by the drawee (buyer) after it has been issued by the drawee's bank, compared to an irrevocable letter of credit, which is totally binding without both parties' written agreement.

Security endorsement: Affirmative document issued by exporter/forwarder to carrier stating goods meet security guidelines.

SGS inspection: Preinspection performed by Societe Generales Surveillance prior to export of goods to designated countries.

Tariff: A tax on imports or the rate at which imported goods are taxed.

Terminal handling charge: Fee assessed by a terminal for handling a shipment.

Through bill of lading: Bill of lading signifying various modes of transportation will be utilized to destination.

Time draft: A draft that matures in a certain number of days, either from acceptance or date of draft.

Tracking: A forwarder or carrier's system of recording movement intervals of shipments from origin through to final destination.

Trade acceptance: *See* acceptance.

Transfer risk: The risk associated with converting a local foreign currency into U.S. dollars.

Transmittal letter: Cover communication outlining details of an export transaction and accompanying documentation.

Twenty-foot equivalent (TEU): Twenty-foot equivalent or standard measure for a 20-foot ocean freight container. Two TEUs represent one 40-foot standard container.

Ullage: Measuring the amount of liquid or dry bulk freight in the hold of a vessel by measuring the height of the stow from the opening on deck.

Uniform Customs and Practice: International rules governing documentary collections.

U.S. Agency for International Development (USAID): A U.S. governmental agency that carries out assistance programs designed to help the people of certain lesser developed countries develop their human and economic resources, increase production capacities, and improve the quality of human life as well as promote the economic or potential stability in friendly countries.

Value-added tax (VAT): An indirect tax assessed on the increase in value of goods from the raw material stage through the production process to final consumption. The tax to processors or merchants is levied on the amount by which they have increased the value of items that were purchased by them for use or resale. This system is used in the European Community.

Warehouse receipt: Receipt given to signify goods have been received into a warehouse.

Weight breaks: Discounts to freight charges are given as the total weight increases at various weight breaks: 50 pounds, 100 pounds, 500 pounds, etc.

Wharfage: Charges assessed for handling freight near a dock or pier.

With average: A marine insurance term meaning that shipment is protected for partial damage whenever the damage exceeds an agreed percentage.

Zone: Freight tariffs are often determined by certain geographic areas called zones.

Key Acronyms

ABI: Automated Broker Interface
ACE: Automated Customs Environment
ACS: Automated Commercial System
AES: Automated Export System
AIDC: Automated Identification and Data Collection
AIS: Automated Identification System
AMA: American Management Association
APIS: Advance Passenger Information System
BASC: Basic Antismuggling Coalition
BIS: Bureau of Industry and Security
BTA: Bioterrorism Act
C4ISR: Command, Control, Communications, Computers, Intelligence, Surveillance
       & Reconnaissance
CBP: Customs and Border Protection
CCL: Commerce Control List
CEO: Chief executive officer
CF: Customs form
CFC: Chlorofluorocarbon
CFR: Code of Federal Regulations
COAC: Customs Operating Advisory Committee
CSA: Canada Customs Self-Assessment
CSI: Container Security Initiative
C-TPAT: Customs-Trade Partnership Against Terrorism
DHS: Department of Homeland Security
DOC: Department of Commerce
DOD: Department of Defense
DOT: Department of Transportation
DPL: Denied Parties List
EAR: Export Administration Regulations
ECCN: Export Control Classification Number
EMS: Export Management System

EPA: Environmental Protection Agency
FAST: Free and Secure Trade
FCPA: Federal Corrupt Practices Act
FDA: Food and Drug Administration
FEMA: Federal Emergency Management Agency
FIFRA: Federal Insecticide Fungicide and Rhodenticide Act
FMC: Federal Maritime Commission
FROB: Freight remaining on board
FTSR: Foreign Trade Statistical Regulations
FTZ: Foreign trade zone
GIS: Geographic Information System
GPS: Global Positioning System
HMF: Harbor maintenance fee
HMR: Hazardous Materials Regulations
HSA: Homeland Security Act
HTSUS: Harmonized Tariff System of the United States
IBET: Integrated Border Enforcement Team
ICE: Immigration and Customs Enforcement
ILO: International Labor Organization
IMO: International Maritime Organization
IOMA: Institute of Management and Administration
IRS: Internal Revenue Service
ISA: Importer self-assessment
ISF: Importer Security Filing (10 + 2)
ISO: International Standards Organization
ISPS Code: International Ship and Port Facility Security Code
ISSC: International ship security certificate
ITA: International Trade Administration
ITAR: International Traffic in Arms Regulations
MEI: Marine educational initiative
MOT: Material of trade
MPF: Merchandise processing fee
MSST: Maritime safety and security team
MTSA: Maritime Transportation Security Act
NII: Nonintrusive inspection
NTC: National targeting center
OECD: Organization for Economic Cooperation and Development
OFAC: Office of Asset Controls
OIT: Office of Information and Technology
ORM: Other regulated material
OSC: Operation Safe Commerce
OSHA: Occupational Safety and Health Administration
PACMAN: Professional Association of Import/Export Compliance Managers

PCB: Polychlorinated biphenyl
PFSO: Port facility security officer
PIC: Prior informed consent
PIP: Partners in Protection (CANADA)
PRD: Personal radiation detector
PSC: Port state control
PSN: Proper shipping name
PST: Port security team
RCRA: Resource Conservation Recovery Act
RFID: Radio frequency identification
ROI: Return on investment
RSO: Recognized security organization
RVSS: Remote video surveillance system
SEC: Securities and Exchange Commission
SED: Shippers export declaration
SENTRI: Secure Electronic Network for Travelers Rapid Inspection
SEVIS: Student Exchange Visitor System
SNAP: Simplified Network Application Process
SOP: Standard operating procedure
SOX: Sarbanes-Oxley
SSA: Ship security alert
SSO: Ship security officer
SSP: Ship security plan
SST: Smart and secure trade lane
TPL: Third-party logistics
TSA: Transportation Security Administration
TSC: Transportation security card
TSCA: Toxic Substances Control Act
TWA: The World Academy
TWIC: Transportation worker's identification card
UAV: Unmanned aerial vehicle
UN: United Nations
USCG: U.S. Coast Guard
USML: U.S. Munitions List
USPPI: U.S. principal party in interest
VAT: Value-added tax
WCO: World Customs Organization

Key International Web Sites

1travel.com:
www.onetravel.com
ACW (*Air Cargo Week*):
www.aircargoweek.com
Addresses and salutations:
www.bspage.com
AES Direct (Automated Export System):
www.aesdirect.gov
Africa Online:
http://www.africaonline.com
AgExporter:
http://www.fas.usda.gov/info/fasworldwide/maghome.html
Air Cargo World:
a ircargoworld.com
American Association of Port Authorities (AAPA):
http://www.aapa-ports.org
American Computer Resources:
www.the-acr.com
American Institute for Shippers' Associations (AISA):
http://www.shippers.org
American Journal of Transportation (AJOT):
http://www.ajot.com
American River International:
http://www.worldest.com
American Short Line and Regional Railroad Association (ASLRRA):
http://www.aslrra.org
American Stock Exchange:
http://www.amex.com

Aviation Week:
http://www.aviationnow.com
Bureau of Industry and Security (BIS)
www.bis.doc.gov
Bureau of National Affairs, *International Trade Reporter Export Reference Manual*:
www.bna.com
Cargo Systems:
http://www.cargosystems.net
Central Europe Online:
http://centraleurope.com
Chinese News (in English):
http://www.insidechina.com
Commercial Carrier Journal (CCJ):
http://www.ccjdigital.com
Commercial Encryption Export Controls:
http://www.bis.doc.gov/Encryption/Default.htm
Compliance maven:
www.compliancemaven.com
Country risk forecast:
www.controlrisks.com
Culture and travel:
http://ciber.bus.msu.edu/busres/culture.htm
Currency:
www.oanda.com
Customs-Trade Partnership Against Terrorism:
www.cbp.gov
Daily intelligence summary:
www.pinktertons.com
DC-PRO:
www.iccbooks.com
Diverse languages of the modern world:
www.unicode.org
DOT's Office of Inspector General:
www.oig.dot.gov
Dr. Leonard's health care catalog:
www.drleonards.com
Dun & Bradstreet:
www.dnb.com
Economic Times (India):
http://www.economictimes.com
Economist:
http://www.economist.com

Electronic embassy:
http://www.embassy.org
Embassies and consulates:
www.embassyworld.com
Embassy Web:
http://www.visaha.com
Excite travel:
http://www.excite.com/travel
Export assistant:
www.cob.ohio-state.edu
The Exporter:
http://www.exporter.com
Export-Import Bank of the United States (EXIMBANK):
http://www.exim.gov
Export Legal Assistance Network (ELAN):
http://exportlegal.org
Export Practitioner (export regulations):
http://www.exportprac.com
Export Sales and Marketing Manual, export link:
www.export-link.com
Export Today magazine:
www.exporttoday.com
Far Eastern Economic Review:
http://asia.wsj.com/public/page/opinionasia.html
Federation of International Trade Associations (FITA):
http://www.fita.org
Financial Times:
http://www.ft.com
For female travelers:
www.journeywoman.com
Global Business Information Network:
davidso@indiana.edu
Global Information Network for Small and Medium Enterprises:
www.gin.sme.ne.jp/intro.html
Glossary of ocean cargo insurance terms:
http://www.tsbic.com/cargo/glossary.htm
Hong Kong Trade Development Counsel (TDC):
http://www.tdctrade.com
iAgora work abroad:
http://www.iagora.com/pages/html/work/index.html
IMEX:
www.imex.com

Inbound Logistics:
www.inboundlogistics.com
INCO terms 2000:
http://www.iccwbo.org/home/menu_incoterms.asp
Independent Accountants International:
http://www.accountants.org
Inexchange:
info@inexchange.net
Information on Diseases Abroad:
www.cdc.gov
Inside China Today:
http://www.insidechina.com
Intellicast weather (four-day forecast):
http://www.intellicast.com/LocalWeather/World
Intermodal Association of North America (IANA):
http://www.intermodal.org
The International Air Cargo Association (TIACA):
http://www.tiaca.org
International Air Transport Association (IATA):
http://www.iata.org
International Association for Medical Assistance to Travelers (IAMAT):
www.iamat.org
International Center for Canadian-American Trade:
www.iccat.org
International Chamber of Commerce (ICC):
http://www.iccwbo.org
International Commercial Law Monitor:
http://www.lexmercatoria.org
International Executive Service Corps (IESC):
http://www.iesc.org
International Freight Association (IFA):
http://www.ifa-online.com
International Maritime Organization (IMO):
http://www.imo.org
International Monetary Fund (IMF):
http://www.imf.org
International Society of Logistics (SOLE):
http://www.sole.org
International trade:
http://ciber.bus.msu.edu/busres/inttrade.htm
International Trade Administration (ITA):
http://www.ita.doc.gov

International trade/import-export jobs:
http://www.internationaltrade.org/jobs.html
International trade shows and business events:
http://ciber.bus.msu.edu/busre
Intershipper:
www.intershipper.com
Journal of Commerce Online:
http://www.joc.com
Latin trade:
http://www.latintrade.com
Libraries:
http://www.libraryspot.com/librariesonline.htm
Library of Congress:
www.loc.gov
LLP Business and Trade Publishing:
http://www.llplimited.com
Local times around the world:
http://times.clari.net.au
Logistics:
LM@cahners.com
London Stock Exchange:
http://www.londonstockexchange.com
Medical conditions around the world:
www.cdc.gov/travel/blusheet.htm
NAFTA Customs:
http://www.nafta-customs.org
National Association of Foreign Trade Zones:
www.NAFTZ.org
National Association of Rail Shippers (NARS):
http://www.railshippers.com
National Institute of Standards and Technology (NIST):
http://www.nist.gov
National Law Center for Inter-American Free Trade:
http://www.natlaw.com
National Motor Freight Traffic Association (NMFTA):
New York Times:
http://www.nyt.com
Office of Antiboycott Compliance:
www.bis.doc.gov/compliance and enforcement/antiboycott/compliance.htm
Overseas Private Investment Corp. (OPIC):
http://www.opic.gov
PIERS (Port Import/Export Reporting Service):

www.PIERS.com
Ports and Maritime Service Directory:
http://www.seaportsinfo.com
Professional Association of Compliance Managers (PACMAN):
www.compliancemaven.com
Reuters:
http://www.reuters.com
Russia Export-Import (REI):
http://www.users.globalnet.co.uk/~chegeo
Russia Today:
http://russiatoday.com
SBA Office of International Trade:
http://www.sba.gov/oit
SBA offices and services:
http://www.sba.gov/services
SEAL:
www.untpdc.org
Search engine:
http://www.google.com
Service Corps of Retired Executives (SCORE):
http://www.score.org
Shipping Times (Singapore):
http://business-times.asia1.com.sg/shippingtimes
Small Business Administration (SBA):
http://www.sba.gov
Small Business Development Centers (SBDCs):
http://www.sba.gov/sbdc
Statistical data sources:
http://ciber.bus.msu.edu/busres/statinfo.htm
STAT-USA and NTDB:
http://www.stat-usa.gov
Strategis:
http://www.strategis.ic.gc.ca
Telephone directories on the Web:
http://www.infobel.com
The Times:
http://www.thetimes.co.uk
Tokyo Stock Exchange:
http://www.tse.or.jp
Trade and Development Agency (TDA):
http://www.tda.gov
Transportation Intermediaries Association (TIA):

http://www.tianet.org
Transportation jobs and personnel:
http://www.quotations.com/trans.htm
Travlang:
http://www.travlang.com
UN Conference on Trade and Development:
www.unctad-trains.org
UN International Trade Center (ITC):
http://www.intracen.org
Unibex:
www.unibex.com
United Nations (UN):
http://www.un.org
Universal Travel Protection Insurance (UTPI):
http://www.utravelpro.com
U.S. business advisor:
http://www.business.gov
U.S. Census Bureau:
www.census.gov
U.S. Census Bureau economic indicators:
www.census.gov/econ/www
U.S. Council for International Business (USCIB):
http://www.uscib.org
U.S. Customs and Border Protection (CBP)
www.cbp.gov
U.S. Department of Commerce (DOC):
http://www.doc.gov
U.S. Department of Commerce International Trade Administration:
www.ita.doc.gov
U.S. Export Assistance Centers (USEACs):
http://www.sba.gov/oit/export/useac.html
U.S. export portal:
www.export.gov
U.S. Federal Maritime Commission (FMC):
http://www.fmc.gov
U.S. foreign trade zones:
http://ia.ita.doc.gov/ftzpage/ftzlist.html
U.S. Patent and Trademark Office (USPTO):
http://www.uspto.gov
U.S. State Department travel advisory:
http://travel.state.gov
U.S. Trade Representative (USTR):
http://www.ustr.gov

USDA Foreign Agricultural Service (FAS):
http://www.fas.usda.gov
USDA Shipper and Export Assistance (SEA):
http://www.ams.usda.gov/tmd/tmdsea.htm
Various utilities and useful information:
http://ciber.bus.msu.edu/busres/utility.htm
Wall Street Journal:
http://www.wsj.com
Wells Fargo:
http://www.wellsfargo.com
World Bank Group:
http://www.worldbank.org
World Chambers of Commerce Network:
http://www.worldchambers.com
World Customs Organization (WCO):
http://www.wcoomd.org
World Factbook:
https://www.cia.gov/library/publications/theworldfactbook/index.html
World Intellectual Property Organization (WIPO):
http://www.wipo.int
World newspapers online:
http://library.uncg.edu/news
World Trade Centers Association (WTCA):
http://iserve.wtca.org
World Trade Organization (WTO):
http://www.wto.org

Appendix A: All About AES: The Automated Export System
Best Practices Outline Summary of the Census Bureau

Global Supply Chain Executives can utilize this Appendix Chapter to stay the most current and trade compliant on programs available form various government agencies impacting the process of importing and exporting.

Table of Contents

Overview of the AES Compliance Review Program
Introduction to & Benefits of AES
BEST PRACTICES: Training
    Training Manual
    Cross-Training
    Mentoring Program
    Seminars & Workshops
Creating a Best Practices Manual
Foreign Trade Regulations Basics
Classifying Commodities
Kimberley Process for Rough Diamonds
Guide to Using a U.S. Authorized or Forwarding Agent
Exports from Foreign Trade Zones
AES Process Flow
AES*Direct*/AES*PcLink* Process Flow

Response Messages from the AES
Correcting Export Information in the AES
When to Submit a Voluntary Self-Disclosure
Review Your AES Compliance and Fatal Error Reports
    Compliance Report
    Fatal Error Report
Instructions for Export Data Request
Software Enhancements
    Software Selection
    Daily Reports
Export Checklist
Acronyms
References
    Contact Information
    Useful Websites
    Government Agencies
Regulatory Websites

Overview of the AES Compliance Review Program

In October 2006, the U.S. Census Bureau (Census Bureau), Foreign Trade Division (FTD) developed the Automated Export System (AES) Compliance Review Program. The program seeks to assist companies in correcting reporting practices that are not in compliance with the Foreign Trade Regulations (FTR), Title 15, Code of Federal Regulations (CFR), Part 30. Section 30.10(b) of the FTR authorizes the Census Bureau to visit companies with the purpose of reviewing all documentation pertaining to export transactions. The ultimate goal of the program is to educate and bring all AES filers into full compliance with the FTR. Failure to comply with reporting requirements may result in delayed shipments referrals to export enforcement government agencies, civil fines, and/or criminal penalties.

The Census Bureau began this project by visiting companies that maintained a compliance rate of 95% or higher to learn their best practices. The compliance rate is calculated by dividing the number of compliance alerts (designated on the Compliance Report) by the number of shipments, subtracted from 100%. As a result of these visits, the Census Bureau has compiled this "Best Practices" manual to share with AES filers the variety of effective methods that can be implemented to stay compliant with the FTR reporting requirements. While this document is not all-inclusive, it does provide several excellent examples of best practices that could assist exporting companies in meeting the FTR compliance standards.

Introduction to AES

The AES is a joint venture between the U.S. Customs and Border Protection (CBP), Census Bureau, other Federal partnership agencies, and the U.S. export trade community. The AES collects export information electronically, applying a series of edits, and responding to the filer so that errors are detected and corrected at the time of filing.

The AES is a nationwide system operational at all ports and for all modes of transportation, designed to ensure compliance with the FTR and the enforcement of many export laws. The collection of export data electronically improves trade statistics and ensures timely and accurate filings along with reducing filers reporting burden.

The Bureau of Industry and Security (BIS), the State Department's Directorate Defense Trade Controls (DDTC), and other Federal agencies have identified data fields in the AES that are critical to their agency's mission. The AES serves as the central point for multiple Federal government agencies in capturing export shipment data electronically.

Public Law 107-228 now requires mandatory filing of export information via the AES. The Final Rule was published in the Federal Register on June 2, 2008. Mandatory electronic reporting of export information began on October 1, 2008.

Benefits of AES

Ensure Export Compliance. The AES, with its editing system and your subsequent corrections, ensures a company's compliance with current Census Bureau export reporting requirements. The system returns an Internal Transaction Number (ITN) as confirmation that you have successfully filed your export documentation.

Correct Errors as They Occur. The AES generates a response message to the filer when data are incomplete, omitted, or inconsistent. The AES allows you to correct errors early in the process, before your goods are subject to delays or penalties.

Decrease Your Costs. Eliminate the cost of corrections with up-front data edits. Save money by reporting your export information through the free and secure Internet application, AES*Direct.*

Eliminate Paper Review of Licenses against Shipments. The interface between the Department of Commerce's BIS and DDTC electronically validates data on export shipments against previously approved licenses and transmits the transaction to the appropriate Partnership Agency.

BEST PRACTICES: Training

Training Manual

It is strongly recommended that companies filing via the AES develop a formal AES Training Manual. A Training Manual provides the basis for achieving consistent results that will support AES filers' efforts in achieving and maintaining compliance. The main purpose of such a manual is to familiarize the user with the AES process. The manual should be reviewed periodically to ensure that it is current with system enhancements, regulatory changes, new business practices, and other export requirements.

Cross-Training

Cross-training is defined as teaching an employee to do different tasks of the organizational unit's work responsibilities. Many companies use cross-training to build depth to cover critical tasks for filing in the AES to be sure the company is filing timely and accurately when employees are on leave, travel, other assignments, or otherwise unavailable. Cross-training employees on both the FTR and how to file via AES will ensure that export transactions are reported accurately and staff will be knowledgeable and equipped to properly file export shipments. For example, staff should be familiar with filing export transactions in the AES and what actions to take for correcting fatal error responses. Cross-training provides improved coverage, increased flexibility, knowledge sharing; additionally, cross-training minimizes or eliminates potential problems that may cause chaotic work conditions.

Mentoring Program

Mentoring allows experienced staff (mentors) to share lessons learned, tips, and suggestions on how to file export transactions accurately and timely. Mentoring also provides ongoing support to new employees, accelerating their learning curve to achieve the level of understanding required to ensure compliance and reporting accuracy. The mentoring section of a company's training manual should include internal as well as external contacts who can offer assistance. Mentors should review the FTR with all new employees and review such concepts as U.S. Principal Party in Interest (USPPI), reporting requirements of an export transaction, routed export transaction, data elements, and export filing exemptions. The ultimate goal of the mentoring program is to have experienced employees share their knowledge and skills with newly employed staff that will be carrying on the company's work in the future. For example, a new employee can shadow an experienced employee throughout the entire process of receiving/verifying documents, entering information into the AES, responding to error responses, and notating loading documents with accurate proof-of-filing citations. By developing a mentoring program, the organization prepares its new employees to better understand the export filing process. Emphasizing employee development will yield positive results for both mentors and new employees.

Seminars & Workshops

A fundamental cause of noncompliance is a lack of understanding of the FTR, other export control regulations, and the AES process. If filing via AES*Direct* or AES*PcLink,* all the AES staff should study the tutorial and take the certification quiz prior to the initial filing of information. Once a year as a refresher, your organization's AES staff should study the tutorial and retake the quiz. The staff should attend sponsored training, such as the AES Export Compliance Seminars and the AES*PcLink* Certification Workshops. Knowledgeable Census Bureau experts lead the seminars and cover information on the FTR, researching commodity classifications, and the proper filing of information via the AES. Seminars and workshops can be offered by the Census Bureau if your company is willing to pay for Census Bureau staff travel expenses, and these seminars and workshops can be tailored to meet the needs of your organization. Also, it is suggested that staff should also attend export seminars and workshops hosted by state and local governments, other federal agencies, trade groups, consultants, and other private companies. The variety of training options will provide employees with an opportunity to learn all aspects of the export process. In addition, companies should conduct in-house forums to share best practices, provide updates on the AES and the FTR, along with information on other government export requirements that are relevant to your company's export process. Furthermore, the mitigation process for penalties takes into consideration if your company attempts to attend export compliance training as well as if you are a new or experienced participant in the business of exporting.

Creating a Best Practices Manual

The Census Bureau's Foreign Trade Division (FTD) publishes monthly trade statistics and ensures the accuracy and completeness of export data. The FTD offers recommendations to those involved in filing Electronic Export Information (EEI) via the Automated Export System (AES). The FTD offers guidance on developing a manual to assist companies in filing accurate, complete and timely export transactions in accordance with the Foreign Trade Regulations (FTR). In the sections to follow, pertinent information has been provided that will assist you in developing an internal best practice manual or adding to an existing manual within your company. The information provided is a guide and additional sections may be added at your discretion that impact your export reporting.

Foreign Trade Regulations Basics

It is vital that employees responsible for export compliance know the requirements of Title 15, CFR, Part 30. The following provides basic information pertaining to the FTR. However, it is strongly recommended that employees access the regulations in its entirety. The FTR can be found at the following Web site: www.census. gov/trade.

Key Terms

- ■ **Electronic Export Information (EEI)**   • **Authorized U.S. Agents**
- ■ **U.S. Principal Party in Interest (USPPI)**   • **Predeparture**
- ■ **Foreign Principal Party in Interest (FPPI)**   • **Postdeparture**

When Is the AES Information Required? (FTR § 30.2(a))

The Electronic Export Information (EEI) must be filed for exports of physical goods valued at more than $2,500 per commodity classification code, when shipped as follows:

- ■ From U.S. to foreign countries,
- ■ Between the U.S. and Puerto Rico,
- ■ From Puerto Rico to foreign countries,
- ■ From Puerto Rico to U.S. Virgin Islands,
- ■ From the U.S. to the U.S. Virgin Islands, and
- ■ Licensable commodities (regardless of value).

What Is an Export Shipment? (FTR § 30.1)

An export shipment is defined as merchandise shipped from one USPPI to one consignee, on the same flight/vessel, to the same country, on the same day, valued over $2,500 per Schedule B/Harmonized Tariff Schedule of the United States Annotated (HTSUSA) number or (any value) where a license is required.

Parties Involved in an Export Transaction (FTR § 30.3(b))

U.S. Principal Party in Interest (USPPI) — the person or legal entity in the United States that receives the primary benefit, monetary or otherwise, from the export transaction. Generally that person is the U.S. seller, manufacturer, or order party, or the foreign entity while in the U.S. when purchasing or obtaining the goods for export.

Authorized U.S. Agent — An individual or legal entity physically located in or otherwise under the jurisdiction of the U.S. that has obtained power of attorney or written authorization from a USPPI or Foreign Principal Party in Interest (FPPI) to act on its behalf.

Foreign Principal Party in Interest (FPPI) — The party shown on the transportation document to whom final delivery or end-use of the goods will be made. This party may be the ultimate consignee.

Types of Export Transactions (FTR § 30.3(c) & 30.3(e))

Standard Export Transaction: In a standard export transaction, the USPPI files the EEI or authorizes a U.S. forwarder or other agent to facilitate export of items out of the United States and/or to file the information in the AES. In the standard export transaction, the USPPI controls the movement of the cargo.

Responsibilities in a Standard Export Transaction

USPPI Responsibilities FTR § 30.3(c)(1):
  - Appoints authorized U.S. agent to facilitate movement of cargo,
  - Provides power of attorney or written authorization to the authorized U.S. agent,
  - Makes a license determination, and
  - Reports required export information or authorizes agent to file report.
Authorized U.S. Agent Responsibilities FTR § 30.3(c)(2):
  - Provides transportation data,
  - Obtains the authorization from the USPPI,
  - Provides the USPPI with a copy of the export information that was filed, if requested, and
  - Reports required export information if authorized by the USPPI.

Routed Export Transaction: In a routed export transaction, the FPPI authorizes a U.S. Forwarder, USPPI, or other Agent to facilitate the export of items out of the United States. In the routed export transaction, the FPPI controls the movement of the cargo.

Responsibilities in a Routed Export Transaction

USPPI Responsibilities FTR § 30.3(e)(1):
  - May file on behalf of the FPPI if a power of attorney or written authorization is obtained from the FPPI,
  - Provides FPPI-authorized U.S. agent with specific export and licensing information,
  - Is entitled to a copy of the required export information that was submitted to the FPPI-authorized U.S. agent to file, and
  - May request in writing from the FPPI (See Export Administration Regulations (EAR) 758.3).
Authorized U.S. Agent Responsibilities FTR § 30.3(e)(2):
  - Obtains a power of attorney or written authorization from the FPPI to move cargo,
  - Completes export information for filing, as authorized by the FPPI, and
  - Provides a copy of the export information to the USPPI when requested.

Classifying Commodities

Overview of the Export Commodity Classification Codes

In order to file your export shipment, you must know the 10-digit Schedule B number(s) for the commodities you are exporting. The Schedule B and its import counterpart, the HTSUSA, are based on the 6-digit international Harmonized System (HS). Before attempting to classify a product, you should have its complete description and knowledge of the product's function, composition, and characteristics. While AES*Direct* and AES*PcLink* offer look up capabilities to classify products, this function provides limited descriptions. Do not rely solely on the limited lookup functions within the AES*Direct* and AES*PcLink* software for classifying merchandise.

After identifying possible codes, closely read the descriptions for the 4-digit heading and subsequent subheadings in the Schedule B number, paying close attention to indentations and alignments. Follow through the detailed descriptions until you arrive at a complete, 10-digit classification code. For further classification guidance, read pertinent section, chapter, and statistical notes in the Schedule B/HTSUSA manual posted at www.census.gov/foreign-trade/schedules/b. An online search of the Schedule B Index produces a list of descriptions and their 6-digit codes or ranges. Selecting a link from this list brings the user directly to the 4-digit heading in the text version of the Schedule B/HTSUSA manual. After reading the heading and verifying that it is the appropriate location for the commodity in question, the USPPI or AES filer should then compare the subsequent subheadings, paying close attention to indentations and alignment. Upon determination of the best 6-digit subheading, repeat the process of comparison to find the correct Schedule B/HTSUSA number.

Use the Schedule B search engine or manual, available at http://www.census.gov/foreign-trade/schedules/b/index.html to assist in your initial classification and for periodic review and updates.

Export Commodity Classification Codes

The 2008 edition of Schedule B supersedes all previous editions as the official schedule of commodity classifications to be used by shippers in reporting export shipments from the United States, and in compiling the official statistics on exports of merchandise from the United States. This edition became effective in January 2008.

The correct commodity number shown in the current edition of the Schedule B must be reported in the EEI. A description of the merchandise, in sufficient detail to permit the verification of the Schedule B number, must also be furnished on the export declaration, as well as other statistical data, in accordance with the FTR. Import classification codes, found in the HTSUSA may be substituted for export codes, with a short list of exceptions noted on the Census Bureau Web site at: http://www.census.gov/foreign-trade/schedules/b/index.html.

Organization of the Schedule B Classification

Schedule B, based on the HS, consists of 22 sections divided into 97 chapters. Chapters 1 through 97 correspond with the International System of Numbering, with Chapter 77 being blank. An additional chapter, 98, is used for special classification provisions that apply only to U.S. exports. The 10-digit Harmonized System-Based Schedule B codes (commodity numbers) comprise these chapters. There are approximately 9,000 of these 10-digit classification codes in the 2007 edition of Schedule B. The definitions for these codes are as follows:

Code	Definition	Example
07	Chapter in which a commodity is classified	Chapter 7, Edible Vegetables and Certain Roots and Tubers
0713	Represents the heading in that chapter	Dried Leguminous Vegetables, Shelled, Whether or not Skinned or Split
0713.10	Represents the Harmonized System code subheading	International Harmonized Code for Peas (Pisum Sativum)
0713.10.4020	Represents statistical subdivisions	Commodity Code for Green Peas

Locating the Correct Schedule B Number

The table of contents of the Schedule B manual lists all of the sections and chapters with their descriptions. This will serve as a guide to the general area in which a commodity may be classified. The Schedule B manual also contains an alphabetical index that indicates the first six digits or six-digit range of the 10-digit Schedule B numbers for the listed item. Although only the first six digits of the Schedule B number are given in the index, the complete 10-digit code must be used in reporting export shipments. The only purpose of the index is to assist in locating the part of the document in which a particular classification can be found. Failure to find the item in the index does not relieve the shipper of the responsibility for locating the correct Schedule B number for the item being reported.

After locating the description and six-digit code for an item in the alphabetical index, the USPPI then searches for that numerical sequence in the body of the Schedule B. After reading all pertinent section, chapter, and statistical notes, the USPPI should assign the appropriate 10-digit Schedule B number.

In cases where the USPPI is unable to locate an item in the alphabetical index, one of two methods of assigning a Schedule B number may be chosen. If the

HTSUSA number is known, in most cases it may be reported in lieu of the Schedule B number. The item also may be located in the Schedule B numeric sequence by referring to the table of contents in the front of the Schedule B and locating the appropriate chapter, and subsequently, the correct Schedule B number. The General and U.S. Rules of Interpretation and Definitions, as well as the notes appearing in the sections and chapters of Schedule B, should be reviewed before attempting to locate the correct commodity number.

If you need assistance with Schedule B classifications call 800-549-0595 and select Option 2.

Reporting Requirements

Not Elsewhere Specified or Included (n.e.s.o.i.). If a Schedule B number has been located that seems to apply to the commodity being classified, but the description for the number carries the limitation n.e.s.o.i., the commodity number should not be used until a check has been made to determine whether there is a classification elsewhere into which the item will fit more specifically. Other classifications under the same general heading should be examined.

Double Units of Quantity. When two units of quantity are specified in the "Unit of Quantity" field for a Schedule B classification, both primary (1st) and secondary (2nd) quantities are required to be reported in the AES.

Shipping Containers. When shipping containers are exported as merchandise for sale or transfer of ownership abroad, they must be reported on export declarations under the appropriate Schedule B commodity number for the particular type of container. However, in accordance with the FTR, shipping containers are not considered to be exported when they are moving, either loaded or empty, strictly in their capacity as carriers of merchandise, i.e., as instruments of international traffic, not for sale or transfer from U.S. ownership or title to foreign ownership or title. Therefore, containers leaving the United States strictly as instruments of international traffic do not have to be reported in the AES. If for any reason a USPPI wishes to report the movements of such containers on export declarations, they may be reported under Schedule B number 9801.20.0000. This classification is not to be used to report the contents of the containers. Contents of such containers are to be reported under the appropriate classification(s) for the merchandise.

Commodities Donated for Relief or Charity by Individuals or Private Agencies. Chapter 98 provides for exports of certain commodities donated for relief or charity by individuals or private agencies. In general, except for bulk grain, such classifications are provided for those commodities that are known to be, or are likely to be, exported for relief or charity in fairly sizable amounts. In addition to chapter notes for Chapter 98, please read the chapter notes for Chapters 1 through 16, 21, 30, and 63, to ensure that relief or charity shipments are correctly classified.

Reporting the Value of Repairs and Alterations. USPPIs and authorized agents must report, under Schedule B number 9801.10.0000, the value of repairs and alterations made on articles previously imported for such purposes. These articles must be reported as domestic merchandise, and the value to be reported must represent the total value of repairs and alterations made in the United States. Even if the customer pays no fees or charges, you must report the actual or estimated cost of repairs to the USPPI. The original or current value of the article that was imported, to be repaired or altered must NOT be reported and therefore should not be included in the value reported for commodity number 9801.10.0000.

Export of Articles Previously Imported for Processing. Articles exported after having been imported temporarily under bond for processing (HTS 9813.00.0520) must be reported as domestic merchandise. The Schedule B number assigned must be selected from Chapters 1 through 97, according to the exported article. The Value reported must be the total value of the article.

Using the Correct Export Information Code. The export information code is a 2-digit code reported in the AES that represents the reporting requirement and nature of the shipment and merchandise being exported. The Export Information Codes are located at the following Web site: http://www.cbp.gov/xp/cgov/trade/automated/aes/tech_docs/aestir/june04_intro/appendices/

The most common Export Information Codes that are misreported:

- Temporary Exports of products that will be returned to the U.S. in the same condition within one year, should be reported as "TE"
- Personal goods and household effects, including furniture, clothing, tools, and other effects should be reported as "HH"
- Shipments to the U.S. Armed Forces for their exclusive use should be reported as "MS"

Using the Correct Country of Ultimate Destination Code. The country of ultimate destination is the country in which goods are to be consumed or further processed or manufactured. The list of valid Country Codes can be found at: http://www.census.gov/foreign-trade/schedules/c/country4.txt

The most common Country of Ultimate Destination that are misreported:

- Country Code for **Ireland** is **IE**
- Country Code for **Italy** is **IT**
- Country Code for **Iran** in **IR**
- Country Code for **Iraq** is **IQ**

Helpful Hints to Avoid Reporting Problems

- Read the full Schedule B Description before selecting a 10-digit code
- Report the correct Unit of Quantity as required in the Schedule B Book
- Select Domestic or Foreign for the Product type

Kimberley Process for Rough Diamonds

What Is the Kimberley Process?

The Kimberly Process is the international initiative launched in 2003 designed to prevent rough diamonds from being used to finance such brutal civil wars that occurred in the diamond-producing countries of Sierra Leone, Liberia, and Angola in the 1990s. The process aims to prevent these "blood diamonds" from entering the mainstream rough diamond market, established while helping to protect the legitimate trade in rough diamonds.

The 74 countries that participate in the Kimberley Process agree to trade rough diamonds only with other countries in the organization. Diamonds must be shipped with a valid Kimberley Process certificate (KPC) and must be in tamper-resistant containers. Natural rough diamonds are those commodities classified under Harmonized System subheadings 7102.10, 7102.21, and 7102.31.

What Are the Requirements of a Rough Diamond USPPI?

- Rough diamonds may only be exported to countries that participate in the Kimberley Process. A current list of those countries can be found at: www.kimberleyprocess.com.
- The FTR require all exports and re-exports of rough diamonds be filed electronically via AES. Furthermore, the regulations state that the KPC number must be entered in the license number field excluding the two-digit U.S. ISO country code.
- The USPPI or brokers of rough diamonds must fax a copy of all Kimberley Process certificates (including voided certificates) to the U.S. Census Bureau at: 1-800-457-7328.
- Rough diamond USPPIs or brokers must retain records of all KPC for five years.
- Rough diamond USPPIs must file an annual report including total export activity and stockpile information via e-mail to: USKimberleyProcess@state.gov. Reports are due annually on April 1.

Do I Need a Kimberley Process Certificate?

The USPPI needs a KPC to export rough diamonds including gem quality or industrial diamonds that are unworked or simply sawn, cleaved, or bruted, which are classified under Harmonized System subheadings 7102.10, 7102.21, and 7102.31.

How Do I Obtain a Kimberley Process Certificate?

KPCs are only available from entities licensed by the U.S. Kimberley Process Authority (USKPA). To obtain a USKPA license, contact the USKPA at the offices of the Jewelers Vigilance Committee at 212-997-2002.

Guide to Using a U.S. Authorized or Forwarding Agent

Definitions of an Authorized or Forwarding Agent

An authorized agent as defined in the FTR is an individual or legal entity physically located in or otherwise under the jurisdiction of the United States that has obtained power of attorney or written authorization from a USPPI or FPPI to act on its behalf, and to complete and file EEI. The FTR defines a forwarding agent as the party in the United States who is authorized by the U.S. or Foreign Principal Party in Interest to facilitate the movement of the cargo from the United States to the foreign destination and/or prepare and file the required documentation. There are situations when an agent or a forwarder is used in an export transaction. However, some companies handle both agent and forwarder responsibilities. The following are examples to show the differences between an agent and a forwarder.

- The USPPI authorizes an agent to file EEI via the AES on their behalf and further selects a forwarder to move the cargo to the port of export;
- The USPPI authorizes an agent to file and that same agent is responsible for facilitating the movement of the cargo to the port of export;
- The FPPI authorizes the U.S. forwarder to facilitate the movement of the cargo only. However, the FPPI may authorize the USPPI to prepare and file the EEI via the AES. The FPPI must provide the USPPI written authorization to file the shipment on the FPPI's behalf;
- The FPPI authorizes their U.S. forwarder to facilitate the movement of the cargo and file the EEI. The USPPI is responsible for providing the U.S. forwarder with their company and commodity information [See FTR 30.3(e)].

Getting to Know Your U.S. Authorized or Forwarding Agent

The USPPI should seek to use agents or forwarders that utilize industry best practices and work toward building and maintaining successful relationships. In addition, it is recommended that the USPPI establish strong communication with the management of the agent or forwarding company. This relationship may assist in resolving issues in a timely manner. This is essential to filing complete and accurate export transactions. The FTR emphasizes that all parties involved are responsible for the export requirements process. If the USPPI and their agent maintain an open line of communication this will help to ensure that companies achieve export compliance. A few ways to do this is by scheduling quarterly visits to see how the agent or forwarder manages its operations. This visit may include conducting a walk through of the daily operations along with reviewing the steps involved in the AES process. If the USPPI cannot visit the agent or forwarder, both parties should maintain contact via the telephone, e-mail, or fax.

In addition to visiting an agent's or forwarder's facility, it is also recommended that the USPPI perform an audit of their export process twice a year. This should involve comparing EEI with invoices and other shipping documents. By auditing, the USPPI is able to reconcile EEI with any discrepancies, which can be resolved through corrections or Voluntary Self Disclosures. Another way to ensure the accuracy of export information is to provide the agent or forwarder with the Schedule B/HTSUSA number and the description of the commodities being shipped.

This is helpful if the same commodities are exported on a regular basis. This commitment to the business relationship ensures that the USPPI, agent, or forwarder maintain compliance with export reporting requirements.

All parties must comply with the FTR record retention requirements of five years for export documents, in accordance with FTR 30.10. The following are examples but not all inclusive:

- Power of Attorney (Either electronic or paper copy)
- EEI reported via the AES
- Invoices
- Licenses
- Pertinent Export Documents

The USPPI should maintain a "checks and balance" system for keeping an account of the number of shipments that the agent or forwarder filed on its behalf. If a working relationship has not been established, it may be difficult to obtain verification for your EEI. The FTR, Section 30.3, grants the USPPI the right to request a copy of the information filed. It is the responsibility of the agent or forwarder to provide such documentation. The agent or forwarder is responsible for providing the documentation to the USPPI in accordance with the FTR. If the agent or forwarder does not want to provide the information, the USPPI should contact the agent or forwarder and inform them that upon request they are required by the above citation. The USPPI should keep a record of all the attempts requesting the AES information. If the USPPI is still unable to obtain your EEI, then contact the Regulations, Outreach, and Education Branch of the Foreign Trade Division at 800-549-5495 and select Menu Option 3. A staff member will work with you to resolve the problem.

In Summary:

■ Build relationships with your agent or forwarder;
■ Schedule quarterly visits;
■ Conduct an export process audit twice a year;
■ Establish a point of contact;
■ Develop procedures for record retention.

The next three pages include a sample power of attorney, written authorization, and invoice. These samples can be used as references for creating or modifying your existing documentation.

POWER OF ATTORNEY TO PREPARE OR TRANSMIT ELECTRONIC EXPORT INFORMATION

Know all men by these presents, that_____, the
(Name of U.S. Principal Party in Interest (USPPI))
USPPI organized and doing business under the laws of the State or Country of
_____ and having an office and place of business at___
_____hereby
(Address of USPPI)
authorizes_____, (Authorized Agent)
(Name of Authorized Agent)
of_____
(Address of Authorized Agent)

SAMPLE

to act for and on its behalf as a true and lawful agent and attorney of the U.S. Principal Party in Interest (USPPI) for, and in the name, place, and stead of the USPPI, from this date, in the United States either in writing, electronically, or by other authorized means to: act as authorized agent for export control, U.S. Census Bureau (Census Bureau) reporting, and U.S. Customs and Border Protection (CBP) purposes. Also, to prepare and transmit any Electronic Export Information (EEI) or other documents or records required to be filed by the Census Bureau, CBP, the Bureau of Industry and Security, or any other U.S. Government agency, and perform any other act that may be required by law or regulation in connection with the exportation or transportation of any goods shipped or consigned by or to the USPPI, and to receive or ship any goods on behalf of the USPPI.

The USPPI hereby certifies that all statements and information contained in the documentation provided to the authorized agent and relating to exportation will be true and correct. Furthermore, the USPPI understands that civil and criminal penalties may be imposed for making false or fraudulent statements or for the violation of any United States laws or regulations on exportation.

This power of attorney is to remain in full force and effect until revocation in writing is duly given by the U.S. Principal Party in Interest and received by the Authorized Agent.

IN WITNESS WHEREOF, _____caused these

(Full Name of USPPI/USPPI Company)

presents to be sealed and signed:

Witness: _____Signature:_____

Capacity: _____

Date:_____

WRITTEN AUTHORIZATION TO PREPARE OR TRANSMIT ELECTRONIC EXPORT INFORMATION

I, _____, authorize

(Name of U.S. Principal Party in Interest)

_____ to act as authorized agent for

(Name of Authorized Agent)

SAMPLE

export control, U.S. Customs, and Census Bureau purposes to transmit such export information electronically that may be required by law or regulation in connection with the exportation or transportation of any goods on behalf of said U.S. Principal Party in Interest. The U.S. Principal Party in Interest certifies that necessary and proper documentation to accurately transmit the information electronically is and will be provided to the said Authorized Agent. The U.S. Principal Party in Interest further understands that civil and criminal penalties may be imposed for making false or fraudulent statements or for the violation of any U.S. laws or regulations on exportation and agrees to be bound by all statements of said authorized agent based upon information or documentation provided by the U.S. Principal Party in Interest to said authorized agent.

Signature: _____

(U.S. Principal Party in Interest)

Capacity: _____

Date: _____

SAMPLE COMPANY INVOICE

XYZ Company

9196 Silver Lane	Job Number: 14451
Jacksonville, FL 32210	Contract order No: JFPR2461
USA	
904.777.1212	Date of sale: MM/DD/YYYY
www.xyzcomp.com	Date of export: MM/DD/YYYY
Federal Tax ID: 511422633	Shipped By: United Airlines, Tampa International

Consignee Address

British Computer Co.

SAMPLE

5556 Victoria Lodge #11

London

Great Britain

ITEM	DESCRIPTION	QTY	UNIT PRICE	TOTAL PRICE
1	Ionographic Printer Unit	10	$2,653.43	$26534.30 U.S.D.
	8443.32.1060			
2	Ink Jet Printer Unit	5	$1,500.00	$7500.00 U.S.D
	8443.32.1040			
	Origin: U.S.			
	Weight: 158.76 KG			

BIS License: B191396			
BIS ECCN: 1A234			
Joe Smith, Customer Administrator			
These goods remain the property of XYZ Company until XYZ Company receives payment in full		TOTAL USD	$34,034.30

Exports from Foreign Trade Zones

A Foreign Trade Zone (FTZ) is a restricted access site in or adjacent to a Customs port of entry. Authority for establishing these facilities is found in the Foreign Trade Zones Act of 1934, as amended 19 USC 81a–81u (Act or FTZA). The purpose of foreign trade zones as stated in the Act is to "expedite and encourage foreign commerce and other purposes." The act is administered in a context of evolving U.S. economic and trade policy and economic factors relating to international competition.

For the Census Bureau statistical reporting purposes, all merchandise removed from FTZs for export out of the United States must be reported in the same manner as all other exports at the Customs port of export electronically using the AES. For exports out of the United States, zone USPPIs must follow the instructions in the FTZ Manual, Chapter 9, subpart 9.12(a), and the Census Bureau's FTR 30.2 and 30.52, which contain provisions for the electronic filing of export information via the AES. There are concerns among the Census Bureau and the CBP Officials that merchandise is being exported from FTZs without the proper export documents being filed with CBP at the port of export. FTZ USPPIs, forwarding agents, and carriers are reminded that, in addition to adhering to the CBP regulations and FTZ operating procedures, they must also adhere to all Federal Government export laws and regulations that apply to the exportation of merchandise from the United States.

For Customs purposes, zone operators are also required to follow appropriate Customs Regulations in Title 19 CFR, Part 146, and the FTZ Manual regarding admission of merchandise into the FTZ and the transfer of merchandise out of the FTZ, either for consumption within the United States or for exports out of the United States. In general, merchandise must be transferred out of the FTZ on a CF-7512, "Transportation Entry and Manifest of Goods Subject to Customs Inspection and Permit." If the merchandise is being exported out of the United States, companies must file their export information via the AES.

AES Process Flow

Below is an illustration of what happens when you transmit EEI from your software into the AES. The AES filer transmits the export information into the AES. It is strongly recommended that the AES filer has upfront edits that will catch missing or incorrect information before the EEI is transmitted to the AES mainframe. Once the EEI has passed your internal edits, the AES will then process your shipment further and send the AES filer a response message, which may include an ITN, fatal response, compliance alert, verify or warning message. Once the AES filer receives the response message, he or she must decide how to proceed based on the instructions entitled "Response Messages from AES."

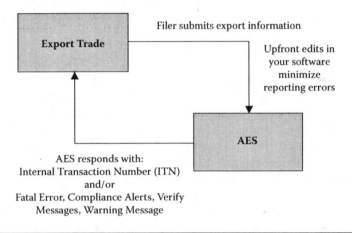

AES Process Flow

AESDirect/AESPcLink Process Flow

Below is an illustration of what happens when you transmit EEI through AES*Direct*. The AES filer transmits the export information into the AES*Direct* and then the EEI is passed to the AES mainframe. AES*PcLink* and AES*Direct* have upfront edits that will minimize your chance of receiving a fatal response. Once the EEI has passed the AES*Direct* and AES*PcLink* edits, the EEI is submitted to the AES for further processing. The AES mainframe will send the AES filer a response message through an e-mail, the shipment reporting center, and the AES*PcLink* software (when automated response is enabled). Once the AES filer receives the response message, they must decide how to proceed, based on the instructions provided in "Response Messages from AES."

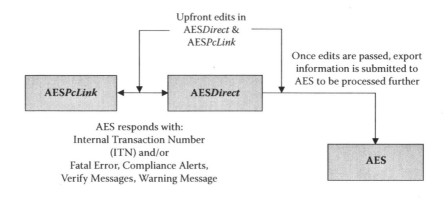

AES*Direct*/AES*PcLink* Process Flow

Response Messages from the AES

In the AES there are filing response messages that are generated to alert the filer when data are accepted, inconsistent, invalid, or incomplete. The possible response messages that can be generated include fatal, warning, compliance, verify, and informational messages. The response messages must be reviewed immediately and appropriate action must be taken, if needed. Instructions on how to resolve the various response messages can be found in the AES Trade Interface Requirements (AESTIR), under June 2004 Appendices, at the following CBP Web site: http://www.customs.gov/xp/cgov/trade/automated/aes/tech_docs/aestir/ titled Appendix A. In this Appendix A you will find a narrative text that gives a description of the error response message, the reason the error was generated, the data elements impacted, and instructions on how to resolve the error.

Shipments successfully reported into the AES will receive a confirmation number, called the Internal Transaction Number (ITN). This number is your proof that your shipment has passed the AES edits and has been accepted. The ITN always begins with an X, followed by the 4-digit year, 2-digit month, 2-digit day, and 6-digit random identifier generated by AES. Although the ITN is linked to your Filer ID and Shipment Reference Number, these are not printed or shown in the response message to protect your privacy and data security. Shipments with compliance alert(s), warning, verify, or informational message(s) will still receive an ITN. Shipments with fatal error messages will not receive an ITN.

Sample ITN: X20080924581949

Below are the AES Response Code Identifiers, the requirement for resolution, and the top responses for each message. These response code identifiers are returned to the AES filer in the AES output record, along with the specific Response Code and message.

F = Fatal Error

Shipments with a Fatal Error Message have not been accepted by AES. The AES output record will display the Response Code "F" and the Response Code Message. Shipments with Fatal Error Message(s) must be corrected prior to the cargo leaving the U.S. or prior to the tenth day after exportation if the USPPI is approved for postdeparture filing.

When you receive notice of a Fatal Error Message from the AES, this means that your export shipment was rejected and you have not actually filed; therefore, your shipment was not added to the CBP database and cannot be viewed by the CBP inspectors. Your cargo may be subject to delay, seizure, fines, or penalties. Immediate attention to correcting such errors is therefore in your company's best interests.

Below are examples of the most common Fatal Error Messages reported via the AES:

Fatal Error 256   USPPI Postal Code Not Valid for State

This error occurs frequently in Routed Transaction shipments, when a Foreign Country Postal Code is reported instead of a U.S. Postal Code. The Postal Code must be the Postal Code for the USPPI address (reflecting a U.S. Postal Code). It must be reported as either five numeric digits followed by four spaces or nine numeric digits. The state code must match the state associated to the postal code.

Fatal Error 649   "Quantity 1" Cannot Exceed Shipping Weight

This error occurs, for example, when the "Unit of Measure 1" requires KG (kilograms) and the net quantity exceeds the shipping weight. The Shipping Weight must always be expressed in kilograms and equal the net kilograms plus the weight of the packing materials. Shipping weight cannot be less than net weight when the unit of measure is expressed in kilograms.

W = Warning

Shipments with a Warning Message must be corrected within 4 days from the date of transmission. The only Warning Message in AES is Response Message 341 — "Ultimate Consignee Must be Reported in Four Days" for shipments flagged as "Sold En Route."

C = Compliance Alert

Shipments with a Compliance Alert Message were filed late and/or a postdeparture change was made to certain elements in the shipment. Receiving a Compliance Alert Message means that your shipment is in violation of the export reporting requirements. You cannot correct a Compliance Alert Message. If a filer consistently receives Compliance Alert Messages, then the filer must identify and correct certain business practices that lead to these alerts. Otherwise, the filer may be subject to delays, fines, and/or penalties.

Below are examples of the most common Compliance Alerts reported via the AES:

Compliance Alert 700   Shipment Reported Late — Option 2 (Predeparture)

This error occurs when the date the EEI was received via the AES is greater or after the Date of Export reported in the shipment.

Compliance Alert 701   Shipment Reported Late — Option 4 (Postdeparture)

This error occurs when the date of EEI was received via the AES is greater than 10 calendar days of the Date of Export reported.

V = Verify

Shipments with a Verify Message receive an ITN, but some information in question must be verified as correct. No further action is required if the information reported is verified and determined to be correct. If not correct, please make the necessary changes and resubmit.

Below are examples of the most common Verify Messages reported via the AES:

Verify Message 8H1   Value/Quantity1 out of range — High

Verify Message 8L1   Value/Quantity1 out of range — Low

The unit price is the value of the goods divided by the first quantity. These Verify Messages occur when the unit price for the goods reported falls outside of the U.S. Census Bureau's expected range. These ranges are determined by historical statistical averages per each Schedule B/HTSUSA number.

I = Informational

Shipments with an Informational message require no action. This is a non-critical response. The information noted is for your records only.

Below are examples of the most common Informational Messages reported via the AES:

Informational Message 176   DDTC License Now exhausted

This Informational Message occurs when the DDTC license DSP5 has been fully decremented.

Informational Message 177   Original license to be lodged with CBP

This Informational Message reminds the AES filer to present the original license to CBP.

Correcting Export Information in the AES

Based on FTR 30.9, the USPPI or their authorized agent is responsible for trans-mitting corrections, cancellations, or amendments to export shipment information previously transmitted using the AES. Corrections, cancellations, or amendments must be made as soon as they are known, whether before or after exportation.

Information known to be true at the time of export must be reported or an esti-mate provided. Should such information change after the export of the commodity, a correction must be made to the EEI filed. Corrections to the EEI can be made up to five years from the date of export. In order for corrected information to be included in a specific statistical year, corrections can be made on a 15-month sliding scale basis from the date of export. That means any shipment filed from January of a statistical year through December of that same year should be corrected in the AES until March 1 of the following year. For example, EEI submitted January 2008 through December 2008, may be corrected until March 2009. Corrections, without the necessity to make a VSD, may be made for changes or errors on a small number of shipments (i.e., 1, 5, 10). Additionally, failure to file export informa-tion on the shipment of goods prior to export may be entered in the AES on the 15-month sliding scale for a small number of shipments. Failure to file electronic export information before the end of the 15-month sliding scale will constitute the need for a VSD. Please refer to the FTR, Section 30.9 for corrections to the EEI. A VSD should not be used to report a routine correction to EEI.

Questions regarding corrections should be directed to the Regulations, Outreach and Education Branch at 800-549-0595, Menu Option 3 or at FTDRegs@census.gov.

When to Submit a Voluntary Self-Disclosure

The Census Bureau strongly encourages companies, without prompting from Federal agencies, to voluntarily and promptly disclose, and expeditiously correct all violations or potential violations of Title 15, Code of Federal Regulations, Part 30, the FTR. The Census Bureau recommends that Voluntary Self-Disclosure (VSD) be made for violations or potential violations going back at least five years. A VSD reflects due diligence by a USPPI or authorized agent in detecting and correcting potential violations when required information was not reported or when incorrect information was provided that violates the regulations. The VSD must be identified and submitted before the Census Bureau or another export enforcement Federal government agency identifies the problem.

Voluntary Self-Disclosures are made for potential violations of electronic export information submission and/or inadvertent recurring non-compliance errors of the regulations. Potential violations or non-compliant practices that are recurring over an extended period of time also should be submitted via a self-disclosure. For example, over a six-month period during 2008, electronic export information not filed for numerous shipments (i.e., 10, 25, 50, 100, etc.) will constitute the need to file a voluntary self-disclosure as soon as the failure to file is discovered. Another example, is the consistent use of the wrong EIN for numerous shipments and/or over an extended period of time (i.e., 2, 3, 6, 9, months, etc.). If the shipment is licensed goods and a potential violation or non-compliant practiced occurs, a self-disclosure may be made regardless of the number of transactions or the time frame involved. Whether or not the non-compliant practice or violation is systematic (recurring), the volume of shipments involved, licensed goods, non-responsiveness to fatal errors, and late filing timeframes should be taken into consideration when determining whether or not to make a disclosure. Please refer to Section 30.74 of the FTR for regulatory requirements on voluntary self-disclosures.

Procedures for submitting a voluntary self-disclosure to the Census Bureau are as follows:

1. Must be in writing, on company letterhead, and addressed to:
Chief, Foreign Trade Division
U.S. Census Bureau
4600 Silver Hill Road, Room 6K032
Washington, DC 20233-6700
2. The letter should include the following information:
    a. The name of the person making the disclosure and contact information: address, telephone number, and e-mail address, if applicable.
    b. A description of the violation(s) or suspected violation(s) including the nature and extent of the violation(s).
    c. An explanation of when and how the violation occurred.
    d. A description of all FTR-mandated information that was either unreported or reported incorrectly.
    e. The complete identities and addresses of all individuals and organizations, whether foreign or domestic, involved in the activities associated with the violation(s).
    f. A description of corrective measures applied to resolve the violation(s) that occurred and steps taken to prevent a recurrence of the violation(s).
    g. A description of any mitigating circumstances that should be considered.
3. Once a VSD is submitted, a staff person in the Regulations, Outreach, and Education Branch, Foreign Trade Division, will communicate with the point of contact listed in the disclosure document to determine actions to be taken.

Please note the following:

1. Disclosures should be made of suspected violations that involve export of items controlled, licensed, or otherwise subject to export control or enforcement jurisdiction by a department or agency of the federal government. These

disclosures should be made to the appropriate federal department or agency, in addition to the VSD required by the Census Bureau.

2. All VSDs will be forwarded to the appropriate agency.
3. Questions regarding when voluntary self-disclosures should be made to the Regulations, Outreach, and Education Branch on 800-549-0595, Menu Option 3 or at FTDRegs@census.gov.

Review Your AES Compliance and Fatal Error Reports

The U.S. Census Bureau monitors and reviews data filed through AES for quality and timeliness. The Foreign Trade Division sends monthly Compliance Reports and bimonthly Fatal Error Reports. It is strongly recommended that companies filing via the AES closely monitor these reports to ensure export compliance. We strongly encourage you to include a section in your manual on the AES reports to stress their importance and effectiveness. Reports should be reviewed and monitored for accuracy.

Compliance Report

On the AES Compliance Report, a compliance rate is calculated for the current statistical month. The compliance rate is calculated by dividing the number of compliance alerts (designated on the report) by the number of shipments, subtracted from 100%. If your compliance rate is below 95%, we strongly recommend that your company implement measures to improve its compliance rate level and prevent or correct identified problem areas. A compliance rate below 80% may trigger a visit from Census Bureau staff as a part of its AES Compliance Review Program.

For example:

Number of shipments for **Month, Year:** 100
Shipments with compliance alerts for **Month, Year:** 3
Compliance rate for **Month, Year:** 97.00%

Receiving a compliance alert means that your shipment is in violation of the export reporting requirements. If a filer consistently receives compliance alerts, then the filer must identify and correct certain business practices that lead to these alerts. Otherwise, the filer may be subject to a visit from the Census Bureau staff, delays, fines and/or penalties. The most common compliance alert is "Shipment Reported Late."

Verify messages generated by the filer are also included in the Compliance Report. The common Verify messages are "Value/Quantity out of range" and

"Shipping Weight/Quantity out of range." Shipments with a Verify message receive an ITN and are not counted against your compliance rate, but some information in question must be verified as correct. No further action is required if the information reported is verified. If not correct, please make the necessary correction and resubmit the shipment.

Fatal Error Report

Another critical issue for maintaining exporting compliance is to promptly correct all fatal errors. To assist AES filers, the AES Branch sends out bimonthly Fatal Error Reports to filers showing their unresolved fatal errors. Under 15 CFR part 30.9, AES filers are required to correct fatal errors prior to exportation of the merchandise or prior to the tenth day after exportation if the USPPI is an approved postdeparture filer. An AES export transaction receiving a fatal error is rejected by AES and an ITN is not generated. Without the ITN, the transaction has not been accepted, and the filer has not met their reporting requirement. It is the filer's responsibility to ensure that all AES transactions receive an ITN.

Many companies develop a database of AES shipments that receive fatal error messages. Other company's software has been developed to stop their process until the fatal error is resolved and an ITN is returned. It is important that fatal error messages are resolved as soon as possible. If your company continues to be noncompliant after repeated warnings, you may be subject to fines, seizures, and/or penalties or revocation of your AES filing privileges.

Instructions for Export Data Request

The FTD's Regulations, Outreach, and Education Branch, upon written request from the AES filers or United States Principal Parties in Interest (USPPI), will provide the filers with validated records of their AES submissions. This initiative will assist companies conducting internal audits, which will result in improved reporting and data in the AES. A company is given 12 months of data free of charge every 365 days. If the filer requests more than 12 months of data in a 365-day time period, the company will be charged a fee for every extra month over the twelve. The encrypted files will be provided to the private companies, via the Census Bureau's File Transfer Protocol (FTP) Server.

Data Requests should include the following:

1. The private company must submit a request on company or agency letterhead.
2. The request must include: Reason for request (ie. internal company audit, agency investigation; Employer Identification Number (EIN)(s); Whether USPPI or Freight Forwarder; Contact Information: Name, Address, Phone Number, Fax Number, and E-mail Address, and Signature

The letter must be dated. Please include the company name for each EIN submitted. Please note if the Company name(s) submitted on the letter does not match the EIN, the data will not be included within the request.

3. The letter should be mailed to:
   Chief, Regulations, Outreach, and Education Branch
   U.S. Census Bureau
   4600 Silver Hill Road - Room 6K125
   Washington, DC 20233
4. The letter can also be faxed on 301-763-8835 (If faxing, please send to the attention of Chief, Regulations, Outreach and Education Branch)
5. The check should be made out to Commerce/Census/FTD and be sent to the attention of:
   Chief, Regulations, Outreach, and Education Branch
   4600 Silver Hill Road, 6K125
   Suitland, MD 20746 (if sent by FedEx) or Washington, DC 20233 (Regular Mail)

Software Enhancements

Software Selection

The software (proprietary or purchased) used to file in AES should contain certain edits that will flag/reject invalid export information before it is submitted. Make sure the software vendor or service center have been authorized by a U.S. Customs Border & Protection client representative. If not authorized, the software vendor must submit a Letter of Intent to the Census Bureau. A client representative will be assigned to test and validate the software. Upon receiving your assigned client representative allow 2–3 weeks for testing.

There should be recommended edits, for example, "Missing value"; if the product value is missing, the selected software should reject the shipment, requiring the filer to correct the error before it is transmitted to AES. Once the errors are identified, correct them immediately. Companies must ensure that they have current updates to code tables, as well as ensuring that the most recent error messages from Appendix A of the Automated Export System Trade Interface Requirements are built in the software. This allows a company to be proactive in identifying errors before the EEI is transmitted.

If you use the standard-edition AES*PcLink* software, you must update the software and tables on all individual computers using the software. If you use the network-edition (LAN) software, your network administrator must update the software and tables for all users. It is recommended that you perform the update functions at least once per month, or more often if you experience coding errors.

Make sure you pay close attention to broadcast messages from the AES Branch and notices placed on the AES*Direct* Web site regarding updates to the *AESPcLink* software. To update the AES*PcLink* software, click on Tools—then, click on Update AES*PcLink* software. To update the AES Code Tables, such as Port of Export, Carrier Codes, etc., click on Tools—then, click on AES Code Tables. If any of the code tables are outdated, then AES*PcLink* will allow you to update those tables.

Daily Reports

Develop or purchase software that has the capabilities of identifying unresolved error responses by running specific reports based on different types of criteria. For example, the software could generate a report for "Shipments without an ITN," "Shipments with an ITN," "Shipments pending response," "Shipments reported over a 24-hour time period," etc.; these reports gives the filer a snap shot of their progress with compliance alerts, fatal errors, verify messages, etc. If you are a USPPI with an authorized agent that files on your behalf, request that your agent provide you with reports of these types.

Export Checklist

Develop a checklist that identifies what the staff must do prior to submitting a shipment transaction via the AES. A checklist provides a tool for collecting information and establishing steps and procedures to ensure that your organization complies with FTR and with export regulations of other government agencies. The following are some examples of the items that should appear on your checklist:

- Ensure that goods have proper licenses, if necessary (See the References section for government agency Web sites),
- Check the consignees name against the Denied Parties List (See the References section for government agency Web sites).
- Verify that the ultimate destination is not a sanctioned country (See the References section for government agency Web sites),
- Confirm that an ITN is received for each shipment submitted (An External Transaction Number can no longer be used),
- Take appropriate action to correct all fatal errors,
- Determine the filing deadline, based upon the estimated date of departure
  - Predeparture filers must file prior to export based on the mode of transportation:
    - Vessel: 24 hours prior to loading cargo
    - Air: 2 hours prior to scheduled takeoff
    - Truck: 1 hour prior to truck arriving at the U.S. border

- Rail: 2 hours prior to train arriving at the U.S. border
- Mail/Other: 2 hours prior to departure
- Note: 'Other' includes passenger/hand carried
- Pipeline: prior to departure or postdeparture on the condition that the pipeline operator provide CBP Port Director proof of filing citations, exemption or exclusion legends within four calendar days following the end of each calendar month.
  - If the USPPI is an approved Postdeparture filer, the USPPI or authorized agent must file within 10 working days of exportation,
- Verify that the commodity classification code is from the current Schedule B/HTSUSA manual,
- If using HTSUSA codes, check to see if the code is not on the "HTS not for us in AES" list located at the following Web site: http://www.census.gov/foreign-trade/aes/documentlibrary/hts-not-for-aes.html
- Ensure the classification code properly identifies the commodity being shipped, and
- Verify that the commodity code is 10 digits with no embedded spaces or characters.

Acronyms

There are many common acronyms and abbreviations used by the trade community and government agencies regarding the export process. Below is a list of the most common acronyms for your reference:

AES	Automated Export System
AESTIR	Automated Export System Trade Interface Requirements
BIS	Bureau of Industry and Security
BOL	Bill of Lading
CBP	U.S. Customs and Border Protection
CCL	Commerce Control List
CFR	Code of Federal Regulations
DDTC	Department of State, Directorate of Defense Trade Controls
DUNS	Data Universal Numbering System (Dun & Bradstreet Number)
EAR	Export Administration Regulations
ECCN	Export Control Classification Number

EEI	Electronic Export Information
EIN	Employee Identification Number
FPPI	Foreign Principal Party in Interest
FTD	Foreign Trade Division
FTR	Foreign Trade Regulations
FTZ	Foreign Trade Zone
HTSUSA	Harmonized Tariff Schedule of the United States Annotated
IATA	International Air Transport Association
ISO	International Standards Organization
ITA	International Trade Administration
ITAR	International Traffic in Arms Regulations
LOI	Letter of Intent
NMFTA	National Motor Freight Traffic Association
OEA	Office of Enforcement Analysis
OEE	Office of Export Enforcement
OFAC	Office of Foreign Assets Control
SCAC	Standard Carrier Alpha Code
Sch B	Schedule B number
USC	United States Code
USITC	U.S. International Trade Commission
USML	U.S. Munitions List
USPPI	U.S. Principal Party in Interest
VSD	Voluntary Self-Disclosure

References

Contact Information

- FTD Census Call Center 800-549-0595
  - AES Help Desk — Option 1
    - For help with AES filings, fatal errors, compliance and fatal error reports, downtime policy, etc.

- Schedule B Classification Assistance — Option 2
  - For help with your classification of Schedule B/HTSUSA numbers for merchandise exported out of the country and information on data discrepancies of published trade statistics
- Regulations Assistance — Option 3
  - For help with clarification of the Foreign Trade Regulations, responsibilities of parties in export transactions
- AES*Direct* Technical Support 877-715-4433, Ext. 6 or 301-562-7790, Ext. 3
- For help with technical problems with AES*Direct* or AES*PcLink*, username, passwords and/or administrator codes

For help with Licensing, License Exemptions, and export requirements issued by the agency

- U.S. Customs & Border Protection — 202-344-3277
- Bureau of Industry and Security
  - Commerce License Help Desk — 202-482-4811
  - Western Regional Office — 949-660-0144 or 408-351-3378
- U.S. State Department, Directorate Defense Trade Controls — 202-663-1282
- U.S. Department of Treasury, Office of Foreign Asset Control — 202-622-2480

Useful Web Sites

AES Data Elements Reference Table
http://www.census.gov/foreign-trade/regulations/forms/sedreftable.pdf
Commodity Filing Response Messages Appendix A (AES Error Messages)
http://www.customs.gov/linkhandler/cgov/trade/automated/aes/tech_docs/
aestir/june04_intro/appendices/apndx_a.ctt/apndx_a.doc
Export Compliance Quick Link to Field Questions on CCL/USML (Brief overview)
http://www.bis.doc.gov/licensing/exportingbasics.htm
Harmonized Tariff Schedule of the United States Annotated
http://www.usitc.gov/tata/hts/bychapter/index.htm
Instructions for Resolving Fatal Errors
http://www.census.gov/foreign-trade/aes/documentlibrary/fatals.html
Lists to Check Before Exporting
http://www.bis.doc.gov/ComplianceAndEnforcement/ListsToCheck.htm
Routed Export Procedures- FTR Section 30.3
http://www.census.gov/foreign-trade/regulations/regs/
regulations20080602-federalregister.pdf
Schedule B
http://www.census.gov/foreign-trade/schedules/b/index.html
Trade Restrictions & Sanctions
http://www.treas.gov/offices/enforcement/ofac/

Appendix B: Supply Chain Security Best Practices Catalog
Customs-Trade Partnership Against Terrorism (C-TPAT)

For importers paying attention to detail is critical to successful trade compliance. This appendix chapter provides intricate information flow and key overview of import regulatory concerns. It is an excellent primer for the import manager for all inbound freight for government compliance.

Table of Contents

Prologue
Introduction
Using This Catalog
Tiered Benefits Structure
    Tier Three Status
    Corporate Governance Structure Supporting Supply Chain Security
Management Support
Advanced Data/Entry Level Data Submission and ACE
Risk Analysis
Self-Assessment
Security Planning and Program Management
Business Partner Requirements
    Manufacturer/Supplier/Vendor Requirements
    Service Provider Requirements

Customer Screening
Customer Outreach
Container/Trailer/ULD Security
    Container/Trailer/Unit Load Device (ULD) Inspections
    Container Seals
    Tracking
    Storage/Inventory
Conveyance Security
    Conveyance Inspections
    Conveyance Storage
    Conveyance Monitoring
Cargo Tracing en Route
Physical Access Controls
    Planning
    Employees
    Visitors
    Deliveries/Cargo Pick-Up (Including Mail)
    Search Vehicles/Persons/Packages (Incoming)
    Challenging and Removing Unauthorized Persons
Personnel Security
    Pre-Employment Verifications, Background Checks, and Investigations
    Personnel Termination Procedures
    Internal Code of Conduct/Employee Evaluations
Procedural Security
    Identifying/Reporting/Tracking Incidents
    Brand Name/Identity Protection
    Manifesting/Invoicing/Electronic Data Interface (EDI)
    Packing/Packaging
    Cargo Discrepancies
    Preventing Collusion
Security Training/Threat Awareness/Outreach
    Awareness
    Specialized Training
    Outreach
    Employee Incentives
    Incident Reporting
Physical Security
    Fencing/Gates/Gate Houses
    Security Guards
    Parking
    Locking Mechanisms
    Lighting
    Alarm Systems

Video Surveillance Cameras
Information Technology Security—Computer Systems
   Access Restrictions (Internal)
   Viruses/Firewalls/Tampering Prevention (External)
   Policies/Procedures/Management Support/Training
   Data Back-Ups and Recovery Plans
   Hardware Security
Emergency Preparedness/Disaster Recovery
Program Memberships to Enhance Supply Chain Security

PROLOGUE

The Customs-Trade Partnership Against Terrorism (C-TPAT) is, beyond question, the largest and most successful government-private sector partnership to emerge from the terrorist attacks on September 11, 2001. C-TPAT was launched in November 2001, with just seven companies—seven major importers who embraced the necessity of supply chain security within the highest corporate management levels of their organizations. Today, more than 10,000 companies—critical players in the global supply chain—have applied for membership, and more than 6,000 have been accepted as certified partners.

Since the beginning, the guiding principles for C-TPAT have been voluntary participation and jointly developed security criteria, best practices and implementation procedures. C-TPAT partners have worked cooperatively with U.S. Customs and Border Protection (CBP) to protect their supply chains from concealment of terrorist weapons, including weapons of mass effect, and global supply chains are more secure today as a result of C-TPAT. In exchange, CBP provides reduced inspections at the port of arrival, expedited processing at the border, and other significant benefits, such as "front of line" inspections and penalty mitigation. Additionally, C-TPAT status is one variable factored into post-incident contingency planning should a terrorist act impact international supply chains. The security commitment demonstrated by C-TPAT members is strong and meaningful, as are the benefits provided by CBP.

Introduction

This catalog of Supply Chain Security Best Practices (Best Practices) is organized based on the Customs Trade Partnership Against Terrorism (C-TPAT) Security Criteria. The best practices included herein are those that have been identified through more than 1,400 validations and site visits conducted by C-TPAT Supply Chain Security Specialists (SCSS). "Best Practices" are defined as security measures that:

   1) exceed the C-TPAT Security Criteria,
   2) incorporate management support,

3) have written policies and procedures that govern their use,
4) employ a system of checks and balances, and
5) have measures in place to ensure continuity.

This catalog is not exhaustive or all-inclusive of best practices in the international supply chain. It is intended to serve as a living document and will be updated periodically to reflect the best practices found during validations.

Best practices are achieved through the effective utilization of people, processes, and technology. Best practices incorporate a system of checks and balances, oversight, accountability, and verification of reliability throughout each aspect of the supply chain in order to ensure that the supply chain cannot be compromised. While many of the best practices listed in this catalog may assist businesses in theft prevention and asset protection, their intended use focuses on the prevention of weapons of mass effect, terrorists, or other contraband from entering the supply chain. A single best practice does not constitute an effective supply chain security program. Security best practices must be applied to appropriately reduce the level of risk associated with any international supply chain. It is of paramount importance to approach the international supply chain in its totality, because a chain is only as strong as its weakest link.

In order for supply chain security best practices to exist, continue to thrive, and be effective, they must have the full support of high-level company management. Security best practices should become an integral part of a company's culture by being incorporated into the company's mission and core business processes. Through the validation process, CBP has found that those businesses whose core philosophy is "continuous improvement" have achieved effective supply chain security and have realized many collateral benefits from analyzing the security of their supply chains. Such benefits include but are not limited to development of standards, elimination of duplicative processes to increase efficiency, and greater supply chain visibility. Most importantly, these companies have made significant contributions to global supply chain security by continually improving their security practices.

CBP recognizes the diverse size and financial abilities of C-TPAT members, and this catalog attempts to provide examples of not only advanced security technologies, but of lower cost security practices as well, both of which may help achieve the same security goals. For example, concerning "conveyance tracking," the intended purpose of accurately tracking conveyance movements and detect deviations can be achieved through the use of GPS tracking systems, or through a lower cost security practice of requiring drivers to follow designated routes with predetermined average travel times, along with periodic communication between the truck driver and company officials. Both of these security best practices help achieve the security goal of conveyance tracking, thus providing a more secure environment.

Using This Catalog

This catalog is written in a generic manner to allow for flexibility, maintaining the confidentiality of C-TPAT partners, and preventing the endorsement of specific technology, services, or products. Generic business entity names are used (e.g., Company, Logistics Provider, Consolidator, Highway Carrier, Port, Terminal Operator, Sea Carrier, and Air Carrier) in order to provide the context in which the best practice was identified. It is important to note that the best practices listed for these entity types are not necessarily exclusive to the entity mentioned. These best practices are applicable to many industries where the process is performed within the supply chain. For example, a best practice for seal control may be listed as being performed by a consolidator, but a factory may be able to use the same best practice, given that seal control also applies to factories. Generic terms referring to time such as "routinely," "randomly," "intervals," "specified period of time," and "periodically" are meant to convey that a definitive time frame should be established for that best practice.

The *Best Practices Catalog* is not designed as a master check list of security practices that must be adopted in order to receive Tier Three Benefits. The C-TPAT program from its inception has taken a flexible approach, where it is recognized that "one size does not fit all," and that customized security measures must be developed and implemented in accordance with the risk present. For example, the adoption of certain best practices in a low risk environment may be sufficient to mitigate the risk present and enable the importer to qualify for Tier Three standing. However, in a high-risk environment, the adoption of the same practices may be viewed as a necessary, minimum security measure, and therefore not elevate the overall security environment to the point at which the importer would be considered for Tier Three. A determination of Tier Three eligibility is thus based on the totality of the security measures employed, not on any specific practice(s), and whether or not the overall security environment effectively addresses the risk adherent to that specific international supply chain.

C-TPAT Supply Chain Security Specialists are committed to working alongside members to help design the security measures necessary to address the risk, exceed minimum security standards, and thus enable the importer to achieve Tier Three standing and receive the greatest benefits afforded by CBP.

Tiered Benefits Structure

To ensure the success of C-TPAT, the security criteria or standards that members must meet or exceed must remain robust, dynamic, and within a flexible security framework, with the overall objective of elevating the security measures employed throughout the international supply chain. As C-TPAT members enhance their security measures to meet these clearly defined security criteria, CBP must also provide enhanced benefits. In May 2005, CBP moved to a three-tiered benefits structure, where C-TPAT importers who do more, receive more.

Under **Tier One,** *certified* importers receive meaningful risk score reductions, resulting in fewer cargo examinations for security concerns, a lower level of random Compliance Measurement examinations than those afforded to non-C-TPAT importers, and the negation of most trade cargo examine selectivity. These three conditions afford Tier One importers with a low level of examinations. Additionally, Tier One importers are also eligible for expedited cargo processing at the border (FAST lanes at the land borders), receive 'front of line' inspection privileges at ports of entry should an examination be required, are entitled to certain penalty mitigation for Trade Act of 2002 violations, become eligible for the Importer Self Assessment program, and may attend C-TPAT training seminars. CBP believes that the level of benefits afforded Tier One importers is commensurate to the level of commitment demonstrated by the C-TPAT member.

With the additional commitment demonstrated as a result of having successfully undergone a *validation,* the validated importer then becomes eligible for Tier Two or Tier Three status. An importer whose validation reveals that *minimum security criteria have been met* will receive Tier Two benefits. **Tier Two** benefits include all the same benefits associated with Tier One, but Tier Two importers are provided with twice the level of risk score reductions received by Tier One importers, resulting in significantly fewer examinations for security reasons than those received by Tier One importers.

Finally, for those importers whose security measures *exceed the minimum security criteria* and have adopted "security best practices" as evidenced by the successful completion of a validation, **Tier Three** status is granted. Under Tier Three, all benefits associated with Tier One and Tier Two are granted, and the most significant risk score reductions available are provided by CBP, resulting in very infrequent examinations for security reasons. Tier Three status is also the precursor for CBP's "Green Lane," which will afford members with zero inspections upon arrival except for an occasional random examination, contingent on meeting other "Green Lane" requirements, such as shipment through a Container Security Initiative (CSI) port, and the use of a container security device. CBP rolled out the "Green Lane" in 2006 when effective container security technology became available.

Tier Three Status

To help importers achieve the highest level of benefits provided, Tier Three benefits and the precursor to the "Green Lane," CBP has committed to outline "Security Best Practices" and work with members to adopt, modify, and implement those security best practices that will help take the member's security practices to the next level.

This edition of the *C-TPAT Best Practices Catalog* is intended to categorize specific security measures that C-TPAT Supply Chain Security Specialists have identified as 'best practices' resulting from the more than 1,400 validations conducted to date. This catalog will be a living document, updated periodically as additional validations are conducted and new security best practices are noted. The outlined "best practices" pertain to security procedures used throughout an international supply chain, such as conveyance monitoring and tracking, cargo tracing, preventing collusion, employee awareness, physical security and surveillance, and other areas crucial to supply chain security.

Corporate Governance Structure Supporting Supply Chain Security

As C-TPAT Supply Chain Security Specialists conduct security validations, one common, essential practice has emerged which is so significant to the overall supply chain security environment, that Tier Three status can only be obtained by the presence of this practice. That practice is a corporate governance structure through which supply chain security is embraced at the highest levels of the company— the CEO, the COO, the President, etc. The security of a company's supply chain should be a required topic of discussion in corporate boardrooms. Security of supply chains is often as important to the financial survival of a company as the accuracy of a company's financial statements. Supply chain security practices must be periodically reviewed for adequacy by CEOs and corporate boards, and noted deficiencies must be addressed timely.

Additionally, a unified corporate governance structure which embraces the importance of supply chain security has proven to be more effective in leveraging their corporate strength to require supply chain security practices and enhancements through their entire international supply chain, from all business partners. These security measures must be pushed back from the point of stuffing of the container or air cargo shipment, through the ultimate arrival of the cargo into a U.S. port of entry. The active engagement by top corporate officials in a company's supply chain security efforts cannot be understated, and as a result, the involvement by senior corporate leaders is a requisite for Tier Three status.

Management Support

Senior management support determines whether or not the appropriate resources (human, financial, and technological) will be dedicated toward improving supply chain security, and ensuring that security is a priority for the company as a whole. This support is demonstrated by senior management's involvement in and understanding of the company's supply chain security program.

Domestic

"Continuous Improvement" Philosophy: Company management integrated supply chain security into its business processes, practices, policies, procedures, and employee job descriptions. The Company considers security part of its "continuous improvement" business philosophy.

Proactively Engaged: Senior management from key departments (Information Technology, Purchasing, Contracting, Finance, Sales/Marketing, Shipping/Receiving, Transportation, Customs Compliance, Human Resources, and Facilities Maintenance) are fully engaged in overseeing and in some cases are actively involved in supply chain security initiatives. This support is demonstrated by their allocation of resources to security related programs and their participation in monthly security assessment meetings. Senior management is proactively engaged in seeking ways to improve security measures for the company and its business partners.

Weekly Briefings: A President of a Highway Carrier provides breakfast to his dispatchers and drivers on Saturday. During that time, he conducts a meeting, provides training, and discusses transportation security concerns. The President documents topics discussed and employees who attended. Follow-up is conducted to ensure that absent employees remain informed.

Supply Chain Security Committee: A Supply Chain Security Committee was established by senior company executives to evaluate the Company's overall supply chain security and make recommendations for improvement. The Supply Chain Security Committee is comprised of senior managers, operational supervisors, line employees, and key management from foreign locations who are responsible for international supply chain security.

Top Management Knows Business Partners: Company's senior executive management maintains a high level of familiarity with its overseas agents, their practices, and affiliations by using formal and alternative methods to collect information. In addition, the Company President has conducted extensive international travel to meet with buying agents to discuss factory and transportation provider security requirements.

Full Integration of Supply Chain Security Policies: Company executive management is committed to ensuring that supply chain security procedures are adopted by all of their subsidiaries, suppliers, and service providers worldwide. All Company subsidiaries must develop and implement a sound security plan that addresses terrorist risks in the international supply chain and crisis management. Executive management reviews these plans to ensure their completeness and implementation.

Worldwide

Establishing Security Directors and Country Managers: An International Corporation has established Regional Supply Chain Security Directors and Country Managers worldwide to ensure that supply chain security procedures are implemented and consistently followed by factories and service providers. These Security Directors and Country Managers also are responsible for continual supply chain security risk analysis and contingency planning for the corporation.

Security Councils: Company established a Security Council to formulate global security guidelines, determine methods to evaluate security weaknesses, formulate action plans, and determine methods to control security procedures worldwide. Senior management at all locations is responsible for documenting actions they have taken to support and improve supply chain security practices.

Mission Statement: International Company has incorporated supply chain security into its mission statement.

Advanced Data/Entry Level Data Submission and ACE

Advanced data helps businesses and government detect anomalies and discrepancies prior to the cargo's arrival. In addition, advanced data increases the timeliness of critical information, enhances logistics planning, and helps to ensure an efficient, seamless, and secure supply chain.

Business to U.S. Customs and Border Protection

Advanced Trade Data Initiative/Entry Level Data Submission: To fully realize the reduced cargo inspection benefits afforded to C-TPAT importers, the Company participates in the Advanced Trade Data Initiative (ATDI) and/or transmits entry-level import data to CBP prior to loading the cargo onto the conveyance for shipment to the United States. Advanced trade data allows CBP to more effectively target high-risk shipments, while affording certified C-TPAT importers with reduced cargo inspections.

Automated Commercial Environment (ACE): Company has enrolled in U.S. Customs and Border Protection's Automated Commercial Environment (ACE) program to facilitate the transmission of entry information and automate all aspects of customs information exchange. The Company actively uses the ACE Portal to monitor import transactions for anomalies.

Business to Business

Electronic Data Interchange (EDI): Broker and Company receive entry information electronically from the shipper prior to the cargo's arrival so that anomalies can be detected, discrepancies can be immediately investigated and resolved, and accurate information is declared to CBP.

Secure Electronic Data Transmissions: Company's shipments are traceable through secure electronic data transmissions. Information is updated at various points along the supply chain. All authorized parties have the necessary viewing privileges to plan appropriately for arriving/departing shipments, as well as the ability to immediately identify anomalies.

Advanced Shipping Notices (ASNs): Barcode pack and scan system allows vendors to transmit Advanced Shipping Notices (ASNs) and packing lists electronically to domestic distribution center. This system improves packing accuracy and reduces quantity discrepancies (overages/shortages).

Risk Analysis

Given the complexity of the international supply chain, a risk analysis is necessary to focus resources and prioritize action items. The more complex the supply chain, the more extensive the risk analysis becomes and consideration should be given to using risk models and developing organizational expertise. Risk analysis helps companies identify and address the most immediate threat(s) to their supply chain. As the political climate, business relationships, trade lanes, and modes of transportation change within a company's supply chain, a risk analysis is needed. Risk analysis requires constant communication with business partners and knowledge about their security measures.

Identifying Risks and Creating Remedies: Company conducted a comprehensive risk analysis of its international supply chain by researching terrorist/criminal activity in supplier countries. Company sent security surveys to all foreign suppliers and service providers. The surveys were used to develop detailed flow charts of the various supply chains and analyze the security measures used to secure shipments at each stage of cargo handling. The company's final step involved developing an action plan to address the gaps, vulnerabilities, and weaknesses that were identified and conduct follow-up with business partners. In addition, a risk analysis is performed for all new business partners.

Tapping into Existing Resources: Air Carrier obtains information from CBP and/or the U.S. Department of State Web sites on a regular basis to determine what cargo is of moderate or high risk for smuggling, sabotage, or terrorist attack. Air Carrier has established procedures to handle high-risk cargo, which include thoroughly reviewing customers' security procedures and rejecting cargo from "unknown" shippers in high-risk locations.

Keeping Key Personnel Informed: The Company's risk analysis and threat assessment are posted on the company's intranet, which provides guidance to buyers, logistics managers, and security personnel in determining necessary levels of security to protect corporate assets and prevent shipments from being compromised. In addition, senior management conducts follow-up with key personnel to ensure they are kept up-to-date on potential threats.

Self-Assessment

Self-assessments enable companies to evaluate the effectiveness of the security measures used within their international supply chain. In addition, self-assessments help to identify the need for additional resources, as well as correct gaps, vulnerabilities, and weaknesses.

Domestic Facilities

Conducts Periodic Assessments: Self-assessments include periodic review and audit of security procedures, equipment, training, and other asset protection measures that directly affect the integrity of the Company's supply chain security.

Engaging Employees: Company selects employees in a random lottery to assist with weekly audits of inbound containers. This procedure affords all employees, even those not in cargo-handling jobs, the opportunity to be involved in the company's supply chain security program through first-hand experience. These audits include seal and inventory verifications.

Weaving Security into Business Practices: Company has incorporated supply chain security into its internal management audits. This practice fully integrates security into business practices.

Verifying Container Inspections and Conveyance Tracking: Highway Carrier President periodically conducts audits of container/trailer inspections performed by drivers to ensure they are consistently conducting inspections before leaving the truck yard and the customer's facility. President also periodically follows drivers on their routes and listens in on dispatcher, receptionist, and driver communications to ensure that there is no collusion.

Verifying/Rotating Security Guard Duties: The Company Security Manager verifies that guards are performing their duties, especially during the night shift. A periodic review of the guards' activity logs and incident reports is conducted, and incomplete/inconsistent information is addressed. Guards are also rotated to avoid complacency and internal conspiracies.

Verifying Physical Security: Inspections of the facility's physical security are conducted and documented as part of the guard's routine responsibilities. Each day, the guard is required to verify that alarms, generators, video surveillance camera systems, and access control devices are working, and that fence lines are maintained.

Foreign Facilities

Holding Business Partners Accountable: After the Company's C-TPAT validation, follow-up meetings and site visits were conducted with foreign suppliers and service providers to evaluate their progress against the C-TPAT Security Criteria. As part of its plans to regularly inspect supply chain partners for security compliance, the Company will conduct several unannounced on-site security inspections of its suppliers and service providers. In addition, the Company amended supplier and service provider contracts to incorporate minimum-security requirements and initiated risk-based audits.

Incorporating Security into Factory Audits: To complement the Company's Factory Audit Program, the Company conducts random security audits of high-risk foreign manufacturers. These random audits serve as another check and balance to ensure foreign manufacturers comply with the Company's security policies. These audits also allow the Company to observe the security measures utilized in their supply chain first hand and discuss the contractual supply chain security requirements with their foreign manufacturers.

Utilizing Overseas Resources: Company routinely monitors factory, supplier, and service provider security by using buying agents stationed overseas who have been trained by a security firm on how to conduct security site verifications.

Utilizing External Resources: A certified C-TPAT Partner hired a security firm to physically verify that all primary overseas factories adhere to C-TPAT Security Criteria, as agreed. During factory site visits, the Company's employees participate in the verification to ensure direct company involvement.

Security Planning and Program Management

Effective supply chain security involves a comprehensive and holistic approach to ensure the right people, processes, and technology are in the right place at the right time to prevent a security incident. A comprehensive understanding of the operations, interrelationships, and interdependencies within the supply chain is critical to establishing a supply chain security program. Supply chain security must be integrated into a company's business processes to be effective.

Holistic Approach to Security: Company uses a holistic approach by first determining the business interrelationships among departments within the organization and with foreign suppliers/service providers. With the collaboration of key domestic department managers and employees (Purchasing, Shipping/Receiving, Human Resource Management, Logistics, Information Technology, Facility Maintenance, and Planning/Operations) and foreign business partners, the Company formulated an international supply chain security program and established a system of checks and balances to ensure that security measures are working. The Company incorporated security risk assessments into its supply chain management plan.

Establishing Internal Networks: Sea Carrier has established an internal network of regional security representatives who are responsible for the integration of security procedures into new projects, in addition to their traditional role of responding to security incidents.

Global Security Management: International Consolidator restructured security force to address global supply chain security issues. Responsibility for all security rests with the Global Security Manager who oversees District Security Managers, Field Security Managers, and Investigators. The clear line of authority and organizational structure has increased the visibility and importance of security throughout the organization.

A Plan for Continuous Improvement: To ensure continued compliance and improvement is part of the Company's ongoing and future commitment to supply chain security, the Company created a program consisting of awareness, compliance, and training. First, the Company continuously promotes an awareness of supply chain security measures to their managers, employees and service providers. Second, internal policies have been updated and a checks and balance system has been established. In addition, supply chain security policies, job descriptions, and the vendor guide have been updated, and security measures have been added to service provider contracts. Third, the Company developed training to keep employees and service providers up-to-date on supply chain security issues.

Interpersonal Relationships and Worldwide Networks: To effectively achieve supply chain security worldwide, the Company has established strong interpersonal relationships and networks to understand the culture of their business partners. This understanding enables the Company to work effectively with their business partners to implement supply chain security recommendations.

Business Partner Requirements

Where a company outsources or contracts elements of their supply chain, such as a foreign facility, conveyance, domestic warehouse, or other service, it is imperative that the company work with its business partners to ensure that security measures are in place and adhered to throughout its supply chain. The following Best

Practices illustrate the leverage, influence, and follow-through of C-TPAT Partners to achieve effective supply chain security worldwide.

Manufacturer/Supplier/Vendor Requirements

Requiring Security Adherence: A C-TPAT certified company is promoting supply chain security by conditioning its business relationships on C-TPAT Security Criteria. The Company requires that all business partners accept and implement the C-TPAT Security Criteria if they wish to continue to do business. For example, the Company's new purchase orders include the language "Supplier accepts responsibility for factory and container security until such time as the container/merchandise is delivered to the ocean terminal, authorized yard, or consolidation point. Supplier will immediately report container seal changes and reason for changes to the U.S. Distribution Center Manager."

Holding Buying Agent Accountable: Company established a Vendor Compliance Manual that outlines the security requirements for overseas factories. All overseas buying agents must use the Vendor Compliance Manual when selecting a factory on behalf of the Company. Moreover, the manual lists freight forwarders approved by the Company that must be used to ensure continuity of supply chain security standards.

Contractual Obligations: Company has incorporated into its contracts with foreign suppliers and service providers a requirement that security gaps, vulnerabilities, and weaknesses must be addressed immediately. They also are subject to random security audits to verify compliance.

Requiring business Updates: Company requires semi-annual "business updates" from all of international service providers and suppliers that include identification of changes in business operations (e.g., security measures, management changes, employee turnover, policy/procedural changes with respect to packaging/cargo handling and storage, political climate, financial status, and contract changes with service providers). This information is used to analyze risk, determine contractual compliance, ensure continuity of established supply chain security measures, and identify the need for changes/modifications to security plans.

Factory Certification Requirements: Company's factory certification program has an established rating scale to assess the level of adherence to the Company's security policies and procedures. Only those manufacturers that receive a passing score are permitted to do business with the Company. This system encourages factories and suppliers to comply with the Company's security standards and improve deficient areas.

Supplier Code of Conduct: Company developed and implemented a Supplier Code of Conduct as part of its Supplier Business Requirements. The Supplier Code of Conduct requires suppliers to understand the key integrity performance criteria required of them, including supply chain security.

Collaborating to Select Suppliers and Service Providers: Company's export/ import, transportation, purchasing, and finance departments take part in supplier and service provider selection/renewal. These four key departments work together to ensure that operational and security problems are addressed and corrected by suppliers and service providers before contract renewal. This collaboration creates system of checks and balances for the service provider and supplier selection process.

Managing Non-Compliant Essential Business Partner: If a supplier is unable to meet C-TPAT security criteria or is uncooperative with the Company, but is deemed a "critical" supplier by the Company, measures are taken to address the supplier's security vulnerabilities by closely scrutinizing the shipments from that supplier. The Company will notify its assigned CBP Supply Chain Security Specialist of concerns with the supplier and develop a plan of action to address these concerns.

Service Provider Requirements

Exclusive Representative: An account representative at the foreign freight forwarders office is specifically assigned to the Company's account to ensure continuity and detect unusual or suspicious activities.

Prohibiting Subcontracting: Company included a clause in highway carrier contracts whereby shipments cannot be subcontracted to other carriers without breaching the contract. The contract states that, "Highway carrier will be subjected to legal and financial consequences if subcontracting occurs." This contract clause helps to ensure cargo control and consistent security measures.

Requiring Background Clearances: Company requires that all service providers (janitorial, transportation, personnel, etc.) conduct comprehensive criminal background investigations on contract employees. In addition, the service provider must submit bio-data with pictures and copies of the background investigations conducted on employees referred to work at the Company.

Contractual Obligations: Company has incorporated security into its contracts with service providers. Such requirements include, but are not limited to, conducting an inspection of all empty containers/trailers prior to loading and documenting inspections; establishing seal control, issuance, affixing, and verification policies with appropriate checks and balances; tracking driver movements throughout transport;

establishing access controls to the Company's cargo; and screening the employees who handle their cargo. These requirements are also subject to on-site verifications.

Establishing Procedures for Selection: Extensive written standards specify requirements for the service provider selection process, which include security. Company verifies the veracity of the service provider's security measures, financial solvency, and business references by conducting follow-up both in person and over the phone. The veracity of the service provider's claims will determine whether or not the Company will continue to do business with them.

Customer Screening

Preventing Misuse of Products by Customers: Chemical Company requires that sales representatives screen customers who use its products to ensure purchases are for legitimate use. In addition to financial information, sales representatives must complete an "Indicators of Suspicious Activities" form for each new customer. The sales manager must review the form before the customer is approved.

Requiring Original Power of Attorney: Broker has a procedure for pre-screening customers prior to engaging in business. The Broker verifies business references and runs credit and business reports. The Broker will not accept cash payments or requests made over a cell phone. This practice reduces the chance of the broker-age firm being used by an unknown party for unlawful purposes. In addition, the Broker requires from clients and freight forwarders an original Power of Attorney that must be notarized before initiating transactions.

Keeping Current with Customer Information: The Broker subscribes to a business information service to monitor his clients' business status and identify unusual trends and financial problems.

Managing the Unknown Customer: Air Consolidator has a database that helps to distinguish known shippers from unknown shippers. Measures are in place to closely examine and segregate unknown shipper transactions. Under the supervision of an operations manager, the cargo is examined and a form is completed that documents the type of examination performed along with the results. All unknown shippers must have a verified business referral.

Requiring Customer Registration: Consolidator requires customers to register as "Known Consignors," whereby they must sign a declaration that has legal implications. The declaration also states that specific security measures have been taken before delivering cargo.

Using External Resources to Screen Customers: Before transporting cargo, Highway Carrier President requires all new customers to complete a credit application and verifies commercial and bank references. Certified check or cash transactions are prohibited. In addition, the customer's reputation is checked through the local trucking association and business contacts.

Requiring Business Referral: Freight Forwarder requires that the U.S. Importer of Record introduce all new shippers and will not do business with unknown entities.

Meeting with Customers In-Person: Highway Carrier's management makes it a priority to get to know customers, customers' employees, and their security measures. Customers are required to complete a security questionnaire and a business profile that includes a request for financial information and business references. Highway Carrier's management then makes a personal visit to the premises of each new customer (and periodically to existing customers) to verify security measures, particularly for product packaging, staging, container/trailer inspections, and seal control. In addition, for each new customer, reference checks are conducted and information is verified to ensure the customer is legitimate. If the customer's security is found to be inadequate, the Highway Carrier works with the customer to increase security or may decide to discontinue doing business with those unwilling to participate in supply chain security measures.

Requiring Customers to Inspect Containers: Highway Carrier requires customers to inspect empty trailers prior to loading if the Highway Carrier's drivers are not present to inspect and witness the loading. Highway Carrier also informs the customer that it will use a contracted security company to perform an inspection of the container/trailer prior to crossing the border.

Refusing Pick-Ups from Unknown Locations: Highway Carrier will not pick up cargo at an unknown location and works with customers to establish routine pickup locations. This procedure helps the Highway Carrier to immediately detect deviations, anomalies, and suspicious activities.

Sending Representatives to Meet with New Foreign Customers: Freight Forwarder has integrated into its security program the procedure of sending a representative to meet with and verify the physical location of all new foreign customers. Freight Forwarder's representatives are responsible for inquiring about customer's security, composing information sheets, reviewing references, and conducting financial checks.

Customer Outreach

Reaching Out to Customers: Highway Carrier sent a letter to all customers expressing its commitment to develop and implement a reliable plan to enhance supply chain security. The letter strongly encourages the customers to enroll in the C-TPAT program and specifies the minimum security requirements that customers are expected to meet.

Container/Trailer/ULD Security

Container security is a requirement for many C-TPAT Partners whose companies and/or foreign shippers/suppliers stuff containers at the point of origin. Container security measures involve container inspection, storage, and tracking, as well as seal control, issuance, and verification throughout the supply chain. A 7-point inspection specifically refers to the following areas of container's/trailer's structure: front wall, left side, right side, floor, ceiling/roof, inside/outside doors, outside/undercarriage. As technology becomes available, C-TPAT partners are encouraged to explore the use of technology such as the "Smart Box" to secure their containers. The following best practices have been identified for container security.

Container/Trailer/Unit Load Device (ULD) Inspections

Domestic Highway Carrier Drayage

Inspecting at Domestic Container Yard: Contracts with local drayage highway carriers include the requirement that drivers must thoroughly inspect the exterior of the container, verify the container and seal numbers, and ensure that the seal is intact prior to transporting the container to the distribution center. Before accepting the loaded container, the driver must report anomalies to the distribution center's receiving manager, who in turn will notify CBP of the anomaly.

Foreign Highway Carrier

Securing Empty Containers: Once a customer pick-up order is placed, the driver conducts and documents a 7-point inspection of the container/trailer using a checklist. The driver must sign the inspection checklist and the Highway Carrier's security guard verifies the inspection and signs the checklist. The guard then places a numbered plastic seal on the trailer, documents the seal number on the delivery trailer/container order, and calls the factory to notify the shipping department of the seal number. The driver verifies the plastic seal number that the guard has placed on the container/trailer by initialing next to it. Upon arrival at the factory, the driver presents the pick-up order to the factory security guard. The factory security guard verifies the seal number upon arrival and signs the inspection sheet. The factory conducts another 7-point inspection prior to stuffing.

Securing Container/Trailer after Customs Examination: The driver must notify the factory and his dispatcher if a customs examination of the cargo is required. After the examination, the factory's broker (who is stationed at the border) places a new seal on the container that is verified by the driver. The broker calls in the new seal number to the factory, highway carrier's dispatcher, and distribution center in the United States. The new seal number is annotated on the bill of lading and is initialed by the broker and the driver. The driver calls his dispatcher to confirm the new seal number.

Detecting False Walls/Compartments: A Highway Carrier uses several low cost, commercially available laser measuring devices to detect false walls, compartments, and hidden contraband. One device is used to measure the dimensions of empty containers and compare the findings against standard measurements. A mirror is used to inspect the undercarriage of the container.

Air Carriers

Screening and Inspecting ULDs on Passenger Flights: An Air Carrier has established special security measures for passenger flights carrying cargo. First, the carrier will not accept containers/ULDs from unknown customers. Second, known customers are informed that their cargo is subject to random inspections. Third, the carrier conducts and documents a 7-point inspection on all empty ULDs/ containers and places a seal on the container.

Establishing Written Procedures for ULD Inspections: An Air Carrier has developed a comprehensive written container/ULD inspection procedure that incorporates the use of a checklist to ensure that the container is completely inspected. Individuals responsible for ULD/container inspections must certify their inspection by printing their name, as well as signing and dating the form. Management audits these checklists periodically.

Consolidators

Conducting X-Ray Examinations: In addition to the airport screening process, the foreign Airfreight Consolidator x-rays all incoming cargo.

Factory/Supplier/Vendor

Inspecting and Weighing Empty Containers: The Factory conducts a 7-point inspection and weighs every empty container/trailer prior to stuffing. The security guard, shipping manager, and driver (if present for stuffing) verify these inspections by signing off on the inspection checklist. In rare instances where the empty container is not loaded immediately, a padlock and plastic seal are placed on the door. Later the seal is verified before opening the empty trailer/container for stuffing to ensure its integrity.

Photographing Container and Seal: After the container is loaded at the Factory, a digital picture is taken of the back of the container before the doors are closed and sealed. After the container is sealed, digital pictures are taken of the seal and all sides of the container. The pictures are transmitted to the port terminal operator and to the distribution center in the United States.

Terminal Yards/Operators

A Team Approach to Container Inspections: Terminal Operator organizes a "checker team" to inspect, weigh, and log every container entering and exiting the terminal. An exterior inspection is performed on full containers and a 7-point inspection is conducted on empty containers to ensure their integrity. The checkers input information regarding the container into the terminal's database and cross-check information provided by the shipper to detect anomalies.

Container Seals

Domestic

Utilizing "Smart Box" Technology Sea Containers: As technology becomes available and more reliable, CBP recommends the use of "Smart Box" technology to increase a company's ability to determine whether or not the container has been compromised while moving through the supply chain.

Verifying and Disposing of Seals: Seal numbers are verified at the distribution center by writing the number of the actual seal next to the seal number listed on the shipping documentation. This procedure provides a written record that the actual seal was checked and verified against the seal number listed on the shipping documentation. The shipping supervisor must be present to verify the seal before it is broken. He/she gathers and secures broken seals to prevent their misuse.

Sea Carrier

Logos on Seals: Sea Carrier requires the use of individually numbered high security bolt seals that bear its logo. The Sea Carrier also requires that this seal be placed on all empty containers laden on its vessels. Each dispatched container is assigned a specific seal that facilitates tracking the origin of the container.

Modifying Containers: Sea Carrier requires seal checks at every interchange throughout the container's transport. In addition, the Sea Carrier has modified the structure of its ocean containers. Rather than use the hasps on the door to affix the seal, carrier uses a locking point mounted on the lower sill of the container structure. This prevents the drilling of the round-head bolt used to secure the hasp, a method used to open container doors while keeping the seal "intact."

Highway Carrier

Utilizing Plastic Seals to Secure Empty Containers: Plastic seals are placed on empty inspected containers that are stored in the truck yard. Seals are verified when the guard conducts his rounds. Unused plastic seals are secured in a locked cabinet, logged, and reconciled.

Highway Carrier

Tracking Seals Given to Drivers: During long haul transport, an extra seal is maintained inside the trailer in a tamper-evident envelope in case the trailer needs to be opened for government examinations while en route. If the seal is used, the original seal must be placed inside the trailer, the new seal number is called in to the dispatcher, and all concerned parties are notified of the seal change. If the seal is not used, the envelope must be returned to the dispatcher.

Seal Control and Verification: Highway Carrier issues high security bolt seals and cable seals to its customers before drivers pick up cargo. The seals are secured, tracked, and verified. At cargo pickup, the Company guard, shipping manager, and driver are present when the seal is placed on the container. All parties present for the affixing of the seal must initial the bill of lading to document their verification. The shipping manager then calls in the seal number to the trucking company dispatcher and the customer in the United States. The seal number must be within the range of seal numbers issued to the customer by the highway carrier.

Factory

Establishing Seal Control Policy: Factory has comprehensive written policies and procedures regarding container seals that include: accountability and responsibility for how seals are controlled, issued, secured, affixed, and verified throughout the supply chain. The policy also specifies how the seal inventory is maintained and reconciled.

Holistic Approach to Seal Control: Seal numbers are electronically transmitted by the Factory to the Highway Carrier and the importer of record before the truck's arrival at the Factory. The truck driver and security guard witness the placement of the seal by the shipping manager and check the integrity of the seal. The seal number is documented on the bill of lading. The guard and driver must initial next to the seal number on the bill of lading to attest to their verification of the seal. Before leaving the Factory, the driver calls in the seal number to his dispatcher who verifies the seal number against the electronically transmitted number. The guard stationed at the gate verifies the trailer number and seal number before the driver leaves the Factory. The guard also initials the bill of lading and records the seal number on the truck exit log.

Multi-National Corporation

Global Seal Control: Company established a uniform policy for all its subsidiaries and service providers regarding seal issuance, control, and verification to ensure product integrity and security throughout the supply chain. Tamper evident seals are affixed and repeatedly verified throughout all changes in custody. Seal changes are communicated to all parties (shipper, importer, highway carrier, terminal, freight forwarder, etc.). The seal number is transmitted to each handling point via secure electronic data transmissions and is verified before acceptance at each handling point.

Consolidator

Segregating and Sealing Less Than Truck Loads (LTLs): Consolidator's trailers have been modified with several partitions to segregate each consignee's cargo to enhance the security of LTL cargo while en route from the Factory/Shipper to the Consolidator's warehouse. The seal number is recorded on the pick-up order and the Factory calls in the seal number to the consolidator at the time of pick-up. The Consolidator verifies the seal numbers upon the truck's arrival.

Tracking

Terminal Operator Container Yard

Addressing Unusual Occurrences: Terminal Operator created a system to detect "unusual" requests and time lags for empty containers dispatched and returned to the yard. When customers order containers, the Terminal Operator initiates a screening process. This process involves obtaining information regarding the amount of time the container is needed, type of cargo, credit information, and positive identification of the customer. In addition, the automated container tracking system generates an alert for containers that are "out of time range" and the container is flagged for an inspection upon its return to the container yard.

Highway Carrier

Identifying and Reporting Anomalies: Highway Carrier developed a spreadsheet to track the time that trailers remain at customers' premises to identify unusual delays. For containers that are out of the normal time range, the Highway Carrier contacts CBP to report the anomaly and request a courtesy examination of the trailer.

Controlling Use of Equipment: Highway Carrier will not permit customers to reroute their trailers to another facility. In addition, Highway Carrier maintains strict control of its equipments' use and location.

Storage/Inventory

Container Yards

Managing Container Inventory: Container yard has established a bar code container inventory management system to track and monitor all empty containers staged in the yard. The system ensures that empty containers do not remain in the yard for more than an established period of time and helps prevent exposure to tampering.

Highway Carrier Truck Yard

Storing Containers: Loaded and empty containers are stored door to door and are sealed to prevent unauthorized access.

Assigning Parking Spaces: Highway Carrier has assigned parking spaces for trailers and containers to facilitate equipment inventory. In addition, a plastic seal that is controlled and tracked is placed on all empty trailers. The security guard is given a map of the parking assignments along with seal numbers to conduct inventory and verify the integrity of the seals throughout his or her shift.

Consolidator

Protecting Unsecured Containers: Consolidator invented a steel plate that protects the contents of open containers while cargo is not being loaded/unloaded. A large cement block is placed in front of the steel plate, making it impossible to be moved without mechanical assistance.

Air Carrier

Controlling Access to ULDs: Air carrier stores empty and full ULDs in a secure location where access is controlled and documented. The Air Carrier uses a ULD inventory system to immediately identify the location of its equipment.

Conveyance Security

Conveyance security is critical to ensure that the mode of transportation is not used to facilitate a terrorist or other illegal act. Inspecting, securing, and tracking conveyances are essential measures in preventing the conveyance, container, and cargo from being compromised en route. C-TPAT partners are encouraged to use technology to accurately track conveyance movements and detect deviations.

Conveyance Inspections

Air Carrier

Using Inspection Checklist: Air Carrier developed a comprehensive conveyance inspection checklist that specifies each area of the aircraft that must be inspected. Areas include, but are not limited to, baggage hold areas, overheads, lavatories, galleys and food carts, cockpit and electronics areas, wheel wells, and landing gear. In addition, the inspection must be documented and the individual conducting the inspection must print and sign his or her name and date the form. Management routinely audits these inspection reports to ensure that they are performed.

Highway Carrier

Reinspecting Conveyance While en Route: Highway Carrier's security guards/ drivers inspect conveyances entering and exiting the facility and use a detailed conveyance inspection checklist to identify modifications to the tractor. Re-inspections are required after intermediate stops. The checklist is maintained for an established period of time for each inspection. Management periodically reviews the inspection checklists and participates in inspections to ensure that they are performed thoroughly, consistently, and accurately.

Sea Carriers

Detecting Stowaways: Sea Carrier uses canine patrols and carbon dioxide detectors to detect stowaways on vessels at each port of call before sailing.

Conveyance Storage

Highway Carrier

Assigning Parking: Highway Carrier has assigned parking spaces for conveyances and trailers to facilitate the guard's inventory and ability to quickly identify missing equipment.

Collaborating to Establish a Secure Yard: A group of Highway Carriers established a secure yard to store full and empty trailers, containers, and conveyances.

Conveyance Monitoring

Highway Carrier

Installing Panic Buttons: Highway Carrier installed panic buttons in each tractor. In the event of an emergency or perceived threat, the driver can depress a button that will send an alarm signal to the dispatch office and to the Highway Carrier's top five managers' cell phones. The Highway Carrier identifies the location of the driver by using GPS tracking and dispatches company personnel. It also alerts local law enforcement and CBP at the border.

Establishing Check Points en Route: Highway Carrier has established several physical checkpoints along the 6–8 hour route. Highway Carrier uses these checkpoints to verify the integrity of the seal and the condition of the container. Management periodically verifies that drivers are stopping at established checkpoints and calling in, as required. If the driver fails to stop at a checkpoint or call-in, an escalation matrix is in place that includes procedures to contact the Highway Carrier's management up to and including contact with local authorities and CBP to conduct a full examination of the container upon its arrival at the port of entry.

Establishing Check Points at the Border: Prior to crossing the border, the Highway Carrier contracts with a private security company that uses dogs to detect contraband. In addition, the private security company takes digital photos of all sides of the trailer and a close-up of the seal. The digital photos are e-mailed to the Highway Carrier for verification before releasing the driver to cross the border.

Security Code Words: Highway Carrier assigns each driver a code word in order to alert the dispatcher of a threat so that police can be called. Code words are also used to identify locations along the route where the driver can be found.

Highway Carrier

Utilizing Security Escorts: In high-risk areas, Highway Carrier uses security guards to escort tractor-trailers to provide additional security for the drivers, cargo, and equipment. Throughout the container's transport, the security guard keeps the container in plain view and communicates with the truck driver via radio/cell phone communication.

Stationing Employee at the Border: Highway Carrier has an employee stationed at the border to monitor arrival times. If there is a significant unexplained time variance, the Highway Carrier's employee will contact CBP to "red flag" the shipment for a courtesy examination.

Utilizing Tracking Technology: Highway Carrier has GPS tracking and text messaging on all tractors. The tracking system enables text communication between dispatchers and drivers. Distress messages can be sent through satellite communication to dispatchers who will, in turn, contact the local authorities. In addition, the GPS system is closely monitored to detect anomalies, unscheduled stops, and route variances.

Tracking Incoming/Outgoing Vehicles: Tractor movements into and out of the yard are recorded using a handheld electronic device that captures driver and tractor information.

Periodic Review of GPS Reports: Senior management periodically reviews GPS reports of driver movements.

Maintaining Communication with Drivers: All of the Highway Carrier's drivers are issued radios and are required to call dispatch when they arrive at the client's facility, when they arrive at the border, when they clear foreign and U.S. customs, and when they drop the trailer at the customer's premises. Dispatch will input these times into a spreadsheet and verify that the times reported are accurate by matching the time reported with the time stamped on the paperwork by foreign and U.S. customs. The dispatcher contacts the customer to confirm the driver's arrival time.

Designating Routes: Drivers are given specific routes to follow and are only allowed to stop at designated areas. Average travel times, during peak and non-peak travel periods, are known.

Utilizing Multiple Monitoring Methods: Highway Carrier uses multiple methods of tracking conveyances. Such methods include: timing driver movements in accordance with the standard time it should take from the point of pick-up to the border crossing; examining fuel consumption to detect route deviations; and establishing alternate routes in case of accidents or road construction. In addition, Carrier provides drivers with two-way radio cell phones and requires drivers to call in their location upon arrival and departure from the Factory, periodically en route to the border, upon arrival at the U.S. distribution center, returning to the border, and arrival at the next pick-up point.

Spot Checking by Management: Highway Carrier management conducts spot checks on drivers' routes and dispatcher call-in logs. If a driver fails to check in at any point, the dispatcher is required to follow-up with management and contact CBP to request a courtesy examination.

Monitoring For Collusion: Highway Carrier monitors communication between the driver, dispatcher, and receptionist to detect internal conspiracies. In addition, Highway Carrier rotates dispatcher assignments and administrative staff to prevent collusion.

Responding to Route Deviations: Highway Carrier uses GPS to track driver movements. When a driver deviates from the route and does not communicate with the base station, the Highway Carrier's dispatcher monitoring the movement will shut off the tractor's engine, lock the trailer so that it cannot be detached from the cab, call the police, and send a company guard to the tractor-trailer's location. Highway Carrier also uses air compression devices to automatically release air into the tires to prevent a flat when the driver is en route to a destination.

Traveling in Convoys: All trucks travel in convoys of four to six vehicles. Each driver has a two-way radio/cell phone and can contact every truck in the convoy.

Driver Check-In Alert System: To closely monitor drivers, Highway Carrier hired a programmer to develop an automated system that alerts the dispatcher when the driver has failed to check-in within a specified period of time.

Sea Carriers

Satellite Monitoring: Vessel Operator has a system that is monitored by a third party specializing in satellite tracking systems for vessels. Most noteworthy about this system is the internal code of communication between the vessel operator and the third party. If intruders compromise the vessel, the vessel operator has established a way to communicate the need for help to the third party without alerting the intruders.

Barge Transshipments

Remote Surveillance: Barge Carrier monitors the loading, transport, and unloading of containers from the barge by using CCTV cameras. The barge also is equipped with a GPS satellite system to monitor the barge's location.

Cargo Tracing en Route

Increased supply chain visibility has many benefits. Visibility allows a company to achieve increased supply chain security and control over inventory management, service providers, and cargo flow. Visibility permits the company to immediately identify and correct problems as the cargo moves through the supply chain.

Utilizing Scanning Cards: Details of the transported shipment are transmitted electronically to the Company through the use of a bar-coded plastic card. Carried by the driver, the card is scanned at each location along the supply chain and provides constant updates to the Company's inventory system. This control mechanism provides a real-time snapshot on the status of each shipment.

Tracing Cargo with Driver Data Port: Company is able to monitor over-the-road cross border shipments through the use of technology that transmits data to the Company from the highway carrier's trucks. The truck is equipped with a data port and the driver is able to transmit messages concerning his or her location and delays. This system enhances the Company's ability to monitor its inbound shipments.

Logistics Tracking System: Company uses an automated system to track the status of shipments worldwide. The system allows the Company's representatives to manage orders and track shipments. The system is fully supported by the Company's information technology personnel. The Company also has used this system for security purposes to track unusual delays or anomalies that may point to illegal activity.

Physical Access Controls

Access controls prevent the unauthorized entry to facilities, maintain control of employees and visitors, and protect company assets. In addition, access controls regulate the movement of people and products to meet the operational needs of a facility.

Planning

Diagraming and Analyzing Access: Company diagramed and analyzed all of its facility's entrances and exits. They then identified all access control security features for the entrances and exits and proceeded to identify and correct gaps, vulnerabilities, and weaknesses.

Employees

Utilizing Biometric Technology: Company uses a biometric handprint identification system together with a 4-digit employee code to access work area and authenticate identities.

Color-Coding Uniforms: The Factory uses color-coded uniforms for its employees to easily distinguish employees from truck drivers, contractors, vendors, and visitors. These uniforms also help identify employees outside of their work area.

Monitoring Access Patterns: Company periodically reviews proximity reader system to identify unusual patterns of employee access.

Terminating Facility Access: When an employee is terminated at the Factory, an information notice is issued to workers that the terminated employee is no longer permitted access to the Factory. A list of names and photos of the terminated employees are given to security to aid them in the access control of the facility.

Renewing Identification Cards: Company requires that employee identification cards must be renewed on an annual basis.

Temporarily Suspending Access: During extended absences, the employee's access privileges to the facility and information systems are temporarily suspended until his return.

Restricting Access: Proximity cards with photo identification are used by employees to gain access to different areas of the facility based on their job function. Employees' entry and exit times are restricted according to their work schedule. If an employee scans in and does not scan out of a particular area or vice-versa, the employee will lose access privileges to the entire facility and an alert is generated. Attempts to access work areas outside normal hours are recorded and investigated. The employee must report to the Security Department to regain his access privileges. "Tailgating" is strictly prohibited, and employees are subject to disciplinary action for violation of this policy.

Requiring Employee Identification: Security guards verify that all employees wear their photo identification badges. Employees who do not have identification are detained until their manager can secure a temporary identification badge for them.

Visitors

Establishing Database for Visitors: After the receptionist verifies the visitor's identity and appointment time, the visitor is required to type his or her name, address, and contact information into a database. The receptionist compares the information entered against the visitor's identification. A photo of the visitor is taken and stored in the database along with the visitor's information. A temporary visitor's ID badge is printed and exchanged for the visitor's government issued identification (e.g., driver's license or passport). The visitor's ID expires at the end of the day. Management periodically runs reports to identify unusual visit patterns.

Establishing Multiple Visitor Check Points: Terminal Operator's visitors must stop at the Port Authority to obtain a pass. After presenting ID and a valid reason for being at the port, the visitor's picture is taken and a 1-day visitor's ID badge is issued specifying the area(s) the visitor is permitted to visit. To be eligible for the pass, the visitor must meet an entity that is authorized to do business inside the port and be escorted at all times. Visitor badges are checked at various security points and badges must be returned at the end of the visit.

Requiring Pre-Clearance: Foreign Port requires that all visitors must be pre-cleared at least 3 days in advance of their visit. Pre-cleared visitors must show a government issued photo identification that is exchanged for a port visitor's badge. Visitors also must go through a metal detector and personal bags are x-rayed and searched.

Verifying Authenticity of Identification: Security personnel verify the authenticity of identification by using an I.D. Checking Guide that depicts license designs from all over the United States and the world. The Human Resources Department also uses this guide to verify the authenticity of state documents.

Deliveries/Cargo Pick-Up (Including Mail)
Terminals/Port Authorities

Exchanging Official Identification for Visitor's Badge: Terminal Operator requires drivers to enter the first access gate and exchange their driver's license for a visitor's badge. The Terminal Operator's guard records the driver's identification, truck number, seal number, and container number. The driver must then stop at the Sea Carrier's office to present his job order sheet and pay the entry fee. The driver then proceeds to the second access gate. The Terminal Operator will once again verify the container number and seal number and direct the driver to the yard location.

Scheduling Pick-Ups: To control access, the Terminal Operator established an appointment office to schedule driver pick-ups. The success of this system is dependent on the communication between the Terminal Operator and its business partners. Empty and full containers arrive at the Terminal Operator's checkpoint where the Terminal's employee verifies the driver's appointment time. The driver is not permitted to enter unless the appointment is confirmed and the vessel is ready for loading.

Requiring PIN Number: Terminal Operator requires the use of a PIN number that is issued by the Shipping Line. This PIN number is unique to the Terminal Operator and supplements driver identification procedures.

Transmitting Pick-Up Information to Highway Carriers: Terminal Operator has created a secure transfer yard located on the outer perimeter of the port where inbound cargo from vessels is staged for pickup after inspection and clearance. As the loads are released for pickup, the information is transmitted to the Highway Carrier. Truckers must present documentation upon entry and are then permitted to enter the yard and pick up their pre-staged loads from designated locations. As drivers leave the yard, the guards verify the container, seal, and documentation against information in the computer database. A procedure to handle discrepancies has been established.

Warehouses/Factories

Establishing Driver Waiting Area: When the truck driver arrives at the Factory, he or she must have an appointment, ring a buzzer, and look into a camera. After the driver confirms the appointment, he or she is permitted to enter through a designated side door into a driver's reception area with a restroom. The driver must present the pickup order/delivery documentation and his or her driver's license. The driver's identity is verified against a drivers list with photographs that is provided by the carrier. A large sign is posted in the warehouse stating "NO VISITORS/DRIVERS BEYOND THIS POINT—EMPLOYEES ONLY." There is a gate between the warehouse and driver's waiting area. These controls help to prevent collusion.

Search Vehicles/Persons/Packages (Incoming)

Screening Incoming Packages: Company established an isolated area and pro-cedures to screen incoming packages and mail before distribution. Company also uses the guidelines listed on the U.S. Postal Service's Web site to safely process incoming mail and packages. Each employee who is responsible for this function has been trained.

Randomly Inspecting Incoming Persons and Packages: A sign is posted notify-ing all who enter the Factory (including company managers and security guards), that a random search is conducted of incoming persons and packages. The Factory periodically conducts random searches of all persons and packages entering the facility. During periods of heightened security alerts, the Company inspects all persons and packages. Searches are documented.

Searching Lockers Prohibiting Personal Items: Personal bags are not allowed inside of the Factory and workers are provided with lockers separate from the Factory's production and warehouse areas. Lockers are periodically searched and employees are not permitted to access lockers during work hours.

Inspecting Vehicles: Terminal Operator's security personnel randomly inspect X% of all trucks entering the facility. A plan is established to randomly search X% of all private vehicles entering the facility each day. A log is maintained of all random inspections and management periodically reviews the log.

Challenging and Removing Unauthorized Persons

Responding to Unauthorized Access: The Company has the ability to lock down access points throughout the facility with the press of a button if unauthorized access is detected. There also is a "panic" button that triggers a silent alarm that will alert the guards and local law enforcement in case of an emergency.

Escalation Matrix: Company has an escalation matrix that has been communicated to all of its employees. The matrix shows the various levels of emergency contacts ranging from company management up to and including federal law enforcement. In addition, in-service training has been provided to employees on how to challenge and remove unauthorized persons.

Personnel Security

The purpose of conducting a background check is to ensure that a prospective employee is qualified to perform the job and is a person of integrity. Random background checks on current employees encourage good conduct. Poor hiring practices could result in security breaches, significant financial losses, and reduced productivity. Security breaches all have one thing in common…PEOPLE.

Pre-Employment Verifications, Background Checks, and Investigations

Domestic

Requiring Background Checks for Contracted Employees: Temporary employees, vendors, and contractors (such as security guards) are subject to the same background investigations required of the Company's permanent employees. The Company requests criminal background checks and application materials from vendors, temporary agencies, and contractors to ensure the integrity of persons having access to its facility and assets.

Conducting Comprehensive Investigations and Re-Investigations: Before hiring an employee, Company conducts in-depth criminal and background investigations for a ten-year period. These investigations include checking criminal records (local, state, and federal), court records, financial history, social security number, right to work documents, past employment, education records, and character references. In addition, employees who are promoted are subject to a reinvestigation. All other employees are subject to periodic reinvestigations.

Conducting Psychological Examinations: Prospective employees are administered a series of psychological examinations to determine their propensity toward corruption or illegal activities, as well as their ability to get along with others in the organization.

Verifying Authenticity of Identification: Human Resource Department verifies the authenticity of identification by using an I.D. Checking Guide that depicts driver's license designs from all over the United States and the world. The I.D. Checking Guide also is used to verify the authenticity of federal documents.

Foreign

Conducting Criminal Investigations in Foreign Country: A Factory and its Highway Carrier have contracted a private firm to run extensive criminal record checks to find individuals who have committed crimes in a foreign country. This background check supplements the requirement that prospective employees receive an original certification from the local police department attesting that they do not have a criminal record.

Employing Alternative Methods to Obtain Information: Although personal privacy laws exist in many domestic jurisdictions and various countries in which the International Company operates, the Company utilizes alternative methods to check applicants' backgrounds in instances where the law prohibits criminal background checks. These alternative methods include asking probing yet noninvasive questions to stimulate conversation with the applicant including in-depth questions regarding gaps in employment; verifying an applicant's background by conducting in-depth personal reference checks and requesting additional references from those personal references; conducting personal visits to references and applicants' homes; verifying driving records (as relevant); verifying current and previous addresses; requesting educational transcripts directly from schools; and checking the applicant's reputation through local associations.

Conducting Criminal Investigations when Not Customary: Background investigations are legal but are not customary in the Manufacturer's country. Therefore, all applicants must complete an "authorization to release information." The form authorizes the Manufacturer to conduct a criminal background investigation and obtain information regarding the applicant's character, general reputation, and mode of living. In addition, the Manufacturer obtains a release from current employees to conduct criminal background checks. These in-depth investigations are primarily performed on employees involved in international cargo handling such as shipping, sales/marketing, import/export, logistics, finance, and personnel.

Personnel Termination Procedures

Establishing Employee Termination Procedures: Company has established employee termination procedures that are in writing. To ensure that termination procedures are consistently followed, managers/supervisors are trained on the employee termination process. A checklist is used to ensure that all access is terminated and that all Company property is retrieved. A final check will not be issued to the employee until all property is returned. Human Resource management strictly oversees this process.

Handling Involuntary Separations: Prior planning is conducted with security and key management before involuntary separations are initiated. All facility access is terminated, keys and equipment are retrieved, and the employee is escorted out of the building. A list of names and photos of terminated employees are given to security guards to aid in the access control of the facility. An information notice is issued to all employees when an employee no longer works for the Company.

Internal Code of Conduct/Employee Evaluations

Addressing Security in Code of Conduct and Employee Evaluations: The Company's Code of Conduct specifies the type of disciplinary action taken when employees violate company security. In addition, the Company includes security as part of its employees' job descriptions and annual performance reviews.

Procedural Security

Security measures must be in place to ensure the integrity of the supply chain. Regardless of a company's size, written policies are needed to achieve effective supply chain security. Procedural security requires oversight, accountability, control, and a system of checks and balances. Technology should be used to enhance all aspects of procedural security.

Identifying/Reporting/Tracking Incidents

Brokers

Maintaining Incident Database: Broker has a central "Security Incident Database" that records all incidents such as overages and shortages. Senior management monitors the database to identify trends or patterns that might reveal a potential security risk within the supply chain.

Identifying Suspicious Activity: Broker developed a list of "suspicious activity" indicators and trained employees on what to look for and how to report such activities to management and CBP.

Addressing Unexplained/Unusual Delays: Broker keeps track of inbound shipments. Unusual or unexplained delays are referred to CBP and a courtesy examination is requested.

Carriers

Establishing Written Procedures to Handle Suspicious Activities: Highway Carrier has established a written procedure to identify suspicious shipments by examining documents, observing unusual behaviors or requests, and monitoring activities at pickup locations. The procedure specifies whom to contact, up to and including CBP.

Establishing Global Reporting and Incident Response Procedures: International Logistics Provider has taken steps to globalize security procedures and reporting. The Security Department developed written policies and procedures to ensure that an efficient and reliable system is in place to report, document, and analyze incidents. The Security Department investigates serious incidents, and coordinates with management, local law enforcement, and CBP to resolve issues and improve security. The procedures are reviewed and updated by the Security Department as business practices change.

Assessing Customer Risk: Air Carrier uses a database that tracks cargo and maintains information on the status of shippers. Air Carrier's agents use an information database to determine if the freight will be accepted for processing on passenger flights. Risk indicators are built into the system to perform this analysis. After cargo information is input and a customer's name appears as a "do not load," the cargo will not be accepted. This system allows the Air Carrier to instantly pass on information about high-risk customers to CBP and other law enforcement agencies.

Brand Name/Identity Protection

Safeguarding Company Stationery: Company safeguards forms and stationery by controlling their issuance and securing them in a locked cabinet in an office where access is controlled. A designated company supervisor controls issuance of forms, and the forms are strategically numbered to detect unauthorized use. In addition, the Company's stationery bears a watermark to prevent unauthorized duplication.

Safeguarding Items Bearing Company Logo: Stamps, tape, and cartons bearing the Company's logo are controlled and their use is monitored. Stamps and tape are issued only to employees who are authorized to use them and are secured while not in use. Cartons are counted, and logos on recycled cartons must be obliterated.

Destroying Sensitive Documents: Sensitive documents are shredded when no longer needed. The Company's representative supervises a contractor to ensure that none of these documents leave the premises without being shredded.

Archiving Records: Archived records are secured in a caged area of the warehouse. The warehouse supervisor controls access to the archives and only authorized employees are permitted to enter this area.

Securing Business Documents: All business documents, including purchase orders, invoices, manifests, and customer information are kept under lock and key when the Company is not operating. Employees are required to secure documentation prior to leaving for the day.

Manifesting/Invoicing/Electronic Data Interface (EDI)

Receiving

Domestic Distribution Center

Utilizing Radio Frequency Identification (RFID): RFID technology is used by the Domestic Distribution Center to obtain "real-time" information on the flow of cargo and enables the Center to immediately address inventory discrepancies. In addition, manifest, invoice, inventory, and packing information are electronically transmitted to the Distribution Center's inventory and accounting systems for cross-checking.

Establishing Automated Import Tracking System: Company has established an in-house automated import tracking system. Once the booking is received from the consolidator, it is uploaded into the Company's tracking system. This allows the cargo to be tracked and verified within the shipping, receiving, and traffic departments. Information includes the factory name, container number, seal number, bill of lading number, estimated date of arrival, quantity, and weight of merchandise.

Restricting Access to Documentation: Limited access to Electronic Data Interchange (EDI) has enabled the Company to ensure document security and has eliminated data input duplication. The use of EDI reduces clerical errors and the opportunity to manipulate or alter data. Transactions are traced through user identification numbers.

Shipping

Consolidator

Ensuring Only Manifested Cargo Is Loaded: Consolidator ensures that only properly marked and labeled cargo is loaded. The Consolidator electronically scans each unit prior to placement in the shipping container. A cross-check is conducted in the computer system at the end of loading to ensure that only manifested cargo is shipped.

Factory/Shipper

Transmitting Advanced Information to Company: Shipper generates documents after stuffing the container and transmits all packing, invoice, container, and seal number information to its customer via Electronic Data Interchange (EDI). An e-mail containing this information also is sent to the customer confirming the details of the shipment. Once received, the customer verifies the shipment before the cargo leaves the shipper's premises.

Weighing Product: For each product, the Factory has a preestablished weight and each package is bar coded for inventory tracking. The product is weighed several times during the production and packing process. If the weight exceeds or is significantly less than the preestablished weight, the system will issue an alert prompting Factory officials to remove the product and investigate the cause of the weight variance.

Restricting Access to Cargo: After the Factory packages the goods for export, they are staged in a highly secure fenced area in the warehouse where access is restricted. At the time of container stuffing, the warehouse manager, shipping supervisor, and a security guard are present; each have backups when absent. Responsible parties must sign-off on the security "check sheet." The Factory General Manager reviews this "check sheet" daily.

Verifying Inspection, Seal, and Manifest upon Departure: Factory does not allow the truck driver to leave the factory until exit procedures are followed that include the issuance of a signed "exit pass" by the shipping department. The "exit pass" can only be signed-off by a limited number of shipping managers and must be verified by security personnel. The "exit pass" is used to verify that the container was inspected, the cargo was loaded, and that the seal and trailer numbers are correct.

Freight Forwarder

Establishing Booking and Manifesting Procedures: A detailed Standard Operating Procedure (SOP) exists between the Freight Forwarder and the Shipper in accordance with their service agreement. The SOP details how to make a booking, what personnel are authorized to make a booking, manifesting requirements, discrepancy reporting, protocol for making changes, and other essential information to ensure the accuracy and security of cargo information.

Air Carrier

Limiting Cargo Hold Time: Air Cargo Consolidator minimizes the time cargo is maintained in the warehouse by matching the schedule of delivery trucks with aircraft departure times to limit the amount of time available to tamper with cargo.

Sea Carrier

Establishing System of Checks and Balances: Sea Carrier has a system of checks and balances to ensure the accuracy of its shipping information. For example, the container number in the automated documentation system is reconciled against the container records in the equipment system, and the stowage plan is reconciled against the equipment and container records.

Packing/Packaging

Utilizing Special Packaging Material: Factory uses a special compressed packaging material that once opened, cannot be repacked.

Specialized Packaging: Factory seals each carton with tape that has the Factory's name imprinted on it. In addition, each pallet is color-coded shrink wrapped, stamped with the Company's seal (that is controlled by the shipping manager), and labeled with the Factory's and Consignee's names. The label is clearly visible from a distance and also contains a barcode with packing and shipping information that is readable using a handheld barcode scanner. Barcode scanners may only be used by authorized personnel and are stored in a secure location when not in use.

Factory

Unique Shipping Mark: A unique shipping mark is generated for each purchase order that gives the shipper, logistics provider, and consignee the ability to verify that each shipment is legitimate. The shipping mark serves as an additional safeguard to ensure that no unauthorized cargo has been introduced into the shipment. If a carton has an incorrect or missing shipping mark, it is rejected and immediately investigated. The same shipping mark is never used twice.

Employing Anonymous Observers: Company employs "anonymous" observers who are considered regular employees in the packing and shipping departments.

The immediate supervisors of these employees are unaware that they report directly to company executive management.

Conducting Random Inspections: Factory conducts random documented examinations of cartons prior to palletizing. After cartons are examined, they are stamped with an "EXAMINATION" stamp, and resealed with tape bearing the Factory's logo. The cartons are then palletized and shrink wrapped.

Cargo Discrepancies

Bar Coding and Scanning to Reduce Cargo Discrepancies: Company utilizes a bar code/scan and pack system. This system allows overseas vendors to electronically transmit shipping information including packing list data to the Company's distribution center. The barcode system ensures product accountability from the time of packing until its delivery to the distribution center in the United States. This system has reduced the number of quantity discrepancies experienced by the Company's distribution center.

Weighing Contents: Factory uses a computerized line production system that generates an itemized record of the contents of each box. The weight of each item is recorded and transmitted to the distribution center in the United States. Each carton's weight is checked at various stages throughout the supply chain. Weight discrepancies are flagged by the system and investigated.

Preventing Collusion

Rotating Dispatchers and Customer Assignments: Each dispatcher is assigned a specific set of customers so that he or she can become familiar with customer and cargo movements to identify anomalies. Assignments are periodically rotated to prevent collusion.

Rotating Shipping/Receiving Personnel: Factory periodically rotates shipping, receiving, and inventory management personnel in order to prevent collusion.

Security Training/Threat Awareness/Outreach

The tragic events of September 11, 2001 and other terrorist acts were well planned, organized, and carried out by individuals or groups. Some of the precursors include conducting surveillance, eliciting information, testing security, obtaining supplies, conducting trial runs, and deploying assets/getting into position. A threat awareness program should be established and maintained by security personnel to recognize and foster awareness of a threat posed by terrorists at each point of the supply chain. Additional training should be provided to employees in the shipping and receiving areas, as well as those receiving and opening mail.

Awareness

Initial and Periodic Training: Company has integrated security training into its new employee orientation, and periodic refresher training is given to existing employees.

Using Alert Levels: Company provides employees with information received from government alerts to ensure that they are aware of the current security alerts. Company then adjusts its alert levels to coincide with those of Homeland Security.

Communicating Terrorism Information to Employees: Company created a terrorism information bulletin board where its employees can view photographs of terrorists and the latest information on terrorist activities throughout the world.

Training Video: Terminal Operator has created a training video that illustrates the techniques used to breach containers. This video has raised security awareness throughout the trade community.

Online Security Courses: Sea Carrier has a mandatory security awareness program for its employees and has developed a course on how to recognize internal conspiracies, maintain cargo integrity, and spot unauthorized facility access. This training consists of a series of online courses where the employees' enrollment and completion are recorded. The Carrier's security department ensures that all employees complete this course and generates a report that details the completion status of every employee.

Intranet and Company Magazine: Highway Carrier has established a formal security-training course and has set-up its own intranet "University" to train drivers on theft, security, and terrorism issues. Company also publishes a magazine to address new policies and security requirements, as well as commend employees for positive work contributions. All training is documented by department supervisors and is periodically reviewed to ensure that all employees have been trained.

Continuing Education: Highway Carrier management keeps abreast of the latest cargo security procedures and technology by reading periodicals and attending security conferences. Information acquired is passed on to employees to keep them up-to-date on global security issues. A system of accountability ensures that information is passed on to employees.

Specialized Training

Training in Areas of Specialty: Employees must complete mandatory training courses that focus on their area of specialty. Training coincides with changes within the global supply chain, including trade lanes used. Company requires all employees to take antiterrorism courses. Attendance is documented in an automated system to facilitate supervisory reviews and identify employees who have not been trained.

Product Tampering, Collusion, Loss Prevention, Handling Breaches: All employees at the Company's foreign factories, shippers, and service providers have been provided with seminars on such subjects as product tampering and smuggling, methods to prevent and detect collusion, the importance of loss prevention policies, effective response techniques, and how to report and handle security breaches.

Conducting Background Investigations: Employees in the Human Resource Management Office receive specialized training on how to conduct employment, reference, driving record, education verifications, and criminal background investigations. In addition, specialized training is given to human resource employees on how to spot fraudulent documents, verify work eligibility, and investigate gaps in employment. They also are trained on techniques to elicit information from applicants without appearing invasive or rude.

Segregating and Reporting Suspicious Containers: Company has trained its personnel to profile container appearance and conditions. If anything suspicious is detected, the container must be segregated into a designated "safe and secure" area. A reporting procedure is in place to contact company management, local law enforcement, and CBP when anomalies are identified.

Conducting 14-Point Trailer and Conveyance Inspections: Highway Carrier has trained all drivers in a 14-point conveyance and trailer/container inspection. Drivers are trained to document inspections and immediately report discrepancies and anomalies to company management, local law enforcement, or CBP, as appropriate.

Highway Watch: Highway Carrier requires every driver to participate in the Highway Watch security orientation and training sponsored by the Department of Transportation and Department of Homeland Security. Highway Watch trains drivers to identify and report suspicious activities while on the highway.

Utilizing External Resources: Highway Carrier invites a private security representative to attend monthly meetings with drivers. The security representative briefs drivers on the latest schemes used by smugglers and how to avoid getting involved with suspicious people and companies.

Security Guards: Security Guards are professionally trained to immediately identify, confront, and report any situations of unauthorized access or other unusual activities; perform patrols; use self-defense techniques; and exercise emergency/crisis management. Specialized training includes: CCTV monitoring techniques, non-lethal weapons training, and methods terrorists use to infiltrate legitimate businesses. Guards are required to receive periodic specialized training to maintain their state issued "Guard Card." The Chief of Security oversees the training, education, and awareness for the facility's guards.

Dual-Use Awareness: Chemical Factory formally trains its sales representatives, drivers, and shipping personnel to identify terrorist threats. This training covers indicators of suspicious activities such as large orders of chemicals by unknown customers or unusual requests by known customers.

Outreach

Collaborating with Local Law Enforcement: Company works closely with local law enforcement and other businesses to maintain an awareness of criminal activities.

Training Business Partners: Foreign manufacturers, suppliers, and service providers are given formal onsite supply chain security training sponsored by the U.S. Company to ensure that supply chain security expectations are fully understood and met. This training is documented and participants are tested to ensure their understanding of the information taught.

Translating Training into Multiple Languages: International Logistics Provider has published its security policies and procedures on the intranet. Security policies and procedures have been translated into several languages. A computer-based reference library allows immediate access to corporate policies and procedures concerning security. In addition, employees are given periodic security training via the intranet. Supervisors are required to review and follow-up if necessary. Some training focuses on "general security awareness" while other training is specifically tailored to key areas such as container and transportation security.

Receiving Updates from Association: Highway Carrier receives continual security updates from its association and provides information to its drivers regarding hazards and security risks.

Employee Incentives

Providing Incentives: Company has incorporated security into its "Business Improvement" incentive program. Employees are given incentives for reporting security anomalies and recommending ways to improve the Company's security.

Incident Reporting

Establishing a Hotline: Company implemented a 24/7 anonymous "hotline" that is available to all employees and vendors (globally) to report suspicious or criminal conduct within the organization, as well as questionable business ethics.

Outsourcing Hotline: The Company's incident reporting hotline is outsourced to a third party so employees are assured of anonymity. In addition, there are posters displayed throughout the facility and handouts regarding reporting procedures that are distributed to employees.

Issuing Emergency Contact Information: Highway Carrier has given each driver a card that lists Company emergency contact phone numbers, including the CBP FAST Office, and the CBP hotline 1-800-BE-ALERT.

Issuing Business Integrity Cards: Company issues business integrity cards to all associates worldwide. The cards provide contact information and instructions for employees to discreetly report suspicious activities and security violations to the corporate security staff and terrorist threats to CBP via 1-800-BE-ALERT.

Physical Security

The physical security of a facility is its first line of defense from intruders. In particular, cargo handling and storage facilities in domestic and foreign locations must have physical barriers and deterrents that guard against unauthorized access.

Fencing/Gates/Gate Houses

Secure Loading: The factory has a caged area that encloses the top and side of the truck in order to restrict access to the truck during loading. The caged area is locked when not in use. Signs posted stating "restricted access" are placed on the fence, and a guard is present to ensure that no unauthorized people approach the truck as it is being loaded.

Magnetic Sensors: The fence surrounding the cargo handling and storage area is equipped with magnetic sensors that are activated if pressure is applied.

Controlling Gate Access: Company issues a time-controlled exit card for departing truckers to ensure compliance with loading and unloading intervals.

Utilizing Technology to Monitor Gates: Company's foreign facilities have electronic gates, perimeter fences with infrared and magnetic sensors, motion detectors, and alarms.

Security Guards

Equipping Security Guards with Adequate Resources and Orders: Guards are given appropriate uniforms and equipment for their work environment (e.g., communication devices with appropriate range, self-defense gear, search equipment, etc.). Post orders/standard operating procedures exist, are periodically updated, and are clearly defined. Guards have a clear understanding of the organization, receive site-specific training, and are familiar with the facility's physical layout, security features, and vulnerabilities. Security Guards are periodically rotated to prevent collusion and predictability.

Procedures for Selecting Contracted Security Guard Services: A comprehensive plan exists when selecting contracted security guard services. The plan includes evaluating the service provider's selection, training, and supervision of the guards.

Supervising Contracted Security Guards: A Company manager has overall responsibility and supervision for both Company and contracted security guard services, including review of guards' performance, daily patrol logs, and adherence to post orders and patrol schedules.

Ensuring Shift Coverage and Accountability: Guards' shifts overlap to provide a briefing period; periodic meetings are held with guards to discuss facility security and alerts. Company management conducts routine verifications of guards' performance on all shifts.

Establishing Patrols: Company has a system that is based on random checkpoints. It establishes critical checkpoints throughout the facility. Security personnel are given several different routes that change randomly. This system helps to decrease guards' predictability.

Preparing and Reviewing Reports: Company's security guards prepare security reports on all three shifts. The reports include the name of the security officer on duty, hours worked, areas patrolled, and the time areas were patrolled. The report also includes unusual incidents that do not appear to be suspicious on the surface (e.g., company truck broke down, driver had to take to shop). The Security Director reviews all security reports and uses them to identify security breaches or other unusual events that may be a precursor to a security incident.

Parking

Procedures for Issuing Parking: Employees have decals on their cars to determine which vehicles belong to employees. Employees must obtain a temporary parking pass if they do not have their decal. Company maintains a list of all decals issued, including decal number, employee name, department, vehicle make and model, department, etc. Lost or stolen decals must be reported.

Locking Mechanisms

Changing Locks: Keys are only issued to individuals who have a need to access the facility or designated area. Issuance of keys is recorded and controlled. If an employee no longer works in a particular area, his or her key is retrieved. If a key is lost, misplaced or stolen, it must be reported immediately and the lock is changed. Periodic inventory of keys is conducted to ensure none have been lost or misplaced.

Lighting

Verifying Functionality of Lighting: Company has a procedure to immediately replace lights that burn out. Company conducted a survey of the facility's interior and exterior lighting to ensure uniformity and appropriate brightness for the facility's size and operations. Company has designated personnel who routinely visit the facility at night to identify which areas an intruder would attempt to enter. Company also consulted with the local police department on appropriate facility lighting.

Alarm Systems

Configuring Alarms: Alarm zones were carefully configured to maximize their effectiveness. Company identified areas of greatest traffic, vulnerability, and use, and worked with security specialists to select an appropriate alarm system. Company's alarm system is equipped with a cell phone backup.

Utilizing Long Range Sensors: The cargo warehouse is protected with an alarm system that is equipped with several sets of long-range infrared sensors. A set of infrared sensors includes both functional and redundant sensors to ensure a backup in case of failure.

Assigning Individual Deactivation Codes: Codes to deactivate the building's alarm system are individually assigned and restricted to those with a need to have access to the building. Company management keeps track of the assigned codes. Company will periodically review reports to identify patterns of unusual access and immediately deactivate codes when an employee is terminated.

Monitoring Exits: All exits from the facility are equipped with an alarm system that is monitored. If the doors are opened without proper card key access or propped open for a period of time, an alarm will sound and the guards will immediately respond.

Video Surveillance Cameras

Storing Recordings: Video surveillance recordings are maintained for a minimum of 30 days and are stored in a secure location with restricted access. Management periodically reviews the recordings.

Maximizing Recording: The digital video surveillance cameras adjust to night lighting, are motion activated, and record high quality images to ensure their usefulness when conducting investigations.

Detecting Intruders: Terminal Operator has a digital video surveillance system that will record anyone who attempts to access a restricted area. The video surveillance system will capture the intruder's image and send it to the security database for immediate response by the guard. The system is equipped with cameras that will record intruders as they set off an alarm or as they move through the area.

Monitoring, Maintaining, and Upgrading System: Port has a surveillance camera system that is staffed 24/7 by security officers. The system features high resolution of key areas so that potential breaches can be identified and recorded with great clarity. All images are projected on wall mounted plasma screens and the camera control panels are situated in conjunction with the communications and dispatch system. This comprehensive system ensures problems are handled expeditiously and efficiently. The system is continually upgraded and expanded. Fiber-optic capability and motion detectors are deployed throughout the Port.

Remote Monitoring: Company senior managers have remote Internet access capability to view recorded activity captured on the video surveillance camera system. In addition, Company also provides the local police department with this capability.

Strategic Placement: Company has several video surveillance security cameras strategically located throughout the facility, including at the loading docks, cargo handling/storage areas, and at facility entrances and exits. These cameras have telescopic and night vision capability. Some exterior cameras have the capability to scan the entire property. Security personnel and company management monitor the cameras.

Information Technology Security—Computer Systems

Access Restrictions (Internal)

Changing Passwords: Individual passwords are used which consist of a combination of letters, numbers, and symbols that cannot be personal identifiers. Passwords must be changed at least every 90 days, cannot be reused, and are deactivated if the password is not changed. An alert message is generated a predetermined number of days before the password expires.

System Lock Out: All users have a login code, station number, and password to access the system. After three unsuccessful attempts to login, the user is locked out of the system and the IT administrator, with the authorization of the user's supervisor, must reinstate the user's access to the system.

Monitoring and Limiting Internet Access: Company limits the number of employees who can access the Internet and requires that they sign an agreement that outlines system security requirements and site access restrictions when using the Internet. Company has software to track Internet usage and is able to identify abuse.

Establishing and Reviewing Access Levels: Levels of access to the computer system are assigned by job category and established by the corporate office. Access levels are reviewed when there is a job change within the organization. In addition, management periodically evaluates access levels of current users and will change access levels as job responsibilities change.

Temporary Access Suspension: During an employee's extended absence (e.g., disability), access to the information system is suspended until the employee's return.

Viruses/Firewalls/Tampering Prevention (External)

Maintaining System Integrity: Company's IT system contains multilevel safeguards, allowing the system to both log and detect viruses, security violations, and tampering. This system allows the IT department to identify weaknesses and initiate efforts to safeguard the Company's IT systems worldwide.

Educating Employees on System Vulnerabilities: IT personnel maintain a constant awareness of cyber attacks and counterattacks that are occurring with automated systems throughout many industries to ensure the Company's system is protected from a breach. Alerts are given to system users to prevent virus attacks and improper release of information.

Utilizes Data Encryption: Wireless communication devices use state-of-the art data encryption technology to prevent unauthorized system access.

Virus Quarantine Software: Company has a "virus quarantine" software program to view file content, origin, and type of virus without infecting the rest of the system.

Securing Remote Access: Company implemented a Virtual Private Network (VPN) for users to communicate within the Company. Each employee that has access to the VPN is issued an access card and unique PIN number. The access card has a random sequence of numbers that changes every minute in order to protect the system from unauthorized access.

Testing System Security: Company contracted a reputable, highly qualified, thoroughly screened service provider to hack its computer system in order to identify vulnerabilities and weaknesses.

Policies/Procedures/Management Support/Training

Comprehensive Approach to IT Security: Company regularly holds meetings that are attended by senior management to address information technology issues, including system security. Company has conducted a thorough analysis of system vulnerabilities, developed a data recovery plan; routinely identifies and responds to virus threats with the most up-to-date anti-virus software, and trains employees in information system security principles and data integrity. The IT security policy is fully documented and addresses access controls and system protection. Updates are communicated to employees. Employees are required to take a basic security awareness course for IT. Company fully supports the continuing education of its IT workers and gives them the opportunity to attend specialized training and conferences to keep up-to-date on information technology security.

Data Back-Ups and Recovery Plans

Contingency Planning: Company has a contingency plan to protect its IT systems, which include a full IT disaster recovery plan to prepare for any unforeseen incidents. It also utilizes Uninterruptible Power Supplies (UPS) for power surges/failure.

Data Storage: Company conducts system back-ups daily that are stored in a safe that is fireproof and only accessible to the IT Manager and senior company executives. Additional back-ups are stored off-site weekly with a bonded company.

Hardware Security

Controlling Workstation: Employees are required to swipe their ID cards and enter their passwords before they can use their workstation.

Securing Server: System server is stored in a fireproof locked room where access is restricted and tracked.

Password Protected Screen Savers: Employees are required to use password-protected screensavers on their workstations. Screensavers must be activated when employees leave their workstations. Screensavers are automatically activated within a specific period of time when there is no activity at the workstation.

Emergency Preparedness/Disaster Recovery

Emergency Generators: Factory has a disaster recovery plan that includes an emergency generator for back-up power to ensure that security systems continue to work.

Disaster Plan: Company has a disaster plan to ensure the continuity of its operations in the event of a man-made or natural disaster. The plan includes mock-disaster exercises to ensure that employees are well prepared and the plan is kept up-to-date as organizational changes occur.

Building Evacuations: In the event of a building evacuation, a plan has been established whereby security personnel and management are assigned by section to account for employees and visitors and conduct an "area sweep" of work locations and restrooms to ensure that all areas are secured in the event that the alarm was falsely initiated. Security also verifies that all computers are logged-out or password protected screensavers have been activated.

Alert Levels: Company developed a threat level response system consisting of three tiers. Each threat level (low, medium, and high) has a specific set of security measures. Threat levels are communicated to staff by management so that all personnel can respond accordingly.

Supply Chain Continuity Plan: Company developed a "Supply Chain Continuity Plan" which consists of policies and procedures to handle a variety of disasters or a terrorist incident; identify the potential impact of a disaster/terrorist incident on supply chain security; conduct mock incident exercises to ensure staff preparedness; and collaborate with government entities, supply chain partners, and industry colleagues.

Program Memberships/Certifications to Enhance Supply Chain Security

Government/Industry Partnership: Company is a member of a foreign government's industry supply chain security partnership program.

Associations: Company is actively involved in promoting supply chain security through its professional association and has encouraged others in the industry to become actively engaged.

Business Certifications: Company has business certifications that support and enhance supply chain security efforts.

U.S. Customs and Border Protection

Office of Field Operations/C-TPAT
Room 5.4C
1300 Pennsylvania Avenue, NW
Washington, DC 20229
www.cbp.gov

Appendix C: Foreign Corrupt Practices Act Antibribery Provisions

Documentation for importers is the backbone of regulatory compliance. This appendix provides a crucial outline of all necessary import documentation, particularly the commercial invoice, which is a cornerstone of all commercial transactions in global trade.

United States Department of Justice

Fraud Section, Criminal Division
10th & Constitution Avenue, NW
Bond Building
Washington, D.C. 20530
phone: (202) 514-7023
fax: (202) 514-7021
internet: www.usdoj.gov
e-mail: FCPA.fraud@usdoj.gov

United States Department of Commerce

Office of the Chief Counsel for International Commerce
14th Street and Constitution Avenue, NW
Room 5882
Washington, D.C. 20230
phone: (202) 482-0937
fax: (202) 482-4076
internet: www.ita.doc.gov/legal

Introduction

The 1988 Trade Act directed the Attorney General to provide guidance concerning the Department of Justice's enforcement policy with respect to the Foreign Corrupt Practices Act of 1977 ("FCPA"), 15 U.S.C. §§ 78dd-1, *et seq.*, to potential exporters and small businesses that are unable to obtain specialized counsel on issues related to the FCPA. The guidance is limited to responses to requests under the Department of Justice's Foreign Corrupt Practices Act Opinion Procedure and to general explanations of compliance responsibilities and potential liabilities under the FCPA. This text constitutes the Department of Justice's general explanation of the FCPA.

U.S. firms seeking to do business in foreign markets must be familiar with the FCPA. In general, the FCPA prohibits corrupt payments to foreign officials for the purpose of obtaining or keeping business. The Department of Justice is the chief enforcement agency, with a coordinate role played by the Securities and Exchange Commission (SEC). The Office of General Counsel of the Department of Commerce also answers general questions from U.S. exporters concerning the FCPA's basic requirements and constraints.

This text is intended to provide a general description of the FCPA and is not intended to substitute for the advice of private counsel on specific issues related to the FCPA. Moreover, this material is not intended to set forth the present enforcement intentions of the Department of Justice or the SEC with respect to particular fact situations.

Background

As a result of SEC investigations in the mid-1970's, over 400 U.S. companies admitted making questionable or illegal payments in excess of $300 million to foreign government officials, politicians, and political parties. The abuses ran the gamut from bribery of high foreign officials to secure some type of favorable action by a foreign government to so-called facilitating payments that allegedly were made to ensure that government functionaries discharged certain ministerial or clerical duties. Congress enacted the FCPA to bring a halt to the bribery of foreign officials and to restore public confidence in the integrity of the American business system.

The FCPA was intended to have and has had an enormous impact on the way American firms do business. Several firms that paid bribes to foreign officials have been the subject of criminal and civil enforcement actions, resulting in large fines and suspension and debarment from federal procurement contracting, and their employees and officers have gone to jail. To avoid such consequences, many firms have implemented detailed compliance programs intended to prevent and to detect any improper payments by employees and agents.

Following the passage of the FCPA, the Congress became concerned that American companies were operating at a disadvantage compared to foreign companies who routinely paid bribes and, in some countries, were permitted to deduct the cost of such bribes as business expenses on their taxes. Accordingly, in 1988, the Congress directed the Executive Branch to commence negotiations in the Organization of Economic Cooperation and Development (OECD) to obtain the agreement of the United States' major trading partners to enact legislation similar to the FCPA. In 1997, almost ten years later, the United States and thirty-three other countries signed the OECD Convention on Combating Bribery of Foreign Public Officials in International Business Transactions. The United States ratified this Convention and enacted implementing legislation in 1998. See Convention and Commentaries on the DOJ Web site.

The antibribery provisions of the FCPA make it unlawful for a U.S. person, and certain foreign issuers of securities, to make a corrupt payment to a foreign official for the purpose of obtaining or retaining business for or with, or directing business to, any person. Since 1998, they also apply to foreign firms and persons who take any act in furtherance of such a corrupt payment while in the United States.

The FCPA also requires companies whose securities are listed in the United States to meet its accounting provisions. See 15 U.S.C. § 78m. These accounting provisions, which were designed to operate in tandem with the antibribery provisions of the FCPA, require corporations covered by the provisions to make and keep books and records that accurately and fairly reflect the transactions of the corporation and to devise and maintain an adequate system of internal accounting controls. This material discusses only the antibribery provisions.

Enforcement

The Department of Justice is responsible for all criminal enforcement and for civil enforcement of the antibribery provisions with respect to domestic concerns and foreign companies and nationals. The SEC is responsible for civil enforcement of the antibribery provisions with respect to issuers.

Antibribery Provisions

Basic Prohibition

The FCPA makes it unlawful to bribe foreign government officials to obtain or retain business. With respect to the basic prohibition, there are five elements that must be met to constitute a violation of the Act:

  A. Who — The FCPA potentially applies to *any* individual, firm, officer, director, employee, or agent of a firm and any stockholder acting on behalf of a firm. Individuals and firms may also be penalized if they order, authorize, or assist someone else to violate the antibribery provisions or if they conspire to violate those provisions.

Under the FCPA, U.S. jurisdiction over corrupt payments to foreign officials depends upon whether the violator is an "issuer," a "domestic concern," or a foreign national or business.

An "issuer" is a corporation that has issued securities that have been registered in the United States or who is required to file periodic reports with the SEC. A "domestic concern" is any individual who is a citizen, national, or resident of the United States, or any corporation, partnership, association, joint-stock company, business trust, unincorporated organization, or sole proprietorship that has its principal place of business in the United States, or that is organized under the laws of a State of the United States, or a territory, possession, or commonwealth of the United States.

Issuers and domestic concerns may be held liable under the FCPA under *either* territorial or nationality jurisdiction principles. For acts taken within the territory of the United States, issuers and domestic concerns are liable if they take an act in furtherance of a corrupt payment to a foreign official using the U.S. mails or other means or instrumentalities of interstate commerce. Such means or instrumentalities include telephone calls, facsimile transmissions, wire transfers, and interstate or international travel. In addition, issuers and domestic concerns may be held liable for any act in furtherance of a corrupt payment taken *outside* the United States. Thus, a U.S. company or national may be held liable for a corrupt payment authorized by employees or agents operating entirely outside the United States, using money from foreign bank accounts, and without any involvement by personnel located within the United States.

Prior to 1998, foreign companies, with the exception of those who qualified as "issuers," and foreign nationals were not covered by the FCPA. The 1998 amendments expanded the FCPA to assert territorial jurisdiction over foreign companies and nationals. A foreign company or person is now subject to the FCPA if it causes, directly or through agents, an act in furtherance of the corrupt payment to take place within the territory of the United States. There is, however, no requirement that such act make use of the U.S. mails or other means or instrumentalities of interstate commerce.

Finally, U.S. parent corporations may be held liable for the acts of foreign subsidiaries where they authorized, directed, or controlled the activity in question, as can U.S. citizens or residents, themselves "domestic concerns," who were employed by or acting on behalf of such foreign-incorporated subsidiaries.

B. Corrupt Intent — The person making or authorizing the payment must have a corrupt intent, and the payment must be intended to induce the recipient to misuse his or her official position to direct business wrongfully to the payer or to any other person. You should note that the FCPA does not require that a corrupt act *succeed* in its purpose. The *offer* or *promise* of a corrupt payment can constitute a violation of the statute. The FCPA prohibits any corrupt payment intended to *influence* any act or decision of a foreign official in his or her official capacity, to induce the official to do or omit to do any act in violation of his or her lawful duty, to *obtain* any improper advantage, or to *induce* a foreign official to use his or her influence improperly to affect or influence any act or decision.

C. Payment — The FCPA prohibits paying, offering, promising to pay (or authorizing to pay or offer) money or anything of value.

D. Recipient — The prohibition extends only to corrupt payments to a *foreign official, a foreign political party or party official*, or any candidate for foreign political office. A "foreign official" means any officer or employee of a foreign government, a public international organization, or any department or agency thereof, or any person acting in an official capacity. You should consider utilizing the Department of Justice's Foreign Corrupt Practices Act Opinion Procedure for particular questions as to the definition of a "foreign official," such as whether a member of a royal family, a member of a legislative body, or an official of a state-owned business enterprise would be considered a "foreign official."

The FCPA applies to payments to *any* public official, regardless of rank or position. The FCPA focuses on the *purpose* of the payment instead of the particular duties of the official receiving the payment, offer, or promise of payment, and there are exceptions to the antibribery provision for "facilitating payments for routine governmental action" (see below).

E. Business Purpose Test — The FCPA prohibits payments made in order to assist the firm in *obtaining* or *retaining business* for or with, or *directing business* to, any person. The Department of Justice interprets "obtaining or retaining business" broadly, such that the term encompasses more than the mere award or renewal of a contract. It should be noted that the business to be obtained or retained does *not* need to be with a foreign government or foreign government instrumentality.

Third Party Payments

The FCPA prohibits corrupt payments through intermediaries. It is unlawful to make a payment to a third party, while knowing that all or a portion of the payment will go directly or indirectly to a foreign official. *The term "knowing" includes conscious disregard and deliberate ignorance.* The elements of an offense are essentially the same as described above, except that in this case the "recipient" is the intermediary who is making the payment to the requisite "foreign official."

Intermediaries may include joint venture partners or agents. To avoid being held liable for corrupt third party payments, U.S. companies are encouraged to exercise due diligence and to take all necessary precautions to ensure that they have formed a business relationship with reputable and qualified partners and representatives. Such due diligence may include investigating potential foreign representatives and joint venture partners to determine if they are in fact qualified for the position, whether they have personal or professional ties to the government, the number and reputation of their clientele, and their reputation with the U.S. Embassy or Consulate and with local bankers, clients, and other business associates. In addition, in negotiating a business relationship, the U.S. firm should be aware of so-called "red flags," *i.e.*, unusual payment patterns or financial arrangements, a history of corruption in the country, a refusal by the foreign joint venture partner or representative to provide a certification that it will not take any action in furtherance of an unlawful offer, promise, or payment to a foreign public official and not take any act that would cause the U.S. firm to be in violation of the FCPA, unusually high commissions, lack of transparency in expenses and accounting records, apparent lack of qualifications or resources on the part of the joint venture partner or representative to perform the services offered, and whether the joint venture partner or representative has been recommended by an official of the potential governmental customer.

You should seek the advice of counsel and consider utilizing the Department of Justice's Foreign Corrupt Practices Act Opinion Procedure for particular questions relating to third party payments.

Permissible Payments and Affirmative Defenses

The FCPA contains an explicit exception to the bribery prohibition for "facilitating payments" for "routine governmental action" and provides affirmative defenses that can be used to defend against alleged violations of the FCPA.

Facilitating Payments for Routine Governmental Actions

There is an exception to the antibribery prohibition for payments to facilitate or expedite performance of a "routine governmental action." The statute lists the following examples: obtaining permits, licenses, or other official documents; processing governmental papers, such as visas and work orders; providing police protection, mail pick-up and delivery; providing phone service, power and water supply, loading and unloading cargo, or protecting perishable products; and scheduling inspections associated with contract performance or transit of goods across country.

Actions "similar" to these are also covered by this exception. If you have a question about whether a payment falls within the exception, you should consult with counsel. You should also consider whether to utilize the Justice Department's Foreign Corrupt Practices Opinion Procedure.

"Routine governmental action" does *not* include any decision by a foreign official to award new business or to continue business with a particular party.

Affirmative Defenses

A person charged with a violation of the FCPA's antibribery provisions may assert as a defense that the payment was lawful under the written laws of the foreign country or that the money was spent as part of demonstrating a product or performing a contractual obligation.

Whether a payment was lawful under the written laws of the foreign country may be difficult to determine. You should consider seeking the advice of counsel or utilizing the Department of Justice's Foreign Corrupt Practices Act Opinion Procedure when faced with an issue of the legality of such a payment.

Moreover, because these defenses are "affirmative defenses," the defendant is required to show in the first instance that the payment met these requirements. The prosecution does not bear the burden of demonstrating in the first instance that the payments did not constitute this type of payment.

Sanctions against Bribery

Criminal

The following criminal penalties may be imposed for violations of the FCPA's antibribery provisions: corporations and other business entities are subject to a fine of up to $2,000,000; officers, directors, stockholders, employees, and agents are subject to a fine of up to $100,000 and imprisonment for up to five years. Moreover, under the Alternative Fines Act, these fines may actually be higher—the actual fine may be up to twice the benefit that the defendant sought to obtain by making the corrupt payment. You should also be aware that fines imposed on individuals may *not* be paid by their employer or principal.

Civil

The Attorney General or the SEC, as appropriate, may bring a civil action for a fine of up to $10,000 against any firm *as well as* any officer, director, employee, or agent of a firm, or stockholder acting on behalf of the firm, who violates the antibribery provisions. In addition, in an SEC enforcement action, the court may impose an additional fine not to exceed the greater of (i) the gross amount of the pecuniary gain to the defendant as a result of the violation, or (ii) a specified dollar limitation. The specified dollar limitations are based on the egregiousness of the violation, ranging from $5,000 to $100,000 for a natural person and $50,000 to $500,000 for any other person.

The Attorney General or the SEC, as appropriate, may also bring a civil action to enjoin any act or practice of a firm whenever it appears that the firm (or an officer, director, employee, agent, or stockholder acting on behalf of the firm) is in violation (or about to be) of the antibribery provisions.

Other Governmental Action

Under guidelines issued by the Office of Management and Budget, a person or firm found in violation of the FCPA may be barred from doing business with the Federal government. *Indictment alone can lead to suspension of the right to do business with the government.* The President has directed that no executive agency shall allow any party to participate in any procurement or nonprocurement activity if any agency has debarred, suspended, or otherwise excluded that party from participation in a procurement or nonprocurement activity.

In addition, a person or firm found guilty of violating the FCPA may be ruled ineligible to receive export licenses; the SEC may suspend or bar persons from the securities business and impose civil penalties on persons in the securities business for violations of the FCPA; the Commodity Futures Trading Commission and the Overseas Private Investment Corporation both provide for possible suspension or debarment from agency programs for violation of the FCPA; and a payment made to a foreign government official that is unlawful under the FCPA cannot be deducted under the tax laws as a business expense.

Private Cause of Action

Conduct that violates the antibribery provisions of the FCPA may also give rise to a private cause of action for treble damages under the Racketeer Influenced and Corrupt Organizations Act (RICO), or to actions under other federal or state laws. For example, an action might be brought under RICO by a competitor who alleges that the bribery caused the defendant to win a foreign contract.

Guidance from the Government

The Department of Justice has established a Foreign Corrupt Practices Act Opinion Procedure by which any U.S. company or national may request a statement of the Justice Department's present enforcement intentions under the antibribery provisions of the FCPA regarding any proposed business conduct. The details of the opinion procedure may be found at 28 CFR Part 80. Under this procedure, the Attorney General will issue an opinion in response to a specific inquiry from a person or firm within thirty days of the request. (The thirty-day period does not run until the Department of Justice has received all the information it requires to issue the opinion.) Conduct for which the Department of Justice has issued an opinion stating that the conduct conforms with current enforcement policy will be entitled to a presumption, in any subsequent enforcement action, of conformity with the FCPA. Copies of releases issued regarding previous opinions are available on the Department of Justice's FCPA web site.

For further information from the Department of Justice about the FCPA and the Foreign Corrupt Practices Act Opinion Procedure, contact the Fraud Section, Criminal Division, U.S. Department of Justice,

ATTN: FCPA Coordinator
Bond Building, 4th Floor
10th and Constitution Ave. NW
Washington, DC 20530-0001
(202) 514-7023.

Although the Department of Commerce has no enforcement role with respect to the FCPA, it supplies general guidance to U.S. exporters who have questions about the FCPA and about international developments concerning the FCPA. For further information from the Department of Commerce about the FCPA contact Eleanor Roberts Lewis, Chief Counsel for International Commerce, or Arthur Aronoff, Senior Counsel, Office of the Chief Counsel for International Commerce, U.S. Department of Commerce, Room 5882, 14th Street and Constitution Avenue, N.W., Washington, D.C. 20230, (202) 482-0937.

Appendix D: INCO Terms 2000

Incoterms make international trade easier and help traders in different countries understand each another. These standard trade definitions that are most commonly used in international contracts are protected by ICC copyright.

Correct use of Incoterms goes a long way to providing the legal certainty upon which mutual confidence between business partners must be based. To be sure of using them correctly, trade practitioners need to consult the full ICC texts, and to beware of the many unauthorized summaries and approximate versions that abound on the Web.

Why Incoterms?
Incoterms are international rules that are accepted by governments, legal authorities, and practitioners worldwide for the interpretation of the most commonly used terms in international trade. They either reduce or remove altogether uncertainties arising from differing interpretations of such terms in different countries.

What do they cover?
The scope of Incoterms is limited to matters relating to the rights and obligations of the parties to the contract of sale with respect to the delivery of goods sold, but excluding "intangibles" like computer software.

Why do Incoterms need revising periodically?
As the guardian and originator of Incoterms, ICC has a responsibility to consult regularly all parties interested in international trade to keep Incoterms relevant, efficient, and up-to-date. It is also translated into 31 languages. This is a long and costly process for ICC, which is a non-governmental, self-financed organization. The work is financed out of sales of Incoterms 2000 and related publications, which are protected by copyright.

What are the 13 Incoterms?

Each Incoterm is referred to by a three-letter abbreviation. Here is a complete list, with the meanings spelled out.

The Preambles to Incoterms 2000 do not spell out the obligations of buyer and seller, which are essential to correct use of Incoterms. This information may be obtained by consulting the full published texts of the 13 Incoterms, available only from ICC Publishing.

EXW EX WORKS (...named place)
FCA FREE CARRIER (...named place)
FAS FREE ALONGSIDE SHIP (...named port of shipment)
FOB FREE ON BOARD (...named port of shipment)
CFR COST AND FREIGHT (...named port of destination)
CIF COST, INSURANCE AND FREIGHT (...named port of destination)
CPT CARRIAGE PAID TO (...named place of destination)
CIP CARRIAGE AND INSURANCE PAID TO (...named place of destination)
DAF DELIVERED AT FRONTIER (...named place)
DES DELIVERED EX SHIP (...named port of destination)
DEQ DELIVERED EX QUAY (...named port of destination)
DDU DELIVERED DUTY UNPAID (...named place of destination)
DDP DELIVERED DUTY PAID (...named place of destination)

Appendix E: Sample Documentation for an Export and Import Shipment

In order of appearance:
Example 1
- – Freight quotation request
- – Commercial invoice
- – Packing list
- – Airway bill of lading
- – Certificate of conformity
- – AES transmission copy

Example 2
- – AES transmission copy
- – Ocean freight bill of lading
- – Commercial invoice
- – Packing list

Kelly's Kreatures
19 Benjamin Avenue
East Moriches, NY 11940
516-236-5716

To: Roe
From: Kelly
Date: 11/13/08
Re: Quote to UK

Ro,

Please provide our office with a quotation for 2 boxes (22x23x25) 300 lbs for air export from JFK to London.

No special handling instructions, the freight should be ready for pickup tomorrow.

Thanks,
Kelly

Kelly's Kreatures
19 Benjamin Avenue
East Moriches, NY 11940
516-236-5716

Invoice #1207   *Dated 11/15/08*   *Terms: FCA JFK Airport, NY*

Sold to: *Sam's Salamanders*
               525 Shoreham Village
               Essex, England 2BH 35Z
               44-1230987

Qty	Description	Unit Price	Total
10000	Plastic Litter Pans	0.25	$2500.00
900	Strawman Covers	3.11	$2799.00

Packed in 2 boxes   *Made in the U.S.A.*

                    Invoice Total   USD $5499.00

Ship via Airfreight London Heathrow Airport

Payment Terms: Net 30 Days

These commodities are being exported from the United States in accordance with the Export Administration Regulations. Diversion contrary to U.S. law prohibited.

Kelly's Kreatures
19 Benjamin Avenue
East Moriches, NY 11940
516-236-5716

Packing List #1207   Dated 11/15/08

Ship to: Sam's Salamanders
                  525 Shoreham Village
                  Essex, England 2BH 35Z
                  44-1230987

Qty	Description	Weight	Style No.
10000	Plastic Litter Pans	45 kgs	#2355
900	Strawman Covers	91 kgs	#5523

Packed in two (2) boxes

Shipment by Airfreight

Terms of Payment: Net 30 Days

Country of Origin: U.S.A.

These commodities are being exported from the United States in accordance with the Export
Administration Regulations. Diversion contrary to U.S. law prohibited.

125	JFK	1234 5678					HAWB# JFK KR111808	

Shipper's Name and Address	Shipper's Account Number	Not Negotiable
KELLY'S KREATURES 19 BENJAMIN AVENUE EAST MORICHES , NY 11940		**Air Waybill** AMERICAN RIVER LOGISTICS, LTD. 1229 OLD WALT WHITMAN ROAD Issued by MELVILLE, NY 11747

Copies 1, 2 and 3 of this Air Waybill are originals and have the same validity.

Consignee's Name and Address	Consignee's Account Number
SAM'S SALAMANDERS 525 SHOREHAM VILLAGE ESSEX , 2BH 35Z	

It is agreed that the goods described herein are accepted in apparent good order and condition (except as noted) for carriage SUBJECT TO THE CONDITIONS OF CONTRACT ON THE REVERSE HEREOF. ALL GOODS MAY BE CARRIED BY ANY OTHER MEANS INCLUDING ROAD OR ANY OTHER CARRIER UNLESS SPECIFIC CONTRARY INSTRUCTIONS ARE GIVEN HEREON BY THE SHIPPER, AND SHIPPER AGREES THAT THE SHIPMENT MAY BE CARRIED VIA INTERMEDIATE STOPPING PLACES WHICH THE CARRIER DEEMS APPROPRIATE. THE SHIPPER'S ATTENTION IS DRAWN TO THE NOTICE CONCERNING CARRIER'S LIMITATION OF LIABILITY. Shipper may increase such limitation of liability by declaring a higher value for carriage and paying a supplemental charge if required.

Issuing Carrier's Agent Name and City	Accounting Information
AMERICAN RIVER LOGISTICS, LTD. 1229 OLD WALT WHITMAN ROAD MELVILLE, NY 11747	AES X20081118123456

Agent's IATA Code	Account No.
01-1-9112/0011	

Airport of Departure (Addr. of First Carrier) and Requested Routing
JFK INT'L, NY

To	By First Carrier	Routing and Destination	to	by	to	by	Currency	CHGS Code	WT/VAL PPD COLL	Other PPD COLL	Declared Value for Carriage	Declared Value for Customs
LHR	BA						US$		X	X	N.V.D.	N.V.D.

Airport of Destination	Requested Flight/Date	Amount of Insurance	INSURANCE - If carrier offers insurance, and such insurance is requested in accordance with the conditions thereof, indicate amount to be insured in figures in box marked "Amount of Insurance".
HEATHROW AIRPORT	007/19	NIL	

Handling Information

PLEASE NOTIFY CONSIGNEE UPON ARRIVAL

These commodities, technology or software were exported from United States in accordance with the Export Administration Regulations. Ultimate destination   Diversion contrary to U.S. law prohibited.   SCI

No. of Pieces RCP	Gross Weight	lb/kg	Rate Class / Commodity Item No.	Chargeable Weight	Rate / Charge	Total	Nature and Quantity of Goods (incl. Dimensions or Volume)
2	136 KG 300 LB			136 KG 300 LB	2.25		PET PRODUCTS 2 BOXES
2	136 KG 300 LB					306.00	

Prepaid	Weight Charge	Collect	Other Charges
	306.00		

Valuation Charge

Tax

Total Other Charges Due Agent

Shipper certifies that the particulars on the face hereof are correct and that insofar as any part of the consignment contains dangerous goods, such part is properly described by name and is in proper condition for carriage by air according to the applicable Dangerous Goods Regulations.

AMERICAN RIVER LOGISTICS, LTD.

Total Other Charges Due Carrier
25.00

11/19/08   Roseann Esposito

AS AUTHORIZED AGENT FOR SHIPPER

Signature of Shipper or his Agent

Total Prepaid	Total Collect
331.00	

AMERICAN RIVER LOGISTICS, LTD.

11/19/08   JFK Roseann Esposito

AS AUTHORIZED AGENT FOR CARRIER

Currency Conversion Rates	cc Charges in Dest. Currency	Executed on (date)	at (place)	Signature of Issuing Carrier or its Agent

For Carrier's Use Only at Destination	Charges at Destination	

HAWB# KR111808

Certificate of Conformity

The undersigned, **Kelly's Kreatures**, declares that the following mentioned goods shipped under **British Airways #125-1234-5678**, on the date of **11/19/08**, consigned to **Sam's Salamanders**, are the product of the United States of America.

Marks/Numbers	No. Packages	Weight/kgs	Description
Addr:	2 Boxes	136 kgs	Litter pans
			Pan covers

Certified True and Correct

Signed:
Kelly Raia

AESDirect Shipment Record: KR111808

Shipment Information		USPPI	
Filer ID	#11-12345678	**Name**	Kelly's Kreatures
Shipment #	KR111808	**ID Number**	#11-12345678
ITN:	X20081118123456	**Contact**	Kelly Raia
Current Date/Time:	Wed Nov 18 17:32:03 2008 EST	**Phone**	6313966800
		Cargo Origin	East Moriches, NY

Departure Date 111908

Trans Ref #125 12345678

Origin State NY

Country of Dest GB

Export Port 4701 JFK

Mode of Transport Air (40)

Carrier SCAC/IATA British Airways

Routed Transaction No

Related Companies No

Hazardous No

Ultimate Consignee

Name Sam's Salamanders

Contact Edward Cullen

Phone 011 2345678899

Address 525 Shoreham Village

Essex, London, UK 2BH 35Z

Freight Forwarder

Name American River International

ID Number 11-12349876

Contact Rosanne Esposito

Phone 631-396-6800

Address 1229 Old Walt Whitman Road
Melville, New York 11747

Commodities

Item	EIC	Schedule B/HTS	Qty	Gross Wt	Value	Origin	License	Vehicle
1		3923290000	10000	45 kgs	$2500	D	C33	No
2		4602900000	900	91kgs	$2800	D	C33	No

SHIPPER/EXPORTER ZACK'S ZOO 10 GEORGE AVENUE		BOOKING NO.	BILL OF LADING NO. MAEU111122222

EXPORT REFERENCES
EXPORT FILE # MAEU111122222
KR

CONSIGNEE
TOUCANS BY TACAMOTO
MAIN DRIVE
TOKYO

FORWARDING AGENT
AMERICAN RIVER LOGISTICS FMC#171861

NOTIFY PARTY
TOUCANS BY TACAMOTO
MAIN DRIVE

POINT AND COUNTRY OF ORIGIN GOODS
LOS ANGELES

PRE-CARRIAGE BY*	PLACE OF RECEIPT BY PRECARRIER* LOS ANGELES	ROUTING AND INSTRUCTIONS
EXPORT CARRIER (VESSEL/VOY/FLAG) MIAMI #1118	PORT OF LOADING LOS ANGELES	LOADING PIER/TERMINAL
PORT OF DISCHARGE YOKOHOMA	PLACE OF DELIVERY BY ON CARRIER* LOS ANGELES	TYPE OF MOVE

PARTICULARS FURNISHED BY SHIPPER

MARKS & NO.'s/CONTAINER NO.'s # OF PKGS.	DESCRIPTION OF PACKAGES AND GOODS	GROSS WEIGHT	MEASUREMENT
5	PET PRODUCTS	476.3 K	1.3

These commodities, technology, or software were exported from the United States in accordance with the
Export Administration Regulations. Diversion contrary to U.S. law prohibited.

SHIPPERS DECLARED VALUE $

SEA LION SHIPPING, LTD.

FMC# 4124N

BILL OF LADING

SHIPPER	BOOKING NUMBER	Master No.:
ZACK'S ZOO 10 GEORGE AVENUE	MAEU111122222	20081118-MAEU111122222

	SHIPPER'S REFERENCES KR	ETD: 11/18/2008 ETA: 12/01/2008

CONSIGNEE (Non-Negotiable unless consigned to order)	FORWARDING AGENT (References)
TOUCANS BY TACAMOTO MAIN DRIVE TOKYO	AMERICAN RIVER LOGISTICS FMC#17186F

PORT AND COUNTRY OF ORIGIN
LOS ANGELES

VESSEL MIAMI V# #1118	PORT OF LOADING LOS ANGELES	NOTIFY PARTY: TOUCANS BY TACAMOTO MAIN DRIVE TOKYO
PORT OF DISCHARGE YOKOHOMA	FOR TRANSSHIPMENT TO	

	PARTICULARS FURNISHED BY SHIPPER	

DESCRIPTION OF PACKAGES AND GOODS	NO.	MARKS AND NUMBERS	WEIGHT	MEASUREMENT
PET PRODUCTS	5		476.3 K	1.3

FREIGHT RATES, CHARGES, WEIGHTS AND/OR MEASUREMENTS
SUBJECT TO CORRECTION

	US Rate	PREPAID	COLLECT
FREIGHT CHARGE			

Received from the aforenamed shipper, the goods as described above by the shipper in apparent external good order and condition unless otherwise indicated herein or hereon to be transported in accordance with all of the terms printed, written, typed or stamped in or on this B/L of two (2) pages to which the merchant agrees by accepting this B/L, any local privileges or customs notwithstanding.

In witness whereof, three (3) original BS/L have been signed, and if one (1) is accomplished by delivery of the Goods, issuance of a delivery order or by some other means, the others shall be void if required by the carrier, one (1) original B/L must be surrendered, duly endorsed in exchange for the goods or a delivery order.

DATED AT: _____

BY: _____

TOTAL PREPAID		::::::::::::::::::	FOR DELIVERY, APPLY TO:
TOTAL COLLECT	::::::::::::::::::		
TOTAL USD DOLLARS		.00	

Zack's Zoo
10 George Avenue
Raiaton, NY 11786
631-396-6819

Invoice #ZR212
Invoice Date: 11/01/08
Terms: EXW Raiaton

Sold to:

Toucans by Tacamoto
Main Drive
Tokyo, Japan
39-89890909

Qty	Description	Unit Price	Total
1000	Fido Blankets	$12.50	$12500.00
500	Sandy's Sweaters	9.00	4500.00
500	Canine Clippers	5.25	2625.00
3000	Flying Discs	1.00	3000.00

Packed in 5 boxes   Made in the U.S.A.

Invoice Total USD $22625.00

Ship via Oceanfreight

Port of Yokohoma

Payment Terms: 20 days

These commodities are being exported from the United States in accordance with the Export Administration Regulations. Diversion contrary to U.S. law prohibited.

Zack's Zoo
10 George Avenue
Raiaton, NY 11786
631-396-6819

Invoice #ZR212
Invoice Date: 11/01/08
Terms: EXW Raiaton

Sold to:

Toucans by Tacamoto
Main Drive
Tokyo, Japan
39-89890909

Qty	Description	Weight	Box
1000	Fido Blankets	170 kgs	Box 1 & 2
500	Sandy's Sweaters	95 kgs	Box 3
500	Canine Clippers	147 kgs	Box 4
3000	Flying Discs	64 kgs	Box 5

5 boxes total   476 kgs

Ship via Oceanfreight

Port of Yokohoma

Payment Terms: 20 days

PAPERLESS

173

Form Approved OMB No. 1651-0022

DEPARTMENT OF HOMELAND SECURITY U.S. Customs and Border Protection **ENTRY SUMMARY**	1. Filer Code/Entry No. KH5 0038848-4	2. Entry Type 01 ABI/A	3. Summary Date 01/15/2009
	4. Surety No. 365	5. Bond Type 8	6. Port Code 1104	7. Entry Date 01/05/2009

8. Importing Carrier OOCL SINGAPORE	9. Mode of Transport 11	10. Country of Origin MY	11. Import Date 01/06/2009
12. B/L or AWB No. OOLU3020188730	13. Manufacturer ID MYABCMET80PEN	14. Exporting Country MY	15. Export Date 12/06/2008
16. I.T. No. V1621647323	17. I.T. Date 01/06/2009	18. Missing Docs	19. Foreign Port of Lading 55735	20. U.S. Port of Unlading 4601
21. Location of Goods/G.O. No. D106-NORFOLK SOUTHE	22. Consignee No. SAME	23. Importer No. 12-1374222	24. Reference No.

25. Ultimate Consignee Name and Address	26. Importer of Record Name and Address XYZ METALS CORPORATION 123 BAYVIEW STREET
City State NY Zip	City TURNE State NY Zip 11096

27.	28. Description of Merchandise			32.	33.	34.
Line No.	29. A. HTSUS No. B. AD/CVD Case No.	30. A. Gross Weight B. Manifest Qty.	31. Net Quantity in HTSUS Units	A. Entered Value B. CHGS C. Relationship	A. HTSUS Rate B. AD/CVD Rate C. IRC Rate D. Visa No.	Duty and I.R. Tax Dollars Cents
001	M 3020188730 H 09241PGPIT INVOICE 00001 WELDED METAL PIPES 3241008(1) T,P,SS,=>1.65,CR,NO114.3MM,NI 7306.40.5064 2086 1669KG HARBOR MAINTENANCE FEE MERCHANDISE PROCESSING FEE			NOT RELATED 19489 C2 19489	8 PCS FREE 015877128 0.125% 0.21% CARRIED FORWARD	0.00 24.3 40.93 65.29

Other Fee Summary for Block 39 MPF 499 40.93 HMF 501 24.36	35. Total Entered Value $ 19,489.00 Total Other Fees $ 65.29	CBP USE ONLY	TOTALS
		A. LIQ CODE	B. Ascertained Duty	37. Duty 0.00
		REASON CODE	C. Ascertained Tax	38. Tax
36. DECLARATION OF IMPORTER OF RECORD (OWNER OR PURCHASER) OR AUTHORIZED AGENT		D. Ascertained Other	39. Other 65.29

I declare that I am the ☐ importer of record and that the actual owner, purchaser, or consignee for CBP purposes is as shown above, OR ☒ owner or purchaser or agent thereof. I further declare that the merchandise ☒ was obtained pursuant to a purchase or agreement to purchase and that the prices set forth in the invoices are true, OR ☐ was not obtained pursuant to a purchase or agreement to purchase and the statements in the invoices as to value or price are true to the best of my knowledge and belief. I also declare that the statements in the documents herein filed fully disclose to the best of my knowledge and belief the true prices, values, quantities, rebates, drawbacks, fees, commissions, and royalties are true and correct, and that all goods or services provided to the seller of the merchandise either free or at reduced cost are fully disclosed. I will immediately furnish to the appropriate CBP officer any information showing a different statement of facts.

E. Ascertained Total	40. Total 65.29

41. DECLARANT NAME TITLE	SIGNATURE DATE

42. Broker/Filer Information (Name, address, phone number) American River Brokerage Svcs. Ltd. 614 Progress Street ELIZABETH, NJ 07201 908-354-7746 x121	43. Broker/Importer File No. 0038848

CBP Form 7501 (04/05)

EDITRADE   RECORD

Page: 2

DEPARTMENT OF HOMELAND SECURITY ENTRY SUMMARY CONTINUATION SHEET   OMB No. 1651-0022
U.S. Customs and Border Protection

1. Filer Code/Entry No.
KH5   0038848-4

27. Line No.	28. Description of Merchandise			32.	33.	34.
	29. A. HTSUS No. B. AD/CVD Case No.	30. A. Gross weight B. Manifest Qty.	31. Net Quantity in HTSUS Units	A. Entered Value B. CHGS C. Relationship	A. HTSUS Rate B. AD/CVD Rate C. IRC Rate D. Visa No.	Duty and I.R. Tax Dollars Cents
		BROUGHT FORWARD		19489		65.29
	INVOICE VALUE	20714.40				
	ADDITION	0.00				
	LESS NDC	1225.00				
	NEV	19489.40				
			TEV$	19489		65.29

EDITRADE   RECORD   CBP Form 7501 (04/05)

3461 CONTINUATION SHEET
FOR ENTRY#: KH5-0038848-4

BROKER FILER: KH5   BROKER BOX 101

AMERICAN RIVER BROKERAGE SVCS. LTD.
614 PROGRESS STREET
ELIZABETH, NJ 07201 US

CODE	IT/BL/AWB NO.	QUANTITY	H.S. NO.	C/O	MID	CONTAINER
						OOLU7654320

FILER 101

U.S. DEPARTMENT OF HOMELAND SECURITY
Bureau of Customs and Border Protection

Form Approved
OMB No. 1651-0024

ENTRY/IMMEDIATE DELIVERY

AMERICAN RIVER BROKERAGE SVCS. LTD.
614 PROGRESS STREET
ELIZABETH, NJ 07201 US

CST # 173   19 CFR 142.3, 142.16, 142.22, 142.24   *** ABI CERTIFIED ***

1. ARRIVAL DATE	2. ELECTED ENTRY DATE	3. ENTRY TYPE CODE/NAME	4. ENTRY NUMBER
010709		01	KH5-0038848-4

5. PORT	6. SINGLE TRANS. BOND	7. BROKER/IMPORTER FILE NUMBER	
1104		0038848	

	8. CONSIGNEE NUMBER		9. IMPORTER NUMBER
	12-1374222		SAME

10. ULTIMATE CONSIGNEE NAME	11. IMPORTER OF RECORD NAME
XYZ METALS CORPORATION 123 BAYVIEW STREET TURNE, NY 11096	SAME

12. CARRIER CODE	13. VOYAGE/FLIGHT/TRIP	14. LOCATION OF GOODS-CODE(S)/NAME(S)
OOLU	88E	D106-NORFOLK SOUTHERN CORP

15. VESSEL CODE/NAME
OOCL SINGAPORE

16. U.S. PORT OF UNLADING	17. MANIFEST NUMBER	18. G.O. NUMBER	19. TOTAL VALUE
4601			19489

20. DESCRIPTION OF MERCHANDISE

WELDED METAL PIPES

21. ITBL/AWB CODE	22. ITBL/AWB NO.	23. MANIFEST QUANTITY	24. H.S. NUMBER	25. COUNTRY OF ORIGIN	26. MANUFACTURER NO.
I	V1621647323		7306405064	MY	MYABCMET80PEN
M	OOLU3020188730				
H	VGLT09241PGPIT	8			

27. CERTIFICATION	28. CBP USE ONLY
I hereby make application for entry/immediate delivery. I certify that the above information is accurate, the bond is sufficient, valid, and current, and that all requirements of 19 CFR Part 142 have been met. SIGNATURE OF APPLICANT X PHONE NO. / DATE	**ELECTRONIC ENTRY - NEWARK, NJ DISTRICT** I certify that this cargo has been authorized for delivery by CBP **American River Brokerage Svcs. Ltd.** COMPANY NAME X SIGNATURE / DATE DELIVERY AUTHORIZED: SIGNATURE / DATE

29. BROKER OR OTHER GOVT. AGENCY USE

CONTAINER #: OOLU7654320 FCL
ONLY FOR DIRECT TRANSFER TO:
VIA CHL TRUCKER: CHL#
IN LIEU OF CHL, IMPORTER SECURES
PERFORMANCE OF ALTERNATE CARTAGE BY
ENTRY BOND PER 113.62 (f) C.R.
DO NOT BREAK SEAL.
ALTERNATE TRUCKING COMPANY:
TRANSFER AUTHORIZED:
INSPECTOR-BADGE-DATE
DATE/TIME CARTAGE BEGAN:

EDITRADE   CBP Form 3461 (01/89)

01/08/2009   **American River Brokerage Svcs. Ltd.**   Page: 1
01:45:36 PM   **CARGO/MANIFEST STATUS QUERY RESULTS**   GPINO

File No: 0038848	**Entry No:** KH5-0038848-4	**Entry Type:** 01
Imp IRS: 11-346579000	**Vessel:** OOCL SINGAPORE	**Carrier:** OOLU
Voy/Flt/Trip: 88E	**Arrival Date:** 01/05/2009	**Entry Port:** 1104

Status

Msg Type	Release Date	Message	Date	Time
ACTION		PAPERLESS	01/05/2009	01:28:00 pm
REL. BY	01/05/2009	RELEASE DATE UPDATE	01/05/2009	01:28:00 pm
Addl. Msg:		SELECTIVITY PROCESSING DATE	Lines: ABI/OGA Thru ABI/OGA	

Bill Of Lading

IT No.	Master Issuer	Master	House Issuer	House	Sub-House	Quantity	UOM
V1621647323	OOLU	3020188730	VGLT	09241PGPIT		30	PCS

ABC Metal Trading

80 Lorong Perusahaan Maju 6, Prai Industrial Estate IV, 13600 Prai, Penang, Malaysia
Contact: Lucy Edo Email: Lucy.Edo@ABC.com   www.abcmetaltd.com

COMMERCIAL INVOICE

Consignee XYZ Metals Corp 123 Bayview Street Turne, NY 11096 Tel: 562-235-8965 Fax: 562-235-7528 Contact:Ana Good www.xyzmetalscorp.com Email: Agood@xyz.com	INVOICE NO. 200811/02	DATE 3-Jan-09
	Contract No. SC/SP-080051	P/O NO. 324/001008
	L/C No.	L/C Issuing Date
Vessel/Voyage OOCL SINGAPORE 88E	Sailing on or about 5-Jan-09	L/C Issuing Bank
Loading port Penang	To: Pittsburgh PA Port of Entry: 1104	
Unlading Port: 4601 NY		

Marks & Nos.	Description	Quantity	Unit Price	Amount
				CIF Pittsburgh PA USA
	Welded Metal Pipes ASTM A3.12/ASME SA312	FT	(USD) (Per feet)	TOTAL (USD)
Container No: OOLU7654320	4" SS Welded Metal Pipes S/10 TP304/304L 2" SS Welded Metal Pipes S/40 TP304/304L	1,080 1,080	11.63 7.55	12,560.40 8,154.00
Seal No: OOLP 900936	US HTS# 7306.40.5064 Country of Origin/Export: Malaysia Gross Weight : 2,086kg Net Weight: 2,003kg			
Marking: 324/001008 PO 08-2330 JM Malaysia Pittsburgh	CIF Value Freight Insurance FOB Value			20,714.40 900.00 325.00 19,489.40

Prepared by: _____

ABC Metal Trading

80 Lorong Perusahaan Maju 6, Prai Industrial Estate IV, 13600 Prai, Penang, Malaysia
Contact: Lucy Edo Email: Lucy.Edo@abc.com   www.abcmetaltd.com

Packing List

Consignee		INVOICE NO.		DATE	
XYZ Metals Corp		200811/02		3-Jan-09	
123 Bayview Street					
Turne, NY 11096		Contract No.		P/O NO.	
		SC/SP-080051		324/001008	
Tel: 562-235-8965					
Fax: 562-235-7528					
Contact: Ana Good		L/C No.		L/C Issuing Date	
www.xyzmetalscorp.com					
Email: Agood@xyz.com					

Vessel/Voyage	Sailing on or about	L/C Issuing Bank
OOCL SIGNAPORE	5-Jan-09	
88E		

Loading Port	To: Pittsburgh PA
Penang	Port of Entry: 1104

Unlading Port: 4601 NY

Marks & Nos.	Description	Bundle	Quantity	Net WT	Gross WT
	Welded Metal Pipes		CIF Pittsburgh PA USA		
	ASTM A3.12/ASME SA312		(FT)	(KGS)	(KGS)
Container No:	4" SS Welded Metal Pipes S/10 TP304/304L	6	1,080	267	278
OOLU7854320	2" SS Welded Metal Pipes S/40 TP304/304L	2	1,080	1,736	1808
Seal No:					
OOLP 900936					
Marking:					
324/001008					
PO 08-2330 JM	Total:	8	2,160	2,003	2086
Malaysia					
Pittsburgh					

Prepared by: _____

XYZ Metals Corp. - 123 Bayview St., Turne, NY 11096

Tel:562-235-8965
Fax:562-235-7528

Date: 13-Jan-09	Contact: Ana Good	XYZ Ref: 324/001008 (1)
	Email: Agood@xyz.com	Cust PO# 08-2330JM

Letter of Instructions

Customs Broker   Dated: 5-Jan-09

America River	Tel: 908-354-7746 x122
614 Progress Street	Fax:908-354-9114
Elizabeth, NJ 07201	Email:Cdavila@americanriverintl.com
Contact: Carolina Davila	

Container: OOLU7654320

Vessel: "OOCL SIGNAPORE V 88E

MAWB# OOLU3020188730
AWB# VGLT09241PGPIT

Via: Malaysia/NY/Pittsburgh
ETD:Penang / 06-Dec-08
ETA: Pittsburgh / 7-Jan-09

IT#V1621647323 / 6 -Jan-09
Shipment Available: Norfolk Southern Corp
D106

No. of Bundle(s): 8   Weight/LBS: 4,599   US HTS# 7306.40.5064 / Duty Free

Shipping Marks: 324/001008
PO# 08-2330JM
C/NO. 1-30

Enclosures:
- Bill of Lading
- Suppliers Comm. Invoice   COPY
- Suppliers Packing List   COPY
- Arrival Notice
- Certificate of Origin
- Freight Invoice
- Import Steel License

Delivery Address:
Better Pipes & Tubes
895 Tope Street
Allentown PA 15942
Tel: 310-549-5126
Fax: 310-549-3257
Contact: Ted Strong

Special Handling Instructions
Customs Clearance Charges To Be Billed to: XYZ Metals Corp.
Trucker: Easy Trucks   **Tel:** 562-464-2531
ON FLAT-BED TRUCK (Dray/Devann & Deliver at XYZ Acct)
***INLAND FREIGHT: **PREPAID (XYZ's ACCT)**
Note: Deliver According to Marks & Nos. Only.

AMERICAN RIVER BROKERAGE SVCS. LTD.
614 PROGRESS STREET
ELIZABETH, NJ 07201 US

Tel: 908 354-7746
Fax:

DELIVERY ORDER

XYZ METALS CORPORATION
123 BAYVIEW STREET
TURNE, NY 11096 US

DATE	OUR REF.NO.
01/05/2009	0038848

THE MERCHANDISE DESCRIBED BELOW
WILL BE ENTERED AND FORWARDED AS
FOLLOWS:

IMPORTING CARRIER		LOCATION		FROM PORT OF / ORIGIN AIRPORT
OOCL SINGAPORE-88E		NORFOLK SOUTHERN CORP- PITTSBURG, PA		PENANG; PINANG, MALA

B/L OR AWB NO.	ARRIVAL DATE	FREE TIME EXP.	LOCAL DELIVERY OR TRANSFER BY (DELIVERY ORDER ISSUED TO)		
OOLU 3020188730	01/02/2009		EASY TRUCKS		

INLAND CARRIER		ISWAB NO.	ENTRY NO.	CUST.REF.NO.
EASY TRUCKS		09241PGPIT	KH5-0038848-4	3241008(1

FOR DELIVERY TO	ROUTE
BETTER PIPE & TUBES 895 TOPE STREET ALLENTOWN, PA 15942 US Contact: TED STRONG 310-549-5126	NOTIFY: CAROLINA DAVILA 908 354 7746 X122

NO. OF PKGS.	DESCRIPTION OF ARTICLES, SPECIAL MARKS & EXCEPTIONS	WEIGHT	DO NOT USE
8 PCS	WELDED METAL PIPES 324/001008(1) PO# 08-2330JM C/NO. 1-30 ***DELIVER ACCORDING TO MARKS AND NOS. ONLY*** ISSUER__MASTER_____HOUSE OOLU 3020188730 09241PGPIT Containers:OOLU7654320 3241008(1) ***. INLAND FREIGHT PREPAID: XYZ'S ACCT. **** DELIVER ON A FLAT BED TRUCK (DRAY/DEVANN & DELIVER)	4599 LB	

INLAND FREIGHT ➤

PREPAID / COLLECT
PREPAID

Received In Good Order
By:

DELIVERY CLERK: DELIVER
TO CARRIER SHOWN ABOVE

PER CAROLINA LOPEZ

ORIGINAL

FALCON LOGISTICS INC.

PO Box 1067
Secaucus, NJ 07096
(201) 123-7000 201-123-7001 (fax)

SHIPPING ADVICE	
Reference No..:	45001403 PIM
Date..........:	12/22/2008
Page..........:	1

License No. 16311N

Customer
XYZ Metals Corporation. 123 Bayview Street. Turne, NY 11096. Tel# 562-235-8965 Fax# 562-235-7528

Reference	
Account.....:	NOIN
Vessel......:	OOCL SINGAPORE
Voyage......:	88E
Customer Ref:	SUPERINOX INT'L
Container...:	OOLU7654320
Service Date:	12/22/2008

MBL #OOLU3020188730,   HBL #09241/PGPIT
E.T.D.   E.T.A.
11/26/08 PENANG   1/2/08 PITTSBURG, PA
I.T. #V1621647323, 12/30/08 NEWARK
1X40', TOTAL 30 PKGS, 17920 KGS, 25 CBM
WELDED STAINLESS STELL PIPES
AMS #VGLT 09241PGPIT
CARGO LOCATION: NORFOLK SOUTHERN, FIRM #D106
TEL: 412-893-5525, FAX: 412-893-5526
OBL REQUIRED !!!!!!!!

Qty	U/M	Description	Rate	Total
1.0	Each	Ocean Freight	.01/EA	.01
1.0	Each	Handling Fee	65.00/EA	65.00

TOTAL   65.01

Frankie.
X131

Office Copy

FALCON LOGISTICS INC.

BILL OF LADING

09241/PGPIT

Shipper: ABC Metal Trading
80 Lurong Perusahaan Maju 6.
13600 Penang, Malaysia

Consignee: XYZ Metals Corp
123 Bayview Street
Turne, NY 11096

AMERICAN RIVER INTERNATIONAL
614 PROGRESS STREET, ELIZABETH, NJ 07201
PHONE: +1(908)354-7748 EXT.121 FAX: +1(908)354-8114

** CONTACT :
HENRY MORALES-HMORALES@americanriverintl.com
EMMA BRAVO-EBRAVO@americanriverintl.com
RENNIE ALSTON-ralston@worldest.com

LYRA V.082E	CY PENANG, MALAYSIA	
OOCL SINGAPORE V.88E49	PENANG, MALAYSIA	
NEW YORK	CY PITTSBURGH, USA	

PARTICULARS FURNISHED BY SHIPPER

CNTR. NOS./SEAL NOS OTHER NUMBERS	QUANTITY PACKAGES	H M	DESCRIPTION OF PACKAGES AND GOODS	GROSS WEIGHT	MEASUREMENT
324/001008 PO.OR-2330 IN MALAYSIA PITTSBURGH ✓ FREIGHT PREPAID			"SHIPPER'S LOAD AND COUNT" 1X40' CONTAINER 30 BUNDLES (6,140 FT) OF WELDED STAINLESS STEEL PIPES ASTM A312/ASME SA312 FUMIGATED WOOD SPACER USED (2INCH X 3 INCH X 4 FEET) TOTAL 50 PIECES TO STACK BUNDLE OF PIPES	✓ 17,920.00 KGS	25.000 M3
CONTAINER / SEAL NO. OOLU7654320 / OOLP900936			SHIPPED ON BOARD LYRA V.082E IN PENANG, MALAYSIA 26/11/2008 AND TRANSHIPMENT TO OOCL SINGAPORE V.88E49 IN SINGAPORE TOTAL : ONE FORTY FOOTER CONTAINER ONLY		

LIMITATION ON CARRIER'S LIABILITY / SHIPPER'S AD VALOREM OPTION. The Carrier shall in no event be or become liable for any loss or damage to or in connection with the transportation of Goods in an amount exceeding US $500 per package, or in the case of goods not shipped in packages per customary freight unit, or the equivalent of that sum in other currency, for such other limitation imposed by a Carriage of Goods by Sea Act, statute or law in force according to the provisions hereof, unless the nature and value of such goods have been declared by the Merchant before shipment and inserted in the Bill of Lading. Such declaration of value shall not, however, be conclusive on the Carrier for purposes of determining the extent of the Carrier's liability. If the Merchant desires to be covered for a valuation in excess of said US $500 per package or customary freight unit or any other applicable limitation, the Merchant must so stipulate in this Bill of Lading and such additional liability only will be assumed by the Carrier upon payment of the Carrier's ad valorem freight charge.

Declared Cargo Value $_____ . If Merchant enters a value, Carrier's limitation of liability shall not apply, and the ad valorem rate will be charged.

FREIGHT & CHARGES PAYABLE AT / BY			TARIFF NUMBER	ROUTE CODE	COMMODITY CODE

2008	TARIFF ITEM	PREPAID/ED KG	R'A'E	U.S $ PREPAID	U.S $ COLLECT	LOCAL CURRENCY

26 NOV 2008

COPY NON-NEGOTIABLE

Index

A

ACE, *see* Automated Commercial Environment
Acronyms, 127–129
Advanced Shipping Notices (ASNs), 180
Advanced Trade Data Initiative (ATDI), 179
AES, *see* Automated Export System
ASNs, *see* Advanced Shipping Notices
ATDI, se Advanced Trade Data Initiative
Automated Commercial Environment (ACE),
    179
Automated Export System (AES), 139–169
    acronyms, 167–168
    authorized or forwarding agent, 151–156
        becoming acquainted, 151–152
        definitions, 151
        power of attorney, 153
    benefits of, 141
    best practices manual, 139, 143
    classifying commodities, 146–150
        export commodity classification codes,
        146
        reporting requirements, 148–150
        Schedule B classification, 147
        Schedule B number, location of,
        147–148
    compliance report, 163–164
    compliance review program, overview of,
    140
    contact information, 168–169
    correcting export information, 161
    daily reports, 166
    definition of, 120
    export checklist, 166–167
    export data request, 164–165
    fatal error report, 164
    Foreign Trade Regulation basics, 143

    Foreign Trade Zones, 156
    introduction, 141
    key terms, 144–145
        Electronic Export Information, 144
        export shipment, 144
        export transactions (parties involved
        in), 144
        export transactions (responsibilities),
        145
        export transactions (types of), 145
    Kimberley Process for rough diamonds,
        150–151
        certificate (need for), 150–151
        certificate (obtaining), 151
        process definition, 150
        rough diamond USPPI requirements,
        150
    logistics expertise, 106
    process flow, 157–158
    response messages, 158–160
    routed export, 31
    software selection, 165–166
    table of contents, 139–140
    training best practices, 141–143
        cross-training, 142
        mentoring program, 142
        seminars and workshops, 142–143
        training manual, 141–142
    Voluntary Self-Disclosure, 161–163
    web sites, 131, 169

B

Best practices catalog (supply chain security),
    171–220
    Advanced Shipping Notices, 180
    Advanced Trade Data Initiative, 179

255

Automated Commercial Environment, 179
business partner requirements, 183–188
    customer outreach, 188
    customer screening, 186–188
    manufacturer/supplier/vendor
        requirements, 184–185
    service provider requirements, 185–186
business to business, 179–180
business to U.S. Customs and Border
        protection, 179
cargo tracing en route, 197–198
    driver data port, 198
    logistics tracking system, 198
    scanning cards, 198
    visibility, 197
catalog use, 175
container seals, 190–192
    Consolidator, 192
    domestic, 190
    factory, 191–192
    Highway Carrier, 191
    multi-national corporation, 192
    Sea Carrier, 191
container/trailer/ULD security, 188–194
    container seals, 190–192
    inspections, 188–190
    storage/inventory, 193–194
    tracking, 192–193
conveyance inspections, 194
    Air Carrier, 194
    Highway Carrier, 194
    Sea Carrier, 194
conveyance monitoring, 195–197
    barge transshipments, 197
    Highway Carrier, 195–197
    Sea Carrier, 197
conveyance security, 194–197
conveyance storage, 195
customer screening, 186–187
    keeping current with customer
        information, 186
    management of unknown customer,
        186
    meeting with customers in-person, 187
    preventing misuse of products by
        customers, 186
    refusing pick-ups from unknown
        locations, 187
    requiring business referral, 187
    requiring customer registration, 186
    requiring customers to inspect
        containers, 187

    requiring original power of attorney,
        186
    sending representatives to meet with
        new foreign customers, 187
    using external resources to screen
        customers, 187
data submission, 179–180
Electronic Data Interchange, 179
incident reporting, 213
    business integrity cards, 213
    emergency contact information, 213
    hotline establishment, 213
    outsourcing hotline, 213
information technology security (computer
        systems), 216–220
    access restrictions, 216–217
    data back-ups and recovery plans, 218
    emergency preparedness/disaster
        recovery, 219
    hardware security, 218–219
    policies/procedures/management
        support/training, 218
    program memberships/certifications,
        219–220
    viruses/firewalls/tampering prevention,
        217–218
inspections (container security), 188–190
    Air Carrier, 189
    Consolidators, 189
    domestic Highway Carrier, 188
    factory/supplier/vendor, 190
    foreign Highway Carrier, 188–189
    terminal yards/operators, 190
introduction, 173–174
management support, 177–179
    continuous improvement philosophy,
        177–178
    Country Managers, 178–179
    domestic, 177–178
    integration of policies, 178
    mission statement, 179
    proactive engagement, 178
    Security Councils, 179
    Security Directors, 178
    Supply Chain Security Committee, 178
    top management, 178
    weekly briefings, 178
    worldwide, 178–179
manifesting/invoicing/Electronic Data
        Interchange, 206–208
    Air Carrier, 208
    Consolidator, 207

Domestic Distribution Center, 206
Factory/Shipper, 207
Freight Forwarder, 207–208
receiving, 206
Sea Carrier, 208
shipping, 207
manufacturer/supplier/vendor
requirements, 184–185
collaborating to select suppliers and
service providers, 185
contractual obligations, 184
factory certification requirements,
184
holding buying agent accountable, 184
managing non-compliant essential
business partner, 185
requiring business updates, 184
requiring security adherence, 184
supplier code of conduct, 185
personnel security, 202–204
Code of Conduct, 204
pre-employment checks, 202–204
termination procedures, 204
physical access controls, 198–202
deliveries/cargo pick-up, 200–201
employees, 198–199
escalation matrix, 202
planning, 198
search vehicles/persons/packaging,
201–202
unauthorized persons, 202
visitors, 199–200
physical security, 213–216
alarm systems, 215
fencing/gates/gate houses, 213
lighting, 215
locking mechanisms, 215
parking, 214–215
security guards, 214
video surveillance cameras, 216
procedural security, 204–209
brand name/identity protection,
205–206
cargo discrepancies, 209
collusion, preventing, 209
identifying/reporting/tracking
incidents, 204–205
manifesting/invoicing/Electronic Data
Interchange, 206–208
packing/packaging, 208–209
prologue, 173
risk analysis, 180–181

identifying risks and creating remedies,
180
keeping key personnel informed,
180–181
tapping into existing resources, 180
secure electronic data transmissions, 180
security planning and program
management, 182–183
continuous improvement, plan for, 183
global security management, 183
holistic approach to security, 182–183
internal networks, establishment of, 183
interpersonal relationships and
worldwide networks, 183
security training/threat awareness/outreach,
209–213
alert levels, 210
awareness, 210
background investigations, 211
business partners, 212
company magazine, 210
continuing education, 210
conveyance inspections, 211
dual-use awareness, 212
employee incentives, 212
external resources, 211
Highway Watch, 211
incident reporting, 213
International Logistics Provider, 212
intranet, 210
local law enforcement, 212
multiple languages, 212
online security courses, 210
periodic training, 210
product tampering, 211
security guards, 212
specialized training, 211–212
suspicious containers, 211
terrorism information, communication
of to employees, 210
training video, 210
updates from association, 212
self-assessment, 181–182
business partner accountability, 182
container inspections and conveyance
tracking, 181
domestic facilities, 181
engaging employees, 181
external resources, 182
factory audits, 182
foreign facilities, 182
overseas resources, 182

periodic assessments, 181
physical security, 181–182
security in business practices, 181
security guard duties, 181
service provider requirements, 185–186
  contractual obligations, 185–186
  establishing procedures for selection,
    186
  exclusive representative, 185
  prohibiting subcontracting, 185
  requiring background clearances, 185
storage/inventory (container security),
    193–194
  Air Carrier, 194
  Consolidators, 193–194
  container yards, 193
  Highway Carrier truck yard, 193
table of contents, 171–173
tiered benefits structure, 175–177
  corporate governance structure, 177
  Tier Three status, 176–177
tracking (container security), 192–193
  Highway Carrier, 193
  terminal operator container yard,
    192–193
BIS, *see* Bureau of Industry and Security
Brand name/identity protection, 205–206
  archiving records, 206
  destroying sensitive documents, 206
  safeguarding company stationery, 205
  safeguarding items bearing company
    logo, 205–206
  securing business documents, 206
Bureau of Customs and Border Protection
    (CBP), 43–44
  advanced manifest notification, 57
  global security issues, 55
  import management, 46
Bureau of Industry and Security (BIS), 31, 35
  Commerce Control List, 87
  definition of, 120
  PACMAN, 106
  responsibility of, 35, 87
Business integrity cards, 213

C

Cargo loss control management, 28
CBP, *see* Bureau of Customs and Border
    Protection
Computer system security, *see* Information
    technology security

C-TPAT, *see* Customs-Trade Partnership
    Against Terrorism
Customs-Trade Partnership Against Terrorism
    (C-TPAT), 54
  ISA Program, 8, 54
  Plus, 100
  purpose of, 100
Customs-Trade Partnership Against Terrorism
    (C-TPAT), best practices catalog,
    171–220
  Advanced Shipping Notices, 180
  Advanced Trade Data Initiative, 179
  Automated Commercial Environment,
    179
  business partner requirements, 183–188
    customer outreach, 188
    customer screening, 186–188
    manufacturer/supplier/vendor
      requirements, 184–185
    service provider requirements,
      185–186
  business to business, 179–180
  business to U.S. Customs and Border
    protection, 179
  cargo tracing en route, 197–198
    driver data port, 198
    logistics tracking system, 198
    scanning cards, 198
    visibility, 197
  catalog use, 175
  container seals, 190–192
    Consolidator, 192
    domestic, 190
    factory, 191–192
    Highway Carrier, 191
    multi-national corporation, 192
    Sea Carrier, 191
  container/trailer/ULD security, 188–194
    container seals, 190–192
    inspections, 188–190
    storage/inventory, 193–194
    tracking, 192–193
  conveyance inspections, 194
    Air Carrier, 194
    Highway Carrier, 194
    Sea Carrier, 194
  conveyance monitoring, 195–197
    barge transshipments, 197
    Highway Carrier, 195–197
    Sea Carrier, 197
  conveyance security, 194–197
  conveyance storage, 195

customer screening, 186–187
keeping current with customer
information, 186
management of unknown customer, 186
meeting with customers in-person, 187
preventing misuse of products by
customers, 186
refusing pick-ups from unknown
locations, 187
requiring business referral, 187
requiring customer registration, 186
requiring customers to inspect
containers, 187
requiring original power of attorney,
186
sending representatives to meet with
new foreign customers, 187
using external resources to screen
customers, 187
data submission, 179–180
Electronic Data Interchange, 179
incident reporting, 213
business integrity cards, 213
emergency contact information, 213
hotline establishment, 213
outsourcing hotline, 213
information technology security (computer
systems), 216–220
access restrictions, 216–217
data back-ups and recovery plans, 218
emergency preparedness/disaster
recovery, 219
hardware security, 218–219
policies/procedures/management
support/training, 218
program memberships/certifications,
219–220
viruses/firewalls/tampering prevention,
217–218
inspections (container security), 188–190
Air Carrier, 189
Consolidators, 189
domestic Highway Carrier, 188
factory/supplier/vendor, 190
foreign Highway Carrier, 188–189
terminal yards/operators, 190
introduction, 173–174
management support, 177–179
continuous improvement philosophy,
177–178
Country Managers, 178–179
domestic, 177–178

integration of policies, 178
mission statement, 179
proactive engagement, 178
Security Councils, 179
Security Directors, 178
Supply Chain Security Committee, 178
top management, 178
weekly briefings, 178
worldwide, 178–179
manifesting/invoicing/Electronic Data
Interchange, 206–208
Air Carrier, 208
Consolidator, 207
Domestic Distribution Center, 206
Factory/Shipper, 207
Freight Forwarder, 207–208
receiving, 206
Sea Carrier, 208
shipping, 207
manufacturer/supplier/vendor
requirements, 184–185
collaborating to select suppliers and
service providers, 185
contractual obligations, 184
factory certification requirements, 184
holding buying agent accountable, 184
managing non-compliant essential
business partner, 185
requiring business updates, 184
requiring security adherence, 184
supplier code of conduct, 185
personnel security, 202–204
Code of Conduct, 204
pre-employment checks, 202–204
termination procedures, 204
physical access controls, 198–202
deliveries/cargo pick-up, 200–201
employees, 198–199
escalation matrix, 202
planning, 198
search vehicles/persons/packaging,
201–202
unauthorized persons, 202
visitors, 199–200
physical security, 213–216
alarm systems, 215
fencing/gates/gate houses, 213
lighting, 215
locking mechanisms, 215
parking, 214–215
security guards, 214
video surveillance cameras, 216

procedural security, 204–209
    brand name/identity protection,
        205–206
    cargo discrepancies, 209
    collusion, preventing, 209
    identifying/reporting/tracking
        incidents, 204–205
    manifesting/invoicing/Electronic Data
        Interchange, 206–208
    packing/packaging, 208–209
prologue, 173
risk analysis, 180–181
    identifying risks and creating remedies,
        180
    keeping key personnel informed,
        180–181
    tapping into existing resources, 180
secure electronic data transmissions, 180
security planning and program
        management, 182–183
    continuous improvement, plan for, 183
    global security management, 183
    holistic approach to security, 182–183
    internal networks, establishment of, 183
    interpersonal relationships and
        worldwide networks, 183
security training/threat awareness/outreach,
        209–213
    alert levels, 210
    awareness, 210
    background investigations, 211
    business partners, 212
    company magazine, 210
    continuing education, 210
    conveyance inspections, 211
    dual-use awareness, 212
    employee incentives, 212
    external resources, 211
    Highway Watch, 211
    incident reporting, 213
    International Logistics Provider, 212
    intranet, 210
    local law enforcement, 212
    multiple languages, 212
    online security courses, 210
    periodic training, 210
    product tampering, 211
    security guards, 212
    specialized training, 211–212
    suspicious containers, 211
    terrorism information, communication
        of to employees, 210

training video, 210
    updates from association, 212
self-assessment, 181–182
    business partner accountability, 182
    container inspections and conveyance
        tracking, 181
    domestic facilities, 181
    engaging employees, 181
    external resources, 182
    factory audits, 182
    foreign facilities, 182
    overseas resources, 182
    periodic assessments, 181
    physical security, 181–182
    security in business practices, 181
    security guard duties, 181
service provider requirements, 185–186
    contractual obligations, 185–186
    establishing procedures for selection, 186
    exclusive representative, 185
    prohibiting subcontracting, 185
    requiring background clearances, 185
storage/inventory (container security),
        193–194
    Air Carrier, 194
    Consolidators, 193–194
    container yards, 193
    Highway Carrier truck yard, 193
table of contents, 171–173
tiered benefits structure, 175–177
    corporate governance structure, 177
    Tier Three status, 176–177
tracking (container security), 192–193
    Highway Carrier, 193
    terminal operator container yard,
        192–193

D

DDTC, *see* Directorate of Defense Trade
        Controls
Denied Party Screening, 35–36
    maintenance, 35
    software, 36
Department of Homeland Security (DHS),
        44–45
    Department of Agriculture, Animal Plant
        Health Inspection Service, 94
    Highway Watch, 211
    importing, 93
    management centers, 45
    organization structure, 44–45

recommendations to, 59
RFID technology, 101
supply chain security, 90
Transportation Security Administration, 91
DHS, *see* Department of Homeland Security
Directorate of Defense Trade Controls
(DDTC), 88

E

ECCN, *see* Export Control Classification
Number
EDI, *see* Electronic Data Interchange
EEI, *see* Electronic export information
Electronic Data Interchange (EDI), 179,
206–208
Air Carrier, 208
best practices, 179
Consolidator, 207
Customs Service, 47
description, 179
Domestic Distribution Center, 206
Factory/Shipper, 207
Freight Forwarder, 207–208
interface development, 99
receiving, 206
restricted access, 206
Sea Carrier, 208
shipping, 207
Electronic export information (EEI), 88
Export Control Classification Number
(ECCN), 167
classification review, 6
determination process, 35
product classification, 32
trade compliance SOPs, 113
Export logistics, compliance management and,
17–41
Bureau of Industry and Security, 35
cargo loss control management, 28
census, 31–33
Denied Party Screening, 35–36
documentation and letters of credit, 41
export compliance, 31
Export Control Classification Number, 35
export documentation, 37–38
export freight forwarding and supply chain
management, 18–19
export logistics, freight forwarding, and
shipping, 17
export packing, 28–30
management policy, 29

managing compliance and
documentation, 30
packaging resources, 30
set packing guidelines, 29–30
FCPA awareness and adherence, 38–40
harmonized tariff schedule/schedule B
number, 34–35
INCO terms in logistics, 26–27
Office of Foreign Asset Controls, 36–37
power of attorney, 24–25
shipping costs, 19–23
price quotations, 19
shipping cost breakdown, 21
terms of payment, 27–28
valuation, 33
value-added services, 23–24

F

Federal Tax Identification Number, 73
Foreign cargo remaining on board (FROB),
65
Foreign Corrupt Practices Act antibribery
provisions, 221–229
background, 222–223
basic prohibition, 223–225
enforcement, 223
government guidance, 228–229
introduction, 222
permissible payments and affirmative
defenses, 226–227
affirmative defenses, 227
routine governmental actions, 226–227
sanctions against bribery, 227–228
civil, 227–228
criminal, 227
other governmental action, 228
private cause of action, 228
third party payments, 225–226
United States Department of Commerce,
221
United States Department of Justice, 221
Foreign principal party in interest (FPPI), 31
authorization, 151
export transaction, 144, 145
Foreign Trade Zone (FTZ), 156
applicant identification number, 64
definition of, 123
exports from, 156
FPPI, *see* Foreign principal party in interest
FROB, *see* Foreign cargo remaining on board
FTZ, *see* Foreign Trade Zone

G

GAAPs, *see* Generally accepted accounting
        principles
GAO, *see* General Accounting Office
General Accounting Office (GAO), 100
Generally accepted accounting principles
        (GAAPs), 12
Glossary, 119–126
Government agencies, 87–95
    electronic export information, 88
    exporting, 87–92
        Department of Commerce, Bureau of
                Census, Foreign Trade Division, 88
        Department of Commerce, Bureau of
                Industry and Security, 87
        Department of Commerce, Office of
                Antiboycott Compliance, 88
        Department of Commerce, Patent and
                Trademark Office, 90–91
        Department of Energy, Natural Gas
                and Electric Power, 89–90
        Department of Energy, Nuclear
                Regulatory Commission Office of
                International Programs (nuclear
                materials and equipment, technical
                data for nuclear weapons), 90
        Department of Health and Human
                Services, Food and Drug
                Administration (drugs and
                biologics, investigational drugs
                permitted, medical devices), 89
        Department of Homeland Security,
                Customs and Border Protection, 90
        Department of Homeland Security,
                Transportation Security
                Administration, 91–92
        Department of Interior, Fish and
                Wildlife Service, 92
        Department of Justice, Drug
                Enforcement Administration, Office
                of Diversion Control (chemicals and
                controlled substances), 89
        Department of State, Directorate of
                Defense Trade Controls, 88
        Department of the Treasury, Office of
                Foreign Asset Controls, 92
        Federal Maritime Commission, ocean
                freight forwarders, 90
    importing, 93–95
        Consumer Products Safety
                Commission, 94
        Department of Agriculture, Animal
                Plant Health Inspection Service, 94
        Federal Communications Commission,
                95
        Food and Drug Administration, 93
        U.S. Customs and Border Protection,
                93
        U.S. Fish and Wildlife Service, 94–95
    strikes, 91
    surprise cargo security inspections, 91
    U.S. Munitions List, 88
GPS tracking, Highway Carrier, 196

H

Harmonized System (HS), 146
Harmonized Tariff Schedule of the United
        States (HTSUS), 64
    export shipment, 144
    import compliance, 52
    number, 64, 86
    web site, 169
Highway Carrier, 195
    border check points, 195
    check points, 195
    code words, 195
    collusion, monitoring for, 197
    communication with drivers, 196
    convoys, 197
    driver check-in alert systems, 197
    employee at border, 196
    GPS tracking, 196
    Highway Watch, 211
    monitoring methods, 196
    panic buttons, 195
    route designation, 196
    route deviations, 197
    security escorts, 195
    spot checking, 197
    tractor movements, 196
HS, *see* Harmonized System
HTSUS, *see* Harmonized Tariff Schedule of
        the United States

I

ICC, *see* International Chamber of
        Commerce
Importer Security Filing (ISF), 64, 101
Importer Self-Assessment (ISA) Program,
        54–55
    Customs involvement, 93

identified risk, 55
quick response audits, 54–55
requirements, 54
self-audit, 8
Import management and inbound logistics,
43–86
best practices, 52–53
commercial invoice requirements, 52–53
country of origin marking, 53
duty payment management, 53
global security management C-TPAT
participation, 52
harmonized classification, 52
informed compliance, 53
internal supervision and control, 52
power of attorney management, 53
record retention, 53
valuation, 53
Bureau of Customs and Border Protection,
43–44
certificate of registration, 73–74
Customs bonds, 82–83
amounts, 83
parties, 82
types, 83
Customs powers of attorney, 68–73
revocation, 69–72
validation, 72–73
Customs-Trade Partnership Against
Terrorism, 54
Department of Homeland Security, 44–45
management centers, 45
organization structure, 44–45
duty drawback, 84–85
Federal Tax Identification Number, 73
focused assessment, 50
foreign shipper's repair/manufacturer's
affidavit, 74
global security awareness, 55–66
advanced manifest notification
programs, 57
Container Security Initiative, 56–57
flexibility of filing, 64
foreign cargo remaining on board, 65
implementation process of final rule,
65–66
methods of filing ISF data, 66
postloading filing privileges, 64
two-hour advanced notification for
ground and rail shipments, 58–64
wheels up or four-hour advanced
notification, 57

harmonized tariff system, 85–86
alphabetical index, 86
chapter notes, 86
format, 85–86
general notes, 85
GRI consideration, 86
HTSUS number structure, 86
techniques of classification, 86
importation and Customs clearance
process, 74–78
Importer Security Filing, 64
Importer Self-Assessment Program, 54–55
identified risk, 55
quick response audits, 54–55
requirements, 54
import management (importer of record vs.
ultimate consignee), 46–51
background, 47–48
consolidated entries with multiple
ultimate consignees, 49
entries initiated by UC but another
entity is IOR, 50
introduction, 47
procedures, 49
unsolicited merchandise on entries
listing company as UC, 49–50
import regulatory issues, 46
invoices, 83–84
Customs entry declaration, 83
invoice requirements, 83–84
statement of fact, 84
reasonable care, 51–52
broker, 52
importer, 51
meeting reasonable care standards,
51–52
record keeping, 78–82
Customs brokers, 80
importers, 79–80
methods of storage of records, 80–82
recommendations of compliance,
79–80
valuation verification, 66–68
assists, 67
commissions, 67–68
methods of valuation, 67
royalties, 67
Incident reporting (supply chain security), 213
business integrity cards, 213
emergency contact information, 213
hotline establishment, 213
outsourcing hotline, 213

INCO terms 2000, 231–232
Information technology security (computer
    systems), 216–220
  access restrictions, 216–217
    access levels, 217
    access suspension, 217
    changing passwords, 216
    monitoring and limiting Internet
      access, 217
    system lock out, 217
  data back-ups and recovery plans, 218
    contingency planning, 218
    data storage, 218
  emergency preparedness/disaster recovery, 219
    alert levels, 219
    building evacuations, 219
    disaster plan, 219
    emergency generators, 219
    Supply Chain Continuity Plan, 219
  hardware security, 218–219
    controlling workstation, 218
    password protected screen savers, 218–219
    securing server, 218
  policies/procedures/management support/
      training, 218
  program memberships/certifications, 219–220
    associations, 219
    business certifications, 220
    government/industry partnerships, 219
  viruses/firewalls/tampering prevention,
      217–218
    data encryption, 217
    educating employees on system
      vulnerabilities, 217
    securing remote access, 217
    system integrity, 217
    testing system security, 218
    virus quarantine software, 217
Internal Transaction Number (ITN), 158
International Chamber of Commerce (ICC), 9
International web sites, 131–137
ISA Program, *see* Importer Self-Assessment
    Program
ISF, *see* Importer Security Filing
ITN, *see* Internal Transaction Number

K

Kimberley Process for rough diamonds, 150–151
  certificate
    need for, 150–151
    obtaining, 151

process definition, 150
rough diamond USPPI requirements, 150

L

Local law enforcement, 212
Logistics
  expertise, 106
  tracking system, 198

M

Management support, 177–179
  continuous improvement philosophy,
      177–178
  Country Managers, 178–179
  domestic, 177–178
  integration of policies, 178
  mission statement, 179
  proactive engagement, 178
  Security Councils, 179
  Security Directors, 178
  Supply Chain Security Committee, 178
  top management, 178
  weekly briefings, 178
  worldwide, 178–179
Manifesting/invoicing/Electronic Data
    Interchange, 206–208
  Air Carrier, 208
  Consolidator, 207
  Domestic Distribution Center, 206
  Factory/Shipper, 207
  Freight Forwarder, 207–208
  receiving, 206
  Sea Carrier, 208
  shipping, 207
Manufacturer/supplier/vendor requirements,
    184–185
  collaborating to select suppliers and service
      providers, 185
  contractual obligations, 184
  factory certification requirements, 184
  holding buying agent accountable, 184
  managing non-compliant essential business
      partner, 185
  requiring business updates, 184
  requiring security adherence, 184
  supplier code of conduct, 185
Mentoring program, 142
Multi-national corporation, 192

N

Non-compliant essential business partner, 185

O

Office of Foreign Asset Controls, 36–37
Outreach (supply chain security), 212
    business partners, 212
    International Logistics Provider, 212
    local law enforcement, 212
    multiple languages, 212
    updates from association, 212

P

Personnel deployment, training, and best
        practices, 105–117
    action plan, 115–116
    benchmarking and best practices, 109–114
        areas included in SOPs, 113–114
        benchmarking, 109–110
        best practices in trade compliance,
            110–114
        reasons for creating SOPs, 113
        SOPs, 112–113
    organized and formal education and
        training, 114–115
    trade compliance officer, 111
    training and education, 106–109
        PACMAN benefits, 107
        U.S. Export Compliance.com, 107–109
    where trade compliance should be
        managed, 105–106
Personnel security, 202–204
    Code of Conduct, 204
    pre-employment checks, 202–204
        domestic, 202–203
        foreign, 203–204
    termination procedures, 204
        establishment, 204
        handling, 204
Physical security, 213–216
    alarm systems
        configuration, 215
        deactivation codes, 215
        long range sensors, 215
        monitoring of exits, 215
    fencing/gates/gate houses
        controlling gate access, 213
        magnetic sensors, 213
        secure loadings, 213
        utilizing technology to monitor gates,
            213
    lighting, 215
    locking mechanisms, 215

    parking, 214–215
    security guards
        patrol establishment, 214
        reports, 214
        resources and orders, 214
        selection of services, 214
        shift coverage and accountability, 214
        supervision of guards, 214
    video surveillance cameras, 216
        detecting intruders, 216
        maximizing recordings, 216
        placement, 216
        remote monitoring, 216
        storage of recordings, 216
        system maintenance, 216

Q

QRAs, *see* Quick response audits
Quick response audits (QRAs), 54–55

R

Racketeer Influenced and Corrupt
        Organizations Act (RICO), 228
Radio frequency identification (RFID),
        99–104
    China compliance, 103
    Domestic Distribution Center, 206
    import-export management, 99
    international acceptance, 104
    mainstream acceptance, 100
    marking on inventory, 102
RFID, *see* Radio frequency identification
RICO, *see* Racketeer Influenced and Corrupt
        Organizations Act

S

Sarbanes-Oxley (SOX) regulations, 6, 7
    revenue recognition, 12
    SOPs, 112
Security, *see* Best practices catalog; Physical
        security
Shipment documentation (export and import),
        sample, 233–254
Smart Box technology, 101
Software
    anti-virus, 218
    Automated Export System, 165
    commodities classification, 146
    daily reports, 166

Denied Party Screening, 36
fatal error report, 164
third-party providers, 98
trade compliance programs, 98
virus quarantine, 217
SOPs, *see* Standard operating procedures
SOX regulations, *see* Sarbanes-Oxley (SOX)
    regulations
Standard operating procedures (SOPs), 6, 109
Customs compliance and security, 56
Customs-Trade Partnership Against
    Terrorism, 100
definition of, 112
establishment, 110
executive development, 40
Freight Forwarder, 207
government benchmark, 6
internal supervision and control, 52
reason for creating, 113
security guards, 214
self-audit, 8
SOX, 7, 112

T

Technology options, 97–104
advantages, 97–98
General Accounting Office, 100
Importer Security Filing, 101
periphery subjective influence, 100
radio frequency identification, 99–104
service providers and technology, 99
Smart Box technology, 101
Threat awareness, 209–213
alert levels, 210
awareness, 210
background investigations, 211
business partners, 212
company magazine, 210
continuing education, 210
conveyance inspections, 211
dual-use awareness, 212
employees, 210, 212
external resources, 211
Highway Watch, 211
incident reporting, 213
International Logistics Provider, 212
intranet, 210
local law enforcement, 212
multiple languages, 212
online security courses, 210
periodic training, 210

product tampering, 211
security guards, 212
specialized training, 211–212
suspicious containers, 211
training video, 210
updates from association, 212
Trade compliance officer, 111
Trade compliance programs, importance of, 1–15
facilities review, 3
global contract management, 8–9
global supply chain, 1–2
INCO, 9
resources outline, 13–15
    associations, 14
    e-mail newsletters, 15
    magazines, 14
structuring and implementing, basics steps,
    2–8
    action plan, 5–6
    analysis and review, 3–4
    awareness, 2–3
    person(s) responsible (team initiative), 4
    resource development, 5
    self-audit, 8
    senior management, 3
    standard operating procedures, 6–7
    training and education, 7–8
terms of sale/INCO terms, 9–13
    compliance, 13
    freight, 12
    insurance (loss and damage), 13
    payment, 11
    revenue recognition (exports only), 12–13
    title, 12
uninformed executives, 3
Transportation Security Administration
    (TSA), 91
TSA, *see* Transportation Security
    Administration

U

USML, *see* U.S. Munitions List
U.S. Munitions List (USML), 88
USPPI, *see* U.S. principal party in interest
U.S. principal party in interest (USPPI), 13

V

Video surveillance cameras, 216
detecting intruders, 216
maximizing recordings, 216

placement, 216
remote monitoring, 216
storage of recordings, 216
system maintenance, 216
Virtual Private Network (VPN), 217
Viruses/firewalls/tampering prevention,
217–218
data encryption, 217
educating employees on system
vulnerabilities, 217
securing remote access, 217
system integrity, 217

testing system security, 218
virus quarantine software, 217
Voluntary Self-Disclosure (VSD), 161–163
need for, 161
questions, 163
regulatory requirements, 162
VPN, *see* Virtual Private Network
VSD, *see* Voluntary Self-Disclosure

W

Web sites, international, 131–137

About the Author

Thomas A. Cook is a seasoned veteran of global supply chain management, with more than 35 years of experience specifically directed to the elements of transportation, importing, exporting, logistics, freight, and overall business management.

Tom is a veteran author of over nine books, such as *Post 9/11 Security and Compliance, Mastering Import and Export Trade*, and *Global Sourcing*.

He began his career as a NYS Maritime Academy graduate with numerous years serving our country in the Navy and in the Dutch and U.S. Merchant Marine.

He has been directly involved in manufacturing, insurance, banking, trading, logistics vendor services, freight forwarding, customs brokerage, 3PL, and many other related services to global supply chains.

He is considered a leader in education, training, and consulting to many of the Fortune 1,000 companies on an array of topics hosted by various government agencies, the World Trade Institute, the American Management Association, the World Academy, CCSMP, the Department of State, ISM, and NAPM, to name a few.

He has been the recipient of numerous awards and accolades—more recently the International Partnership Award bestowed by former President Bill Clinton at the State University of New York in Westbury.

Tom is currently on the New York District Export Council and is managing director of American River International (www.americanriverintl.com).